Kate gained her B.A., Dip Ed and enjoyed 20 years teaching in western Sydney where she especially loved supporting kids lost in the crowd when they started school. During those years she underwent counselling, gained a Master of Education and took time off to write this book. She now lives in the Blue Mountains with her partner, also a homes kid, and satisfies her passions for bushcare, sculpture, social justice and, of course, writing.

THE LONG WAY HOME

The Story of a Homes Kid

KATE SHAYLER

RANDOM HOUSE AUSTRALIA

Random House Australia Pty Ltd
20 Alfred Street, Milsons Point, NSW 2061
http://www.randomhouse.com.au

Sydney New York Toronto
London Auckland Johannesburg

First published 1999
This Random House edition published 2001

National Library of Australia
Cataloguing-in-Publication Data

Shayler, Kate.
The long way home the story of a homes kid.

ISBN 1 74051 050 X.
1. Shayler, Kate. 2. Burnside Homes for Children. 3. Children—Institutional care—
Australia—Biography. 4. Foster children—New South Wales—
Biography. I. Title.

362.733092

Text and cover designed by Gayna Murphy, Greendot Design
Typeset by Midland Typesetters, Maryborough, Victoria
Printed and bound by Griffin Press, Adelaide

10 9 8 7 6 5 4 3

This story is true to my memories and is published without malice. The names of
many people have been changed to protect their privacy. Others have not been
changed in recognition of their contribution to our care.

THANKS

Thanks to Rich and Carla whose love let me tell my story.

Thanks to many other friends, especially Pamela Anne and Necia, who walked with me through the dark adult times.

Thanks to Patti Miller who told me to keep writing and to my writing group friends who made sure I did.

Thanks to my dear Dave, the 'make it happen man', for space and time to weave the threads together into this book.

Thanks to Burnside workers who had the courage to open their eyes and ears and make changes.

Thanks to all who listen to children and act to protect them.

TO ADULTS WHO WERE SEPARATED FROM
LOVE AND FAMILY AS CHILDREN, TO
THE CHILDREN INSIDE THEM STILL AND TO
THE CHILDREN TO WHOM THEY ARE PARENTS
NOW – WE ALWAYS DESERVED LOVE.

CONTENTS

PROLOGUE
SETTING OUT

Little girl. Standing in a cold room. Alone. Sobbing.
A voice from the other side of the door.

'You're not coming out until you stop that crying.'

Thinking at the voice. Shut up you nothing. You big fat skinny stick nothing. You're not in my life. Don't say things to me. You're not in it. You're a nothing.

'. . . very naughty girl . . .'

Shouting, 'I want Daddy. Oh, Daddy, Daddy.'

Knowing he's in my life. He's mine.

Why did he say we have to live here now? Not with him. I don't want to. I told him I don't want to. I shouted at him. To make him know. Shouted at his back. I don't want to stay here. I want to go home with you. He kept walking. Away. The louder I screamed, the further away he went. Couldn't he hear me? Couldn't you, Daddy?

'Daddy. Oh Daddy, Daddy. Don't leave me here. Please.'

They held on to me, those stick hard hands. They wouldn't let me run after his sad old back. Leaving. The skinny stick things took me and Kenny. Kenny didn't cry. He just made his

1

face all hard and he wouldn't talk. He didn't get shut in the room where cry babies have to stay.

Why doesn't Mummy come? She could make things right. She could cuddle me. Rock me. Make this not be happening. Safe and warm. Big and soft. Daddy said Mummy's dead, said she can't come back. 'Course she can. I want her. She's got to.

And Kerry. I want baby Kerry. She's ours. I want her. Where is she? Daddy hasn't got her. Is she with Mummy? Well why can't I go too?

Noises on the other side of the door. Bad noises. Not our noises. I want Mummy.

I had been a perfect child. Not the perfection of the Aeroplane jelly girl on the swing or the angelic toddlers in the Pears soap ads and certainly not the perfection of never being naughty. No, mine was the perfection of being totally lovable. I was so secure in my mother's love that I felt my perfection at the very centre of my being. Memories of that time are few but I want, I need to take the journey back to them. I need to go back to my family.

My father was a plumber then, in his early sixties. He worked in a factory that has long since been pulled down. My mother, who gave birth to us in her forties, cared for us three kids, her three K's Kenny, Kate and Kerry, in our little house at the top of a hill in Marrickville. The pram that took us into the world beyond our house now pushes my memories back into that world where I was perfect.

We always took the pram with us in the tram when we went shopping. The conductor collapsed it and stored it near the driver while we clambered aboard. I hurried to get the window seat so I could chart our progress by the passing of the factory, the butcher's shop, the station and the gate with stone balls on top.

'Oh. Stop that, Kate. It's dirty,' my mother says huffily.

Stop what? I'm just looking at the factory where Daddy is.

'Use your hanky. Look. Here it is.'

Use my hanky! What for?

I love my hankies. They've got brightly coloured doggies, ducks, elephants and clowns! Mummy makes them into stories that I can carry around in my pocket or pinned to my dress. Why is she holding my circus elephant one to my nose and saying 'Blow'? He'll get snot all over him!

'We'll wash it when we get home. The elephants will still be there.'

The problem of shopping with three small kids was solved by arranging us around the pram. Baby Kerry slept inside, I sat on a board across the front while Kenny walked along holding on with Mummy. Sometimes two could sit on the board but not when the shopping was finished and loaded onto the pram. Definitely not when we got to the hill that led up, such a long, long way up to our house.

'I can't push you and the shopping, love. You'll have to walk. Yes you can. Hold on to the rail. See, like Kenny. Follow him . . . Yes you can. I'll be behind you.'

I clutch the handrail for dear life every inch of the way. Things at the top of hills always roll back down, unless something holds them. Something has to stop them hurtling out of control back down, down, down and away.

'Let go now, Katie. You won't fall.'

'You hold me.'

'I can't hold you and the pram.'

'Hold me.'

'I've got to hold the pram. It'll roll if I don't.'

I know. And I'll roll if you don't too. I'm not letting go.

My mother gently coaxes me.

'No. You hafta hold me.'

She tells me firmly to let go.

'You hafta hold on to me.'

She even scolds.

'No. Hold my hand.'

3

We stand arguing, glaring. White knuckles. At last a neighbour, a busybody, who doesn't know anything, comes to see what Mummy is doing.

'Good morning, Mrs Shayler. How are you and the children?'

My mother explains how we are.

'Here, dearie. You hold my hand while Mummy pushes the pram. There's a good girl.'

No. You're not mine. It has to be Mummy.

'Look. Kenny's all the way to the corner.'

No. Only Mummy can stop me rolling down the hill. Big strong Mummy. Not tall skinny other people.

'I want Mummy!'

'Oh for goodness sake! Mrs Jenkins, would you mind taking the pram?'

At last, the hand I need! Bury my face in her dress, feel her, smell her sweat and hide my face from that awful helping person who's saying things to me.

I'm safe. Perfection intact. We reach home. Mrs Jenkins comes in for a cuppa. I hide.

Now I let the pram push my memory back, back to a Humpty Dumpty wall.

'That's a girl. Wait here while we get Mummy off first.'

The conductor helps Mummy down off the tram. She's got Kerry. Next he brings the pram out and Mummy puts our baby in.

'Big jump.' He helps me down too.

He waves goodbye and the tram lumbers away down the track.

We begin the slow journey up the steepest hill in the world. Kenny goes ahead. He's a big boy now. It's been a long day and I'm sleepy. Mummy lifts me onto the pram. Legs dangle. Tummy wobbles. Kerry squirms. Stays asleep.

Mummy, pushing, puffing, pushing, puffing.

It's hot in the sun but we have to go the long way home so we don't have to see Mrs Guy in the shop. We haven't got any money for her today. My cheek falls against Mummy's hand as she keeps pushing. I watch the passing world through drooping eyelids. There goes the paling fence where the bark dog lives. We're not scared of him. He can't get out. We roll slowly past the saggy grass, past the brown stuff with prickles that stick to our socks.

Up and up we roll. Sometimes my eyes fall shut but I force them open. I want to see the Humpty Dumpty wall. My legs dangle looser near Mummy's wobbly tummy. I can hear her puffing as she pushes past the 'Don't touch. Dirty' papers that loll about the edge of the path.

Bump, bump, bump. Up the 'Hold on now' steps. Around the rattly grey path to the Humpty Dumpty wall. Yeah, there it is. All the blocks snuggled into each other. Tufts of grass lean out of cracks. Pink leaves hang down from above and moss sits in the dark places.

The wall stops passing. Everything's still, except Mummy. She's moving slowly downwards. She's holding the pram with one hand and brushing my cheek with the other. She's pushing her fist into her chest while she sits on the path, leaning against the wall. Her eyes squeeze shut. She folds over. I see her knuckles whiten as I fall asleep.

I wake to see we're still near the Humpty Dumpty wall. Little ants hurry along, all in line. Mummy gets up very slowly, stands for a while and finally starts pushing us home past fences and flowers, fences and fences. I nod off to sleep again.

I wake as Daddy is lifting me off my seat.

'Where's Mummy?' I ask dopily.

'Mummy's resting. You go and play with your brother.'

Was this just before the big rest that she never woke up from?

Our pram always brought us home where at the end of each day troubles and dirt are washed away as we're bathed in the laundry tubs.

Baby Kerry was done first and, when she was in her cot, Kenny and I were lifted into the warm soapy water of our adjoining tubs. Suds everywhere, our mother the centre as she played and sang with us, weary but content.

Then came my favourite part. My mother's strong arms lifting me up and out before all the water gurgled down the plughole. Kenny waited. He was big. He wouldn't go down the plughole with the water. My mother wrapped me in a towel and held me close to her big, soft body while she cuddled and crooned and dried me. Nothing has ever felt safer or stronger than being there.

This is the contentment of the perfect child. I waited to be put to bed, to sleep deeply, peacefully, safely.

I've been told that one afternoon, when I was four, my mother mowed the lawn then went to bed before dinner. She was so tired. Daddy got us kids fed and into bed where we all slept peacefully as usual. In the morning I went in to wake up my parents. I couldn't wake my mother. Nor could my father.

I can't remember her cold and lifeless.

Afterwards our house was filled with strangers and confusion. Kerry, Kenny and I were on the edge of the adult whisperings, never a part of what was going on. Never understanding why our mother didn't come to send them all away and make things happy and right. She never pushed our pram past the Humpty Dumpty wall again. Instead we were pushed into a different world, a new cold one where I was lost.

For a long time the only memory I had of my early years was of a little girl, who might be me, standing alone in that huge, cold room sobbing.

I would hear a voice, a little gentler this time, say, 'You can come out now. Look, here's Kenny. He's not a cry baby. No more of that now or you'll have to go back in there, by yourself.'

And the child who came out of that room was not me. Not the whole and perfect child. The child who came out was broken, frightened, secretive. Alienated from the world that gave her life and self. Lost.

Getting lost took moments. Finding the child I was took many years. This story and the writing of it are the journey home.

ONE IN A CROWD

Two days before Christmas 1954, Kenny and I were taken to live at Burnside Presbyterian Homes for Children. I went screaming and was shut in the dining room until I broke. Kenny created an insulation of stony silence for himself. Our baby sister, Kerry, disappeared as surely as our mother had.

I kept looking for them, especially for my mother. I hoped for her, longed for her and I knew she'd come back. Things don't stop being just because you can't see them. They're always somewhere and you can find them if you just keep looking. Like lucky stones, socks or your monkey hanky, nothing just goes nowhere. Especially not Mummy.

Grown ups say words but they don't mean anything. I listen to them carefully. I try to understand what they say about Mummy but they don't say real things. They say, 'Your mother is dead.'

Dead isn't something you can be. What's a dead?

They say, 'Your mother has gone to be with God.'

But where? Where is she? When Mummy comes back I'm gunna tell her she should have stayed here with us. Going to God takes too long and I don't like this place where we have to wait, where people say, 'She can't come back.'

'Course she can. Daddy comes back from work every day so Mummy can come back from God.

Sometimes I understand what these people say: 'Stand over there', 'Hold out your hand', 'Be quiet when I tell you to'.

But they don't understand me. When I say, 'I want to go home,' they say that this is my home now. No. I mean home where Daddy went. I mean real home. They say this is real home.

I don't ask about Mummy any more. They just say words that make me be quiet. I'll keep what I know quiet inside myself. It's not for them. Those stick things don't know anything. Not things that me and Mummy know. They are not ours.

So I waited inside myself for my mother, my centre, to come back; and the waiting became an emptiness that had no name, a search for something unrecognisable to the child.

Thirty children lived at Reid Home with three matrons. Reid was one of Burnside's many castle-like buildings, huge, imposing and nothing like a family home. It was shiny, cold, hard and immaculately clean. There were no nursery rhymes on warm laps, no joyous laughter or noisy chaos. No babies to love or toys in beds. The matrons looked after us in a tradition that was proudly Christian and whose purpose was, first and foremost, to save our souls.

Life was regimented. Onward Christian soldiers! Conform to survive. There were no individuals. There was always plenty of fresh farm food for our bodies, but for our hearts there was mostly starvation. Hard, protective shells formed around perfect centres.

Christmas morning is the first morning I remember here.

I wake to excited whispers from the strangers in the beds around me.

Someone says, 'Presents! On yer bed. Open yours.'

I can't see a present.

'There, silly. On yer bed.'

Presents are colourful. You get them with cuddles and kisses, like when Kerry was two and we had a cake.

Another kid, Kenny perhaps, comes to help me find mine among the bedclothes. It's small and thin. Doesn't look much good but I do like presents. I pull the paper off. A comb? What do I want a comb for? Mummy does my hair. Or Daddy. And we brush it. We don't comb it with a brown comb.

Everything becomes quiet. Mrs Grable has come out of the dark place where the matrons go at night. She says that it's time to put our presents aside now. There are important things to be seen to.

Mrs Grable is in charge. I'm afraid of her. She took me away from Daddy. She stopped me running after him when he left. I try to stay away from her, to be invisible. I listen carefully and I try to obey her so she won't see me. She sees the naughty kids. Perhaps she won't remember I'm here if I be good like Daddy said we had to be. I'm the youngest so I can hide at the back or cringe down in the middle of the crowd. Mrs Grable isn't like the grown ups we know. She doesn't laugh at anything.

Mrs Henderson is a little lady. She's in charge when Mrs Grable goes somewhere. They call it 'off duty'. Little Mrs Henderson talks quietly, like she did on my screaming day. I'm not as afraid of her. Sometimes I even try to get near her because she's a big person. She isn't nice and strong and funny but she's a big person. I don't want her to know that I need her. What if she doesn't want me and sends me away. There won't be anyone who's mine then. No-one here is really mine. We have to share everything. But I pretend Mrs Henderson is mine. If I don't tell anyone that she is then I can keep her. It's my secret. No-one can spoil it.

I hate Miss Thurland. I don't want her to be mine! We only have to see her at meal times. She likes watching us so she can find things to be mean about. She can see all of us from The Staff Table. We sit in fours at little tables and Miss Thurland watches us. She's like Bingo, our cat from my real home, watching, ready to pounce on mice who want to talk. Sometimes it's a mouse who

10

wants to give his turnip to another mouse or it's mice who make too much din with their spoons or too much racket or too much infernal scraping. I wish Miss Thurland would keep her eyes to her own plate, like she tells us to. She never does. She's always watching. I'm always going to be so good at meals and she'll never, ever see me.

It's easy to be good sometimes. Just do what the others do. Line up at the dining room door. Stand still while the matrons comb your hair. Show your hands so they can make sure they're clean. And your nails too. When they say, 'Forward in,' walk in and stand behind the chair next to Kenny's. Wait for them to say, 'All hands together. Heads bowed. Eyes closed.'

Silence, then more words to wait through.

'For what we are about to receive may the Lord make us truly thankful' or 'We thank Thee Lord for this our food and for Thy daily blessings'.

Say 'Amen' when the others say it, then wait.

'All be seated.'

Sit down. Be quiet. Eat. Eat everything on your plate. Don't think you can sneak bits into your pocket or onto your brother's plate. Don't be an ungrateful wretch. What about the starving hordes in darkest Africa. Korea too! Lucky for me, I like most things we get to eat.

I like sitting with Kenny. I feel bigger, safer, when my big brother is near me. Today I want to tell him something important so I kick him. Not hard. Just a little nudge. To make him look at me then I'll whisper it. Ouch! He kicks me back. Hard. I'm so angry that he hurt me. Just because I want to whisper. I kick him back. Hard. We glare at each other and keep kicking.

Oh no! Miss Thurland. We'd forgotten about her. She's raging at us. Leave us alone, you. She drags us to our feet. She shoves us apart, shoves us to stand with our faces to the wall. She keeps slapping Kenny's head when he looks at her with his hard face. I want to shout, 'Leave him alone or I'll tell Daddy on you!' but I'm terrified.

I keep peeping at Kenny. If he's all right, I must be too. But Kenny won't look at me. He keeps his stony face so close to the wall. Please look at me, Kenny.

Miss Thurland catches me looking at Kenny when she's told me not to. She grabs the scruff of my neck and hurls me away.

'Get up there. Go on. Get away from him,' she screeches. 'I'll teach you to do as you're told.'

Kenny, what can we do? He still won't look at me.

The walk to the corner at the other end of the room is a long, lonely walk. I'm walking away from my brother. Kenny isn't mine any more. Daddy said he had to look after me but he can't.

Everyone else has gone now. There's just us, standing in corners. I can hear Miss Thurland crashing about in the kitchen. I turn around. Kenny might smile or even just look at me now. He doesn't. I'm so alone.

What other punishments are we going to get. Has Miss Thurland forgotten us? How long do I have to be alone here? Mummy?

I stand here worrying about what will happen next. Nothing happens for a long time.

Eventually Mrs Henderson comes and quietly tells us to clean our teeth now.

Clean our teeth. That's what we do after meals. When all the plates have been collected into neat piles, we stand to leave the dining room in lines but not before, 'All forward out.'

We march through the playroom to line up at the washroom. We move slowly past Mrs Henderson, hand out to get a spoonful of tooth powder. Sometimes Mrs Henderson smiles. Our toothbrushes hang like columns of little soldiers and they've each got a number to help us find the right one. I haven't learnt numbers yet. I can't remember which little wriggly line is mine, so I don't know which toothbrush is mine. The kids don't care if I get the wrong one but the matrons do.

'Surely you've learnt to count by now!' they tell me. 'What the devil is the matter with you?'

After we clean our teeth at night, we play until we're called upstairs for a bath. Bath time is so different here but I love the bathroom. The walls are tiled and there are three high baths. Girls come from the big girls' home at bath time. They have to help us get in so they can wash us. Sometimes it feels a tiny bit like Mummy is near when the big girls play with me and show me kindness. And when someone strong lifts me up to hold me against a warm place.

Something else makes the bathroom special. It's the painting on the walls. The colours are mostly dull but they're beautiful. I know what they are too. The little fish I saw in the water with Mummy and Daddy once on a holiday at the beach. And there's a mermaid with these fish. They swim around blowing bubbles that float up to the top that we can't see. We're all under the water. Behind the waving sea grass and corals there's a treasure chest with gold and jewels, like we'll get when we're real princesses. A friendly starfish is minding the treasure. A wavy octopus is calling us closer.

Bath time ends too soon. Other kids are waiting.

We're lifted out and sent to Mrs Henderson who helps us into our pyjamas before sending us to bed in the dormitory.

Thirty iron beds with coconut fibre mattresses, very white sheets and grey blankets stand in rows on the polished, wooden floor. No toys, books or mess. Just beds. We're allowed to talk until everyone is in and then the Bible is read to us before lights out.

Now we have to be very quiet. Quiet fills the terrifying darkness. The matrons have gone to their rooms where we're not ever allowed to go. Some kids talk, the brave ones. They'll soon be quiet when warnings come from the matrons' dark place. The matrons' noises mean they're not watching us, they can't see me. I burrow into my blankets and fall asleep quickly, warm in my solitude, tired from loneliness.

Mrs Grable and Mrs Henderson wake us up every morning and get us dressed while Miss Thurland cooks the porridge downstairs. Breakfast is always lovely warm porridge and milk.

13

I have learned to like the brown sugar. Miss Thurland sprinkles it on before she gives us our bowl. I watch to see if I'm getting the most. Good children get more than bad children. Bad children don't deserve it. They're a disgrace.

After breakfast we play. The playroom is big and it has low cupboards that double as seats up the side where the windows are. I like sitting on the seats. That's where I was when Daddy went. So I sit here to see if he's coming back yet. Sometimes I have to move so they can open the seat lid to get the toys out.

Playing with all these people is harder than when it was just Kenny and me and Kerry. If I remember that nothing is mine, it's better. There's always a matron or two watching. I must not make a fuss if someone takes my toy, just let go and stay quiet.

It's better to play by myself. Easier to keep my secret too—that Mrs Henderson is mine. When Mrs Grable is here with Mrs Henderson, I have to keep away. I take a toy to the far end of the playroom. But I long to be close to Mrs Henderson, so I listen all the time for Mrs Grable to go to the off duty place. Then it's time to begin my secret shuffle over to Mrs Henderson. She's usually on her chair darning and mending. I make up ways to get near her that look like playing, not just going straight up to her. She might tell me to go away and play. No-one else is allowed to know what I'm up to either. They might copy and get there first or get in my way and spoil it.

Being near Mrs Henderson is nice. I know what it means. She needn't talk to me or even smile. She just has to be there and be big.

I'll play more happily then, even though most of the toys are broken or they've got bits missing. It doesn't matter. I know what to do with them.

I owned a very special toy once. Really owned it, just for a moment. Kenny and I. Not long after we came here, Daddy bought us a rocking horse. It was dapple grey with a wavy blonde mane and tail. It stood proudly on a red stand, inviting Kenny and me to be its friend. Not the others. Just Kenny and me.

Because it was ours, we got a go first. Girls before boys. I began a clumsy climb on, clutching the reins, foot in the stirrup and . . . Whoa! It was trying to gallop away without me! I'd fall off. I clutched at the wretched neck, pulled the hair. It galloped on.

'I wanna get off!'

I knew Daddy was sad that I was afraid but Kenny was bursting.

'I'll show 'er, Daddy!'

He jumped on and galloped across paddocks and mountains and battlefields. He waved his sword and slayed dragons. He urged the horse on and on. He was almost like our Kenny at home.

Then they said I had to have another try, now that my big brother had shown there was nothing to be frightened of.

Another clumsy climb, a vice grip on the mane, Daddy close by and I was in the saddle. Whoa there! Soon I got used to the rocking. I liked Daddy's smile and the sounds the matrons made. Then I didn't want to get off, not even when I looked at the others waiting. When I got off, this precious thing wouldn't be mine any more. It would be everybody's. It would really be nobody's. I kept rocking.

'You've had your turn now,' Mrs Grable said.

Have not. Don't say things. Daddy's the boss of this.

I'm braver when Daddy's here.

Mrs Grable tried again. 'Wouldn't it be nice if some other children had a turn now?'

No! He's mine. Daddy said so.

'Better let the others have a go now, Princess.'

'But he's mine. You said.'

'There'll be more time later. The horse is yours. He lives here with you and Kenny now.'

But the others will own him too. I want him to be mine, only mine. I want to keep . . .

'Down you get, Princess. That's a good girl.'

I climbed down for Daddy, as slowly as I possibly could.

I don't remember riding the horse much after that.

Most playtime was spent outside so that we wouldn't mess up the inside of Reid Home. It had to be kept clean and shiny in case 'The Church People' came.

Outside toys were scarce so we invented them. If we wanted doll people, we made them out of sticks and scraps of wool that Mrs Henderson gave us after she'd finished the mending. The wool held the sticks together and it was clothing too. Our people were one legged when we couldn't find sticks that split right and bent, without snapping, to make two legs. It didn't matter.

I liked playing gardens most. We each had a patch of dirt out in the yard and, like toothbrushes and towels, these were in rows that needed to be counted along. It was still tricky, even when I'd learnt to count, to find the right garden patch because there were no proper boundaries.

When at last I found my garden I created and ordered a world that no-one else was in charge of. I didn't need anything from anybody. I didn't look at what other kids had so I wouldn't want it, wouldn't have to try and steal it when they weren't looking and wouldn't be sad when they stole it back.

I was satisfied with my dirt. With the dry dirt in my hands, I crushed bad lumps and watched the dust fly away and the heavier grains fall in tiny mountains. I collected little stones, berries, dry worms, dead beetles, grass flowers and whatever else I could find and made intricate patterns according to their colour or size and how many I could find. Sometimes I made pictures or let stick people play in my garden but patterns were best. Everything in its place and always knowing what came next. And me in charge of the whole thing.

Sometimes we could get watering cans to help in our gardening. I watched what water did and I hated it. It washed my patterns away to chaos, it didn't stay where I put it and it bowled my people over. I couldn't control it. I didn't want water. Mud pies were the only good thing about having it but mud pies meant scoldings and angry staff. Patterns was always the best gardening game.

There was another menace besides water. On the other side of our yard was a paddock where Burnside's dairy herd grazed during the day. The dairy supplied fresh milk to the five hundred children who lived in the homes then. Very early every morning, when milking was finished, big boys walked the cows up from the dairy, across Pennant Hills Road and into that paddock around Reid Home.

At home in Marrickville the only cows I'd ever seen were in picture books and on hankies and I'd never heard one moo. The first time I heard that dreadful, deep moaning was in that hazy stage between sleep and waking, that restless time when I struggled out of nightmares into the loneliness of realising where I was. The sound I heard terrified me. It was like all sadness and fear carried in one mighty groan. There was no-one I could ask about it. I felt as if something had followed me out of a nightmare. I couldn't wait to get up.

Then warm and safe in my garden. Leaf, beetle wing, bark. Leaf, beetle wing, bark. Leaf, bee . . .

MOO, booms beside my head.

Head jerks up. Eyes meet huge, hairy monster. Wet slimy nose. Slobbering mouth. Stinking breath chews sideways. Dark pool eyes stare. Watching me. Frozen. Thin bits of wire between me and it. Can't move.

Cow gets bored or hungry, wanders away as quietly as it had come. Head goes down, nuzzles grass.

Always check to see where the cows are before playing gardens. They should have a rule for that. Cows are angry, threatening beasts. They snort and moo at me to warn me that one day, or one night, they'll come right through the wire and get me.

Daylight doesn't dispel my nightmares. There are no grown ups who will make the nightmares stop or the days safe or the cows leave me alone.

Kenny couldn't. I don't remember playing with him much but I know it felt emptier when he left Reid Home to be a big boy. We could only stay in the little kids home until we turned seven, then boys and girls were separated. So a year after we moved to Burnside Kenny was transferred to the big boys home. Big boys learnt farm work and big girls learnt to be domestic servants. Kenny went to live in Worome, a castle across the road and I hardly ever saw him. Later I discovered the real name of his new home was The War Memorial, 'War Home' for short, but for now it was Worome. I was proud to have a big brother there. Big kids were heroes. I missed Kenny but I got to see him on visiting days and at church.

Sundays, church days, were different to other days. After breakfast we were dressed in our Sunday clothes, including hat and gloves for girls and ties for boys. We formed two lines, boys in one and girls in the other and, when everyone was very still and quiet, suitably Christian I suppose, we marched off to Sargood Hall for church.

I liked church. Apart from the chance to see Kenny, I liked the walk there and back, holding hands.

Sometimes Mrs Grable spoilt it. 'Oh dear, oh dear. You should be in straight lines, children, not strolling along like Brown's cows.'

Cows! Where? Hold my partner tight. Walk faster. Get near Mrs Henderson. Put her between me and the brown cows. Don't let them see me.

Kids from each home sat in the same place every Sunday so I knew roughly where to look for Kenny. He started to get embarrassed having a little girl calling him, beaming smiles at him, waving and giggling, but he waved sometimes, a little bit.

Turning around at church was bad. Matrons spat words at you that meant you should keep looking at the people out the front. There might be more trouble when you got home too. I loved seeing Kenny. I tried not to stare in case a big boy teased me with funny faces or made his mouth say, 'Stare, stare like a bear, like a sausage in the air.' That would make me giggle.

The matrons always caught gigglers so I had to peep, just catch a glimpse of Kenny. I wanted to see my brother, really see him, but a glimpse was better than no Kenny at all.

The very best thing about church in winter was that I got to wear my royal blue velvet dress with the cream lace collar. Nanna had made it for me and when I tried it on she'd said I was beautiful. I believed her. Daddy said I was beautiful too, like a princess. That was when he first started calling me 'Princess'. I believed him too, but only when I was with Nanna and Daddy. Daddy knew about royal things. He'd lived in the same country as the queen and not just book queens either. His was the real one.

I wanted to be a royal person. They were the most important people anywhere. They could kill dragons, monsters and probably cows too. I needed there to be kings and queens, princes and princesses who had magical powers.

In 1954 the Queen visited Australia and Mrs Henderson was so excited, even after the Queen had gone back to her palace. I was too! I knew the magic queen would have long wavy, blonde or jet-black hair that fell to just below her tiny waist and she would be wearing a long dress made of silk or royal blue velvet. A crown of jewels would sit on her head and on her face there'd be a radiant smile. Around her long neck would be pearls or diamonds, I didn't mind which though I thought pearls were probably more royal. She would ride in a golden coach pulled by six shiny white horses. She would bestow presents on her loyal subjects and do magical things that would make everyone live happily ever after.

'Children, when you are all very still and quiet, I will show you something very, very special,' announces Mrs Henderson, the queen's most loyal subject.

'Ooh. Show us.'

'Yeah. Let's see. What is it?'

Excitement. Suspense. Mrs Henderson turns her old magazine around.

'This is our queen,' she says in her special Sunday prayers voice.

Where's the queen? There's no queen there. Don't you know what a queen is, Mrs Henderson?

19

'Queen Elizabeth. Isn't she wonderful.'

I look up again, expecting that Mrs Henderson has realised that she'd shown the wrong page and turned to the right one. No. It's the same one. Mrs Henderson's finger points to a very ordinary person.

'That's not a queen!' I blurt out.

Mrs Henderson assures me that it really is Queen Elizabeth but saying a queen name doesn't make her a queen. She's so ordinary! The more I look the more ordinary she becomes. She's got ordinary brown hair, ordinary short brown hair. Her dress is ordinary, like Mrs Henderson's church dress. She hasn't even got a crown. That's just a hat. And where are the horses and the carriage? What's she doing wearing shoes? Where are her glass slippers!

All hope of anything magical happening is dashed. I know which sort of princess I want to be and it's not Mrs Henderson's sort. Nanna and Daddy must have meant the storybook sort when they called me Princess and gave me the velvet dress.

Once a month visitors were allowed to come to see us if they had permission. Alternate visiting days were called 'outing days'. On those days we could be taken away from the homes as long as we were brought back by five o'clock. Visiting days and outing days seemed so far apart. I had no feel for when one was due so I didn't look forward to them, though I was overjoyed, of course, when one came up. Time words couldn't be trusted. 'Soon' and 'shortly' didn't always come quickly. 'One day' could just as easily come quickly or never and 'a month' could feel like a week or a year.

Today is an outing day and Daddy said he's taking us to Buckingham Palace. Even Mrs Henderson knows that's where the queen lives. We go to town on a bus. We walk into a building that doesn't look much like a palace. We meet an old man who tells me to sit on a velvet chair while he talks to Daddy. We must be going to the royal part after we do something here. There is a wall covered with lots of little boxes, all with numbers and writing on them. Must have treasure in them. It's strange that they're only cardboard. The old man opens one, folds back some tissue paper and shows us. Huh? Shoes? He tells me to put my foot on a little stool and we try the shoe on. Daddy is buying me royal shoes! Next Daddy says we'd better get the bus back to Burnside now.

'But when are we going to Buckingham Palace?'

Daddy chuckles and says that we don't have enough time or money to go there today.

'Oh,' he says. 'Oh, I see.' Then he explains that the shop we've been to is called Buckinghams. 'I suppose it could be a bit royal.'

Well, at least I've got a pair of royal shoes to wear to church with my princess dress.

After church, Princess Me and the others walk back, change into play clothes and get ready for lunch before the Sunday school teachers come. We have to be especially Sunday quiet while they talk to us about something, then they give us nice pictures of Jesus or other men in dresses or fairies in the sky to colour in. The teachers say they're angels but I know they're fairies. There are grown ups words under the pictures and we have to try to remember them. 'Suffer the little children to come up to me and I will give them the rest.'

When the Sunday school people have gone, we still have to be Sunday quiet. Folding toilet paper is how we do it. Mrs Henderson sits on her chair cradling a toilet roll gently in her lap. She carefully tears off sheets and sends them wafting down to the disciples at her feet. We collect three sheets at a time, line them up exactly and fold them together. They get neatly stacked into empty prune tins. The tins are kept at the door of the toilet room and we pick up a set as we go in. We're not allowed to have whole toilet rolls in there. Goodness knows what we might do with them!

I don't understand why toilet paper folding is a Sunday job along with church and Sunday school but I like it anyway. I can be near Mrs Henderson and make her happy. It's easy to do the job well too. If we're quick enough there isn't a big pile of squares waiting on the floor and Mrs Henderson is pleased. If we fold the paper properly Mrs Henderson can fit two layers neatly into the tin. Mrs Henderson is happy and I feel safer.

We fold paper at preschool too but it's nice, colourful preschool paper. Mrs Grable and Mrs Henderson take us there in the afternoons. I love it.

Airlee preschool is another castle and it has huge columns at the front and sandstone walls. There's a pathway around three sides where we love to play. One part is blocked off by a steel gate because there are dragons there that have captured brave knights and fair princesses. They're prisoners and we're going to creep around the back way and rescue them with our swords and shields. When soldiers come into the dungeon that we're peering into, we dart around a corner and hide, whispering plans for rescues and sword fights while we wait. The guards punish us if we're caught playing sword fights so we do them where the pathway has no windows. Punishment means no biscuits at rest time.

At rest time we take off our shoes and lie on hessian stretchers. We can make our game keep going by thinking it 'til we drift off to sleep. Waking up here is safer than waking up from night time sleeps. I lie sprawled across my stretcher, feeling the freedom of my toes wriggling in warm socks. I can think whatever I like without cows or wolves disturbing me while I wait for the tray of biscuits or fruit and lovely, cool milk. After the dull clunks of our empty cups going back on the tray stop, we have a story. I always love stories and I hope we can have them over and over again. Sometimes we do.

In Airlee preschool we could be real children, almost normal children, not homes kids. On visiting days we could be real children too but only if we stayed at Burnside with Daddy and didn't go back to our house.

VISITS AND WOLVES

Kids who were getting visitors had to wait quietly in the playroom on the toy cupboard seats. We waited there every visiting day for Daddy. He always came, always on time and we were taught to be very proud of him for that. He wasn't like certain other people who inconvenienced everyone by being late or not coming at all. I don't know what happened to the kids who didn't have visitors. As soon as I saw Daddy I was off, forgetting about everyone and everything else. He was our only certainty now, the only one who loved us, the only one we could trust to be ours.

Daddy always brought his string bag of surprises that he spread between his questions about how our new life was going and how we should deal with things that worried us. We must always tell Daddy if we had a problem. All this, the string bag and the talking, meant we belonged together, like before. On visiting days we could almost be a family. Our family said goodbye to the matrons, Daddy dipping his hat as he had done when he arrived, then we set off to find the best place to sit. We found a safe place for the hat, arranged ourselves on or around our father and then we were ready for our first surprise. The box of Minties. We huddled over it to see the cartoon on the front of the box and Dad read the caption to us. He really wanted us to understand the joke, to be able to laugh. Sometimes we got it before he explained but his chuckles made us laugh anyway. His was the only adult laugh we heard now.

Next we might have a competition to see who could tear their Mintie paper into the longest strip. Kenny and I were both clumsy but Daddy never won that game. He was good at tearing out little animal shapes and tiny Milly Molly Mandy people though. Iced VoVos came out of the string bag next. I only liked the jam strip up the middle and the pink icing. I licked and scraped these off, making ripply patterns with my two front teeth.

Daddy sang, 'All I want for Chrithmath is me two fwont teef,' and we laughed again. I stopped laughing when he said I had to eat the soggy, boring rest of the biscuit. He said it was bad to waste good food, but he didn't say the part about the starving hordes. But when the next VoVo appeared I did the same thing all over again. Daddy did too.

We had turns of his hat and turns on his lap. While I snuggled in he sang about dancing with a dolly with holes in her stocking and he sang about green hills and moonbeams in my eyes. Daddy knew songs and rhymes about hanky characters and he did them whenever we told him to. Pop Goes the Weasel was our favourite.

Round and round the cobbler's bench,
The monkey chased the weasel,
Get a stick and knock him off,
Pop . . .

and Daddy's knees suddenly parted. I fell, giggling uncontrollably, towards the ground, knowing that he would catch me before I landed.

I loved my father's hands. I knew them so well. They were dry and leathery and when he clapped they made a dull thud. Veins stood up on them and you could squish them sideways and watch them wander back to place. When we interwove our fingers I moved mine along the bumps of his knuckles then he'd catch my hand for a tug of war. He pretended I was so strong that I could hold his fingers and he couldn't get away no matter how hard he tried. We'd measure our hands against his and he said he thought we were getting bigger.

If Nanna came with Daddy we would play more gently. We didn't know or care who Nanna was or how she was related to us then. She was just Nanna whose lap we could sit on and who brought princess clothes, kind words and the soft warm pyjamas. She didn't come every visiting day and she could never take the place of Daddy but she was very important.

We talked with our father about whatever came into our heads and he always listened. He asked Mrs Grable about things we told him that we, or he didn't understand or that didn't sound right. If we'd been in trouble he'd ask why. We knew he was our champion so we listened when he told us to try very hard to be good and do as we were told. I always promised to be good but I knew I wasn't sure how to be. For Daddy we didn't have to work at it. We just were good. He didn't understand, and I didn't know how to tell him, that in Reid Home being good meant not needing attention.

I hated my father's leaving every time he went. The first was the worst but none of them ever felt right. The loss I felt as our lollies were tipped into a big anonymous jar, to be shared, echoed my sense of loss of belonging, of being wrenched further and further away. I was nothing again and Kenny turned back into stone. Daddy's promises to come back next month helped a bit but how long would a month take this time? Was Mummy ever coming back?

It's outing day and Daddy says we're going to the cemetery.

'What's a cemetery?'

'It's where Mummy is. Where she's buried.'

No! I don't believe it. You don't bury Mummy. I've buried things in my garden and it's easy to get them out. Mummy wouldn't just be lying around in the dirt instead of coming to get us! And people always say we can't go to where she is. That's why we have to stay with the matrons.

Daddy doesn't say we're getting Mummy back and I'm too mixed up to ask him. I don't think he meant what he said because he seems sad. He wouldn't be sad if we were getting Mummy back. I don't know why he said we're going to her.

We're going on a train and then a bus. At Central station Daddy shows us the big clock that's way up high in a building that's even bigger than Reid Home! He tells us that everyone knows about the clock and if we ever have to meet anyone it's a very good place to wait. I watch people waiting there. Daddy says it's rude to stare.

We have lunch in the dining room at the station. It's much bigger than the dining room at Reid Home. And people talk while they're eating and no-one tells them to be quiet or stand in the corner. Daddy reminds me that it's very rude to stare.

Our pies are here now and a pot of tea. The pies are too hot so Daddy shows us how to take their hats off so they can let off some steam. When we're finished he brushes the crumbs off us and I like him fixing us up to see Mummy. Or something. If it was really Mummy, we'd be running all the way, not looking at the clock and having pies.

Now we have to get on a bus. It finally stops at the end of a dirt road where there are stalls of more bright, happy flowers than I've ever seen. Daddy buys a bunch of all colours.

'We'll get some for Mummy,' he says. He sounds tired and sad, like we're not really with him.

'How are we going to give them to Mummy when she's under the dirt?'

'We'll put them on her grave.'

So many new words at the cemetery. Daddy knows what they mean but I get mixed up.

'What's a grave, Daddy?'

'Come on then,' is all he says.

Kenny and I run along shouting to each other about all the fairies and other gentle stone people we see among the towering gum trees. There are even little castles with fairies on the roofs. But the doors are all locked so the royal fairies must be out today, doing magic.

Daddy gets cross. He says we have to walk, not run, and we have to be very quiet.

'Why do we have to be quiet?' 'Very quiet' is for inside. At Reid.

'Because all these people are sad and they want to be quiet. You'll upset them with your skylarking about. Be respectful in the cemetery.'

'What's that mean?'

'Shh! People can hear you.'

We walk along a dirt road for a while then Daddy calls us back. We're at the row we want. We walk past little fences that Daddy says are graves. We should get some of these for our Reid Home gardens. Some graves have got big smooth rocks with writing on them. Daddy says they're called headstones and the writing is the names of the dead people and the sad people who miss them. Some dead people have got dead flowers in jars and some have got plastic ones in little domes. We're not allowed to play with them because they don't belong to us. We'd make the people who put them there sad if we played with them. Even if we put them back after.

'Here we are. Here's Mummy's.'

Mummy's? But where is she? Nothing about it is anything like Mummy. It's all dry dirt with weeds inside a little fence. Mummy has got flowers too but she mustn't have found them in time. They're dead.

'Who gave Mummy these flowers?'

Daddy says he did, last Sunday. He comes to see Mummy every Sunday. Strange when she isn't even here. He keeps talking as if she is. She hasn't even found her flowers. Can't he see that?

'What are we doing? What are we going to do now?'

Daddy says we have to help him tidy up the grave. We pull weeds out and put them in the bin with the dead flowers. Then we have to go and fill the jar with water but remember to walk because if we fall over the glass might break and there'd be nothing to put the flowers in. We skip away but we can't find a tap. When we get back Daddy is wiping his eyes. Dirt got in them.

'Wait here. I'll go,' he says and he walks away sadly. He must be sad because Mummy isn't here after all.

We put the flowers in the jar and put them inside the grave fence. Daddy wants to sit for a while so he says we can have a walk as long as we go where he can see us. We dash about counting fairies and flowers until Daddy calls us back.

'It's time to say goodbye to Mummy now.'

She isn't here but Daddy wants us to say it. Perhaps the goodbyes wait with the flowers. Or this might be all pretend.

I say a cheery, 'Goodbye Mummy.'

Daddy gets cranky and tells me to say it properly. He doesn't have to say it to me like that.

'Goodbye Mummy.'

Yes. That's how he wants it said. Kenny says it right too.

'Now we'll go and see the stonemason.'

'What's a stonemason?'

'He's the man who does the writing on the headstones. We'll get him to do Mummy's. We'll tell him our names and hers.'

'Will we be on it?'

'Yes. We'll all be on it.'

'Why don't you do it? You can write our names.'

'You need special tools to write on stone. You have to chip bits out then put gold on the words. And you have to have special stone too. It's called marble. If we're very good Mr Stubbs, the mason, might let us watch.'

Mr Stubbs is too busy to show us how he works. He and Daddy talk quietly and Kenny and I get bored.

*

I kept wondering where my mother was and I wondered where Kerry was too. I missed them both. Sometimes I cried without knowing why. Sometimes I cried because I wanted to play with the baby I loved but she was nowhere in my world.

There won't be crying today though. Daddy is taking us to see her! She was too young to come to Burnside with Kenny and me so she's been waiting in the babies' home at Ashfield. I'll burst if we don't get to her soon. I can't wait to cuddle her, tickle her, bounce her up and down and play and laugh just like we used to.

Mummy might be there too but I'm not asking anyone about that. They might say, 'No'. Then she won't be there. I'm not giving them a chance to spoil today. I'll wait and hope.

We walk across a little bridge and up some soft, green grass to a big house. Inside a friendly lady talks to Daddy. Come on. Stop talking. We've got to get Kerry. Another nice lady says to me, 'Are you here to see your baby? It's so exciting isn't it.' She's excited about Kerry too.

At last Daddy's lady takes us to a room full of cots. The lady tells us which one is ours. I run, dance, race along, shouting, 'Is it this one? The next one? This one? This one then?'

'Yes,' Daddy says at last. 'Here's our Kerry.'

But he's wrong. This baby looks like our Kerry but isn't her. When I beam a happy smile in at her, she looks back blankly. Kerry, our Kerry, would gurgle and clamber to her feet and lift her arms up, squealing to be lifted out of the cot to play. She'd know her name and she'd know me. She wouldn't just sit and stare through big empty eyes.

'We'll take her out to the grass,' Daddy says as he lifts the baby out.

'But we have to get ours.' We haven't got time to waste with this one when we still have to get our Kerry.

Daddy says this is Kerry and don't I remember her?

I remember Kerry, not this blank little stranger. Kerry must be where Mummy went. At that dead place. I don't like all these pretend games they play. What's happening? Where will I go now? How will I ever find them? Why does Daddy keep saying silly things?

Words. My words were truthful. This was not my Kerry. My father's words told his truth. She was his Kerry. Well, I would have to wait for my Kerry and my Mummy by myself, without Daddy helping.

In the years that followed I saw quick flashes of my Kerry and then she was gone. I saw our Kenny sometimes too.

Visiting day. On the seats outside Reid Home. Kerry is old enough to live here now that she's four. I'm six, so I'll be moved to the big girls' home next year.

Daddy is bouncing Kerry on his knee and she laughs so much her face glows.

'Look at that little red nose,' says Daddy when he slows down. He likes playing taking our noses off. We hold our breath and wait. Daddy nips Kerry's nose and holds his hand up so she can see that he's got it. Kerry giggles and rubs the place where her nose should be. She plays pretend too.

'Just like a cherry it is,' Daddy grins. 'Yum, yum. A nice little cherry nose.'

'Give it back,' laughs Kerry and she tries to open Daddy's hand to get it. 'Give back Kerry's cherry nose. Kerry cherry's nose. Kerry cherry.' She's laughing so much she can't say it properly.

We all yell, 'Kerry cherry. Cherry nose. Cherry Kerry nose,' and so we make up Kerry's nickname. Kerry Cherry Nose. Cherry for short.

'Call me something funny too,' demands Kenny.

Daddy ruffles his hair and says, 'You silly sausage.'

'Silly soss, silly soss.' And Kenny becomes Soss.

I want a funny name too, one that rhymes like Cherry's does, but princesses can't be Mate or Late or Bate so I settle for Princess in honour of the blue velvet dress.

Our nicknames are only for our family. Only for Daddy, Soss,

Cherry and Princess Me. No-one else is to use them. But if Mummy ever comes back she'll know them.

On most outing days Daddy took us back to the house at Marrickville. I secretly hoped that one day we'd go there and Mummy would be waiting for us. The fact that she wasn't there the first time didn't mean she wouldn't be there the time after or the time after that.

Arriving at the house was wonderful but going into its emptiness was scary, cold. There were comforting things and dark things that I wouldn't begin to understand until many years later.

'Wook adda widdle wizards,' I squealed when I met my old friends again in the back yard. We watched them, then caught them, but their wiry wriggling between our fingers made us drop them quickly. Soon every lizard with any sense had scurried away to hide. Then there was the shed to explore. In the cupboards in the shed there were looms, needles, darning mushrooms, books, old photos and all sorts of strange things that didn't interest me then.

What was far more interesting was the collection of tools that lay on the bench and inside Daddy's work bag. I loved finding out how they worked and what they were for.

The plumb bob was good. I thought it was a spinning top. Why was my Daddy going to work with a toy is his bag? Anyway, didn't the bit of string get in the way when he tried to spin it? No. Daddy explained what it was for and then I didn't see why people couldn't just look down to see where straight down was. The most intriguing tool though was the egg beater drill. Did it mix eggs? Why was it out in the shed not in the kitchen? Aha! A tool with two jobs and two places to be. No, Daddy said. It was called that because to work it you did the same action as you did when you used an egg beater. I watched in wonder as two wheels meshed into each other and turned the other bit around. And there was that fascinating end part that opened out to let you put whatever sized drill you wanted in it. Then close it up and it held onto the drill bit for you. All this and it made a gentle whirring sound when you spun the handle around too.

'What can we drill holes in, Daddy?'

'Hmm. Haven't got much spare timber about. Ah. Here. We'll clamp this on to the bench . . . There. Now give it a whirl. Hold it straight. That's the idea.'

'Oh, wow! What else can we drill? The truck is made of woo . . . er timber. Let's drill that.'

'Ho, ho. I don't think Uncle Jack would be too keen on that!'

'Well he doesn't use it any more. Aw, please.'

'No, Princess. He might want it back one day.'

'The shed then. What about the shed walls.'

'No. Rain will get in. Why don't you play in the truck with Kenny.'

Uncle Jack, whoever he was, had left an old red truck parked in the yard. He became an instant hero. We had many arguments in that truck about who the driver should be and who should pull the stick with the squeeze handle thing and who should move the wobbly stick sideways and press the foot pedals. The driver always got to push the little lever that didn't do anything. But the biggest argument was always about who could sound the horn next. The horn was a Klaxon and it still worked!

'You'll have to stop that tooting now.'

'Why, Dad? We hafta warn the pirates.'

'You'll disturb the neighbours. All right then. Have your turn then find something else to do.'

But our desire to fill the whole of Marrickville with a ridiculous strangled chook sound was irresistible. Dad never had much to do with his neighbours. We never saw them.

We were noisy inside too. The wind-up gramophone and the pile of brittle black records helped. The neighbours couldn't stop us playing the records too fast or too slow or stopping them suddenly and making the needle whiz across to the middle. Daddy reckoned playing them so they sounded like gabble ruined the records. He said that stopping them the way we did would scratch them and then the needle couldn't play them all the way through. It would get stuck and just keep playing in one groove.

We loved those old Scottish songs the best.

'Why don't you kids go out to play for a while. It's nearly time for lunch,' he said when he'd had enough.

Our days at home in Marrickville were times to try to be the children we had once been but we were disoriented here now. We knew we belonged together in this familiar house but it felt strange, foreign, with its soul, its centre missing. Our father tried to make it right and keep our family intact and safe. But sometimes he became a dark threat, intruding on my need for my mother and terrifying me.

Sometimes I would go inside by myself, wander around trying to feel Mummy. Hoping she'd come down the hall or out of her room. I looked for familiar special things of Mummy's that we could look at but not touch and they were still all there. The two green emu eggs that sat in the tops of porcelain vases, the Pekinese dog statues that faced each other on their own little shelves on either side of the dresser mirror.

I crept quietly up the hall to my parents' bedroom to be with more of my mother's things, things that I could touch. Had I understood the price I would pay for needing her, I might not have crept up that hall. But I was a child. The compulsion to be with even the smells of my mother was so great.

I go quietly into the room. I don't want the others to come and spoil it. The clock is ticking on contentedly as if it doesn't know that Mummy has gone. Necklaces and brooches are still in the dish near the clock. Her watch is there and I wind it up because it's stopped. I open drawers and smell her. I hold her clothes as if she might be in them. I close the drawers quietly. In the wardrobe her dressing gown hangs loosely on a hook and her empty dresses are on their hangers. I bury my face in them. Mummy?

The glory box has got a heart shaped cushion tacked neatly on its lid. I open it and try to pretend that the mothballs smell is Mummy's smell. Move the books to one side and see the sheets and tablecloth and the transfers she might sew when she comes back.

Daddy's here now. That's all right. He won't spoil things. He doesn't even talk. I keep looking. Daddy is making strange sounds behind me. I turn around to see what he's doing. He's rocking and groaning and holding something.

'What's that Daddy?' I'm worried about how he's being.

'It's my doodle. Jock. His name's Jock,' he says in a thick voice that isn't his. I'm curious. I go closer. What! Jock is part of Daddy.

'Come closer,' the thick voice says. 'He won't hurt you.'

I don't want to. I'm frightened of this voice and Daddy being so . . . so . . . like that.

'Come on. He won't hurt,' the voice says and Daddy makes a smile that isn't real.

But my Daddy isn't scary. He's good and nice. I go closer.

'Touch him. Go on. It's all right.'

No. I don't know this Daddy. I want to go. He won't let me. He's holding me, making me touch him, showing me how. I don't like this game. Oh Mummy. Mummy. Where are you? I don't know what's happening. I want Mummy. And now he's crushing me on the bed. He says it's good but it's not. It's very, very bad. I tell him he's hurting me but he won't stop. He tells me to be quiet and keeps crushing me. Oh, let me go. I want Mummy. Where is she?

'Oh Katie, Katie,' the thick voice groans.

No. No. Let me go!

'Oh Katie.'

Crushing. Crushing. Then he's still and he's still crushing my breath away. He tells me that only he and I can know about this. He tells me he loves me and he says this is our special secret. I'm not allowed to tell anyone.

That's not my real Daddy in there. My Daddy is kind. He doesn't scare me and hurt me. He listens to what I say. He doesn't make me cry. That one in there is a very dark, thick, scary one who says I can't ever have Mummy back. I don't want that dark Daddy.

But both existed. And I needed my real Daddy so badly that I could not let the other obliterate him. I had to make the dark one a shadow that I couldn't see clearly.

The shadow stays away when Kenny and Kerry are near me. Now I have to be so careful when I sneak inside to be with Mummy. If I hear footsteps coming I dash outside to play. If I don't, dark Daddy finds me and crushes me. Even when I say, 'No. I don't like it,' or 'No. I don't want to,' he stills does it. Sometimes he tricks me into going in there.

Kenny and I have been playing in the truck. I got down to let him be the driver again and I scraped my leg from top to bottom on the door. Kenny said, 'Go and tell Dad. Go on. Tell 'im.'

I can't. Kenny got cranky because I wouldn't go so I pretended I'm really tough.

'Doesn't hurt,' I tell him.

He gets in the truck and I go to the front verandah to cry and try to stop the blood on my own.

At Reid Home the matrons get cranky when they see my leg. I should have got Daddy to clean it up. I let them think I'm stupid. How can I tell them the truth?

I knew when to tell which truth and I was very lonely with my truth. I became a smaller, quieter, shy child whose father was a predator and whose mother never came when she needed her most.

There were always kids about at Burnside who would burst, uninvited, into my loneliness and take me away for a while, but night time always came.

My sleep was often disturbed by a nightmare that stayed with me into my adult life. I am alone in the shelter, a long narrow room that we run into to hide from storms or rain. It's easy to get into because it has no doors to close it off from the outside. It has a door to the play room but in my nightmare that door is locked. I know without trying it. I can hear cows moaning outside. Snarling wolves too. Circling Reid Home. Circling and snarling.

Circling closer and closer. Coming to get me. The wolves absorb the cows and their moaning. Circling closer. Merging into one huge threat. Closer and closer. To get me. Run. Bang on the door. No-one to let me in. Run. Nowhere to run. Have to stay. Wolf. Yellow-green eyes in black shadow. Breathing close. Stand and wait to be torn apart. Terrified. Alone.

I always woke up at this point and lay rigid in my bed waiting for company. Even the matrons' company.

I had a special friend for a while after Kenny moved out. His name was Kevin and I can't remember much about him except this.

If I woke up afraid and lonely in the middle of the night I could go to Kevin. First I'd lie still and listen for wolves hiding under beds before bolting across the dormitory to Kevin's bed. I'd get in and tell him I was frightened. I'd lie there until I felt safe again and then go back to my bed. Sometimes I was so frightened I couldn't bear to wait and listen for wolves. I just dashed across to Kevin so I didn't have to be alone.

One night before bed when we waited for Mrs Henderson to help us put our pyjamas on, a little group, including Kevin, was chatting about girls' bodies and boys' bodies. I told them that if a boy rubbed his doodle on my nipple, creamy stuff would come out of me. Someone else said that only happened when a mummy had a baby.

Suddenly Mrs Henderson is thundering at me. She slaps me and keeps scolding me. Me, not the others. What have I done? I'm confused and frightened.

'Stay right there,' she tells me, then she leaves.

What have I done? The others are very quiet too. They don't know.

Mrs Henderson comes back with Mrs Grable and they both scold me. They tell the other kids that I'm dirty, a liar, a filthy thing that they should all stay away from or I'd make them filthy too. They're not allowed to be friends with me from now on. The matrons dress the others quickly and leave me by myself while they take the others to the dormitory.

I must have done something really terrible. What was it? Who will tell me why I am so bad? I'm so cold.

The matrons are still furious when they come back.

'You filthy, dirty, little thing. You're disgusting. How dare you! How dare you spread your filth around here! Well, we'll see to you. Nobody will like you. No-one will want to play with you.'

I'm so ashamed of myself.

'And what about your poor father? What will he think when he finds out? He'll be ashamed of you. And after all he's done for you too!'

Oh, please don't tell Daddy I'm bad. Please don't tell.

And I don't mind so much that Mrs Grable hurts me but not Mrs Henderson! Please! Not Mrs Henderson!

Tonight I'm so lonely after the wolf comes! I dash across to Kevin's bed and climb in. Suddenly I'm being dragged out and away into the dark place where the matrons go at night. Lights are on. More smacks, shaking me and scolding voices telling me that it's bad enough that I'm filthy in the daytime but it's worse at night. Worse. Worse because I carry on with filth in the dark.

The other kids are warned not to play with me next morning. They are all told that I am so bad that anyone who plays with me will be in danger. Kevin especially isn't allowed to be my friend. I hate Mrs Henderson. She hates me too. I hide from her at the far end of the playroom.

I was so far removed now from the perfect child I had been; I couldn't save myself from the matrons' judgement. Now I knew myself to be worthless. Or worse than worthless. I was a danger to any child I might try to befriend.

And Daddy would be ashamed of me.

I didn't know how to make things right. I couldn't get to the person who would know what to do, the person who would make them know that I was good. That I was perfect. That I was lovable and loved. If I could get to Mummy I would recognise myself.

I didn't want to be bad.

IVANHOE

I was seven and it was time for me to leave Reid Home. My next castle was called Ivanhoe.

I felt ambivalent about the change. Everyone at Reid Home knew me. Getting rid of me must have felt like putting out a particularly putrid lot of garbage. But what would Ivanhoe be like?

I wondered if by staying quiet and obedient, never drawing attention to myself, the matron there mightn't find out about me. After all there was Miss Plumb, my school teacher, who thought I was good. I had been so good at hiding from her. I sent unspoken pleas, urgent prayers to Mrs Grable and Mrs Henderson not to tell the new matron what I was really like.

I'm called for by a stranger who takes me and my things to the office. I didn't know I still owned things but I'm allowed to have some clothes and some toys like the set of penguins Nanna gave me. The rocking horse stays behind.

Miss Brogan, who works with a typewriter and a telephone in the office, talks cheerily to me. She says she knows my Dad. She talks to him every time he comes to see us. She says aren't I lucky to have such a good Daddy. She says that he's so proud of us kids. He's proud? He's not ashamed. And Miss Brogan likes me. Things might be all right from now on.

Miss Brogan says she'll take me to Ivanhoe now. It's just next door, just across the lawn and it's just as well I've got shoes on because there are lots of bindies around here and aren't the gerberas beautiful.

I hear angry shouting coming from the building. No! I don't want to go!

We're heading towards the shouting. I creep along behind Miss Brogan. I peep out from behind her skirt. There's a woman beating someone's legs! With the bristled side of a scrubbing brush! She's screeching, puffing, 'I'll teach you. I'll teach you.'

Oh no! This can't be the right place. Don't leave me here. Take me back. Take me home.

The nasty woman isn't very tall. She's square-shaped with thick brown stockings and black, lace-up shoes. Those shoes try to anchor her to the ground but she has to keep moving to keep up as the girl dances to dodge the scrubbing brush. As the woman lunges, fat bottom in the air, her petticoat dangles between her knees. She lunges again and again at the young, thin legs. She stands up to puff. The blue and white dress only just reaches around the thick, heaving bosom. White hair, parted at the side, a big bobby pin trying to hold it back off a witchy face. Straggly bits of hair have escaped and stick out like stray straws in a broom. The face is sharp and red. The small eyes sink back a long way and the tunnels to them are magnified by glasses. The beating stops when she sees us waiting. I watch from behind Miss Brogan's skirt as the fat woman pulls a white hanky out from the depths of her dress and mops her sweaty face. She adjusts her dress to hide the petticoat and pulls the buttons back into a column down the front.

The two women talk while the old fat hand holds the beaten girl, fingernails digging into the soft part of the arm. I look at the girl's face. She's wild. She's not going to give in to the pain, inside or out. Her jaw is set, chin tilted up. She glares. No tears, just anger. I'm amazed. I've never seen anyone look at a matron like that!

You don't look at their eyes, or speak to them or get in their way. You just obey. You shouldn't ever look at them like that! It makes them angry!

Suddenly Miss Brogan is saying goodbye.

Goodbye? No. Don't go. Don't leave me here. Take me . . . Don't leave me . . .

I don't shout it this time, not so anyone can hear and ignore it. I shout it inside, in my secret place. I feel very small.

Miss Yates, the fat witch, lets go of the girl's arm, grabs her by the earlobe and shoves her roughly into the shelter room in Ivanhoe.

She turns to me and snarls, 'So this is the dirty little thing I've heard about. Well, we'll soon see to you my girl. Don't you dare try any of your nonsense here or woe betide you! Woe betide you. Get! Gorn. Get inside.'

This is my new matron. This is my home.

Miss Yates has been told all about me and she's ready for me. I still don't know what my nonsense is, exactly. I think it must be about my rude body.

So all optimism for a new beginning disappeared in the first minutes of my move to Ivanhoe. I would always be bad. Every part of my being cringed and didn't want to be seen but I was visible by reputation, vulnerable to the bulk and temper of Miss Yates.

New girls were given a few things when they arrived: a number for their towel and toothbrush, a locker and a big girl. The big girl had to look after you, show you where everything was and tell you what to do when. Generally she was expected to keep you in the right place at the right time.

When Miss Yates disposed of me to Analise Vasserman, my big girl, I was relieved. So relieved. I loved Analise instantly. She must surely be a princess. She was tall, slender and blonde. She moved gracefully, spoke to me softly and, although she didn't smile, she had a lovely face and very blue eyes. When she left Burnside she would marry a prince and live happily ever after. In a palace, not a castle. I assumed Analise would be loving, gentle and kind like all princesses in stories were. As she showed me around I began to feel that at last there was going to be a big person who would look after me and make me good.

Analise shows me my locker. This is for keeping my toys, school things, shoes and socks in. Analise warns me to hide my most treasured things at the very back so no-one can pinch them. I put my set of penguins right at the very back. No-one's getting them, ever.

I ask Analise if she knows where my blue velvet dress is. She says it's probably been given to a little kid at Reid Home. My lip trembles but it wouldn't be good to cry. I hold back.

Analise says she's going do something with her friends.

No. Don't leave me. Who'll stay with me? Don't leave me alone.

I'm losing everything too fast. I'm so lonely I can't help sobbing. I sob out my loneliness and my fears. I can't name them but I feel them deeply. I'm frightened that no-one here knows me, really knows me and belongs to me. I'm frightened that I'm too little and stupid to learn all the things I'm expected to do. I'm frightened that I won't be able to avoid the anger that's all around me. I'm frightened of the woe betide woman most of all. My tears aren't just about fear and sadness. They're about anger and frustration too. I'm powerless. I sob for someone to come and tell me who I am.

Analise stands with me for a while. I wish she'd hold me, rock me, tell me everything will be all right. She doesn't. She is only eleven or so herself, too young to mother me and too busy with her own needs.

'Look. You can sit near me for a while but you can't keep hanging around. You'll have to make friends your own age.'

*

Our lives here are ruled by Miss Yates. There's hostility every-where. Two staff look after thirty of us. That should mean two sides in the war—us and them—but the staff don't like each other and girls are in gangs that fight against each other. That makes more sides than I can find my way through alone, so I join a gang. They all want me to join them so it's easy getting in. I pick the most scary one. It's better to be friends with them so they won't pick on me. When they hate Yatesie, I do too. When they hate the older kids' gang, I do too. When they like Miss Perryman, I do too.

Miss Perryman is called the sub-matron. She does the cooking and acts as matron when Miss Yates goes off duty. She wants Miss Yates' job because she thinks Miss Yates does it so badly and she could do much better herself.

I'm amazed! Matrons shouldn't disagree with each other! Right is right and wrong is wrong. Matrons should always know the difference. They're always strong and united against bad children at Reid Home.

Girls talk about waiting until Yatesie's off duty to ask Ma Perro to let them do things that Yatesie has forbidden. Yatesie's day and a half off means mischief.

'Let's ask if we can go for a walk and we'll go up to Ross 'ome an' flirt with the fellas.'

'Ask 'er for the games from the upstairs cupboard.'

'Let's ask if we can have cake.'

It's risky asking Miss Perryman for anything. She is very nasty too sometimes. But the asking is more about defeating Yatesie, so it's worth chancing Miss Perryman's temper. She's usually softer when Yatesie isn't here. Everyone is. It's as if we're balloons whose tops have been let go of, all the air rushing out. After the heady, feverish beginning, we relax, walk more lightly and spend less time hiding and whispering around corners. I worry about all this deceit. I try to keep out of it. How can anyone be safe here? Someone, perhaps everyone, will be punished when Yatesie gets back.

When she comes back there's lots of shouting and groups of girls snigger at the trouble they've caused. Miss Yates clobbers all those who risked a day's pleasure and some who didn't as well. When she blows up, you really need to be invisible. She marches about demanding, 'Where's the culprit? Where is she?' She'll grab you if you're too close. 'You. Girlie. Go and get her. Yes! You. You needn't pretend you can't hear me. I'll give you deaf!'

If I run away, she'll come after me. If she catches me, I freeze hard from her raw rage. It paralyses me. Wait. Terrified. Wanting the first blow to fall to make it real. To get it over with. Holding my hands up to protect myself. Knowing that the blows will fall somewhere that I can't protect. Wishing my hands were big hands. Big, leathery, strong hands. The degradation of the first blow turns me into a wild thing. I struggle as hard as I can to get away, never succeeding. These are terrifying times. Being flogged beats me even further away from my perfect centre. The feeling of worthlessness stays with me, beyond all our tough talk, our empty boasts.

'If she gives it to me, I'll give it to her.'

'Yeah. I'll give 'er the floggin' of 'er life!'

Yatesie builds in me a well of anger and hatred that has no acceptable way out. I don't understand my fits of temper that I'm so ashamed of, yet so unable to control. Why do I get pleasure out of other people getting into trouble? And why the shame after?

To avoid a belting when Yatesie's after a culprit, I have to look as if I'm off to find her a punching bag. If I do find one I'll cop it from the gang for pimping. They'll isolate me, call me horrible names and spread fibs about me and maybe make trouble for me in my gang. Or my locker might be raided and my treasures stolen. My gang mightn't be able to get them back. They mightn't be able to stop me getting bashed up either. Perhaps if I look as if I'm striding away to do exactly as Yatesie told me, I can duck around a corner, hide from her for a few hours and she'll forget about it, or at least forget which girlie she sent to get a culprit. Or, what if I find the culprit, warn her that she's in for a flogging and leave her to it? If she goes, that's her business. If she doesn't, I'll say I told her to and she didn't. But then the gang will get me.

Telling Yatesie I can't find the culprit is a big mistake. She'll tell me I'm useless and she might grab me by the earlobe and make me a substitute victim.

Scabs under the earlobes are status symbols in some gangs but they're common to all of us. I like being able to pull a scab off without my ear bleeding. It's comforting. It means I've avoided Miss Yates for long enough to heal. Scabs prove you're tough and you're not afraid to stand up to her. I am afraid of her but we never admit to that.

The only time I can be alone and safe is when I'm in bed. Perhaps.

The dormitory at Ivanhoe is like the one at Reid. My first bed, down the little kids' end, is in the corner between two windows. I sleep next to Julie McBride who grinds her teeth in her sleep.

'Hey. D'yer wanna see the swaggie?' she whispers early one morning when we're still meant to be asleep.

Big kids threaten little ones that they'll tell the swaggie if they don't do such and such. They'll feed us to the swaggie and his dog. I don't want to see him. Not really. But I'm curious. I get up and peer out the window into semi-darkness. Walking through the morning mist is a man with a long dark coat and a bag over his shoulder. An old hat obscures some of his hairy face. He doesn't look too scary. Just a slow old tramp. Wait on! What's that behind him! That's the real terror! A wolf!

Julie hears me draw my breath in. 'And that's his dog. They go past every morning and every night. They live in the bush and they hunt animals to eat. Or children.'

'The bush down the back?'

'Yeah. They go out every day to catch rabbits but if they can't find any, they catch children.' She waits for me to gulp before she proves her story.

'See that bag. Watcha think he's got in there? Too big for a measly rabbit isn't it! An' he has to feed his dog too.'

'That's not true,' I squeak in the face of the evidence.

'You ask 'im then. Go on. Ask 'im. Trouble is, hardly anyone talks to 'im 'cause you can't understand what 'e's talkin' about.'

Who'd be game anyway! I jump back into bed and pull my blankets up around my neck. I will always do whatever big kids tell me, without question.

Our days begin now not with cows mooing but with Miss Yates' footsteps clunking along the hallway to and from the staff bathroom. When she's ready, at five o'clock on the dot, she comes into the dormitory. Sometimes she sings, 'God is a spirit. Good morning girls. All rise.' If the day begins like this, there's a chance that the morning will be good. However, if God's spirit is not around, the day begins with, 'All rise. Be quick about it.'

As soon as we're up we strip our beds and call, 'Miss Yates, would you pass my bed please?' Miss Yates marches up in her shiny black shoes to bestow her blessing on your bare mattress, though you never knew why it needed her blessing. Then you make your bed as best you can until your big girl comes to help. The big girl might be late though if Yatesie doesn't pass her bed, shouting, 'The sheet! You dolt. Strip your bed,' if she has left a tiny bit of her sheet touching her mattress. Dolts have to stand and wait until Yatesie gets back from the other end of the dormitory to pass their beds. She can target any big kid for a morning of misery by making her late for her other jobs.

'Miss Yates, would you pass my bed please?' Dolts try again.

When your bed is made, you have to get it passed again.

'Miss Yates, I've finished my bed.'

Lumps are intolerable and so are anything but hospital corners. Analise has to help me with them. Sheets must be folded back exactly the right distance and pillows must be plump and smooth. Pyjamas must never peep out from under the pillow or your bed will have to be stripped again so you can get it right this time.

In summer there's mosquito nets to do too. There's no glass in the windows here. Fresh air is healthy for growing children. Shutters are for keeping out the winter cold but in summer mozzies buzz through the wire mesh that keeps possums, birds and bats out of the dormitory. So we each have a lovely white mozzie net tied to a halo above our bed.

I like summer in the dormitory. It's softer beneath the net; I can sit on my bed in my own little cloudhouse and block out the rest of the world. In here it's still and beautiful. If I wake in the night, I'm less worried about scary things under the bed. They might not be real enough to penetrate my white cloud.

Every morning mozzie nets get rolled into long sausages then wrapped around the iron rod that holds their halo up. Ends have to be tucked in so they don't show and squashed mozzies have to be hidden. What if The Church People call in for an inspection and see blood!

Some little kids wet their beds and they always get into trouble from Yatesie. Sometimes their big kids are cranky too because they have to get clean sheets and wash the others before they get to their work. Usually big girls show some compassion though. I don't wet my bed. Analise is pleased with me.

Older girls have to do work before school but little kids don't, unless their big kid tells them to help. Before breakfast we play in the shelter. That's a big room downstairs. It has no doors or windows and the swaggie can see straight in. It's where our lockers are and there's a big table with benches around it where we play and do homework. We only play in the shelter before breakfast and when it rains. Otherwise we stay outside.

When the breakfast bell rings we wash our hands, comb our hair and line up outside the dining room. A big girl checks our hands. Some of them play rhythms, with or without whispered chants, as they clap their hands on yours, supposedly checking for dirt. Breakfast is always porridge then bread and dripping. Sometimes we have honey, treacle or syrup too and cream when there's lots. We make our favourite spread by furiously mixing honey with the dripping until it's white and fluffy. This is against the rules but every now and then, usually on Miss Yates' day off, someone gives it a go and gets away with it. Sometimes there's even a competition to see who gets the whitest, fluffiest mixture. We discuss this with our eyes because talking is forbidden apart from, 'Pass the butter, please' or 'Pass the plate, please'.

'Silence at the table!' booms out and sometimes, 'Get to the corner if you can't obey the rules'.

We have milk with all our meals and it's much nicer than the warm sour school milk. Burnside milk is magic milk. I know. The milkman told me. I've seen the milk being delivered. The slow collop, collop of the horse pulling the cart along the back road begins a daily delight. The horse stops at our home, sometimes even before the milkman croons, 'Whoa there.'

'Whoa there, Dobbin,' I whisper.

The milkman runs up the path, ducks into the kitchen, 'Mornin.' He dips his hat, grabs our cans and runs back down the path to fill the cans from the tank on the cart. He jams the lids on and shuffles back to leave the cans full in the kitchen.

Meanwhile I watch the horse and think about Dobbin from the songs we sing at school and with Dad. This Dobbin seems bored or tired. His head hangs down while he waits for the milkman. It might be because he wears blinkers and he can't see anyone smiling at him. I like him anyway because he brings the best milk. He's so big and warm, not scary like cows. He separates the cows from the milk. He's magic too.

We're not allowed to talk to the milkman but I'm so curious that I creep out and ask him, 'Where does all the milk come from?'

'From the cows at the dairy.'

'But how does so much come out of there?'

'Well, I'll tell you what really happens. In the cart there's a tiny little milkmaid. Every time we pull up she milks a cow and pours the milk out the tap.'

'How can a cow fit in there?'

'Tiny little ones, lots of 'em.'

'But how can tiny little ones make so much milk?'

He climbs up onto his seat and Dobbin collop, collops slowly forward while the milkman smiles and says, 'Magic.'

I suppose I know it's not true but I'm enchanted. I want to believe the story. There's another horse at Burnside. His name is Bon Ami and he belongs to Mr Bergen, one of the farmers. I make these two part of the magic too. Every day Mr Bergen rides Bon Ami to the office to pick up his mail. While he goes inside, Bon Ami waits under a tree out the back. Sometimes Bon Ami leaves fertiliser messages there while he waits for his friend. Girls who are in trouble have to go and pick them up and spread them on the garden. They think Bon Ami is disgusting but I forgive his manure because of the magic.

A rumour spreads that Bon Ami has died. Girls giggle because Mr Bergen cried. I don't see what's so funny. I'm sad too. I supposed they don't know about the magic. Lots of farm things are magic, not just the cow and milkmaid in the milk cart.

Between breakfast and school time big kids finish their jobs if they hadn't been finished before breakfast. They might make the little kids help if they are running late. Then it's out of play clothes and into school uniforms. We walk to school and come home for lunch. Sandwiches and milk. Then back we go to school for the afternoon and home again to change back into play clothes and to do more jobs, then homework and then play.

Summertime is different. We have to go swimming after school. This is never a burden. We get away from Yatesie again. Kids from three homes all go to the pool at once with one or two staff.

Changing to get to the pool was like the metamorphosis of caterpillars into butterflies but more urgent and chaotic. Children dashing about wanting to be turned into real children.

Quickly get your togs on and get away, then there's less chance of your having to walk to the pool with the staff. Bolt across the bindies as fast as you can.

Of course, there are rituals to be performed before we jump into the pool. First the cold shower that we hate, then the footbath where we wash our feet with sloppy, orange Lifebuoy soap that we love the smell of. Next we parade past 'Fat Mac', Mr McLatchey, the pool supervisor, so he can make sure we've had showers. We often just splash a bit of water over our heads and hustle out with the crowd to jump in the icy water. Mr McLatchey sometimes picks someone to go back and have a proper shower but that's just to let us know he's checking. He couldn't check all sixty girls pushing past at once.

Fat Mac is staff so he's automatically the enemy, although we really like him. He has a lovely lilting Scottish accent that we can sometimes understand and for me he brings back memories of the old records at home in the lounge room. He has an enormous belly and he wears big wide shorts. Girls giggle about looking up his shorts to see what's there when he walks around the pool. I pretend this is funny but I'm uneasy. I don't know why. I'm glad Fat Mac leaves me alone. I can have my own secret opinion of him. I like him. He's fair and predictable. Everyone knows that.

Fat Mac always encourages us. We follow his lead and encourage and help each other at the pool. New kids start swimming in the wading pool, then they can ask Fat Mac for a test. If they pass, they're allowed in the shallow half of the big pool. When they think they're good enough, they can ask for another test and then they can use the whole pool. Fat Mac is never mean to kids who are over-ambitious. There are no lessons yet except for the tips he gives us. He seems to always know who should be where. He blows his whistle to send pretenders back to safety. When we call him Fat Mac, we mean it affectionately.

There's only fun in the pool. No threats. We invent underwater games like hidings, secrets, dances, a choir and distance races. I can do twenty-five metres under water easily. We practise lap swimming. I enjoy my skill and strength. Bombing and running are not allowed. If you get caught doing them you're sent straight home. We're easy to discipline here. When the whistle blows long and loud it's time to get out to let the next sixty kids in.

When we get home we put on our play clothes to do more jobs

and then homework or play until the dinner bell rings. After dinner little kids go upstairs for a bath and big kids do more homework and jobs.

We undress at our beds and dash naked to the bathroom. New girls find this immodesty embarrassing. They try to cover themselves but the rest of us don't care. We're used to it and, anyway, it's only girls here.

This bathroom has no pictures on the walls. It has three baths that are filled with clean water every couple of rounds of kids. It's best to try to get there quickly but we're not really fussy about the water. We get in and out so quickly it hardly matters. A big kid is rostered on to supervise and, if you're her pet, she might let you have longer in the bath or run you some extra hot water.

Sometimes Miss Yates comes in to make sure the unlucky bathers are scrubbing their necks and behind their ears properly. Or does she have to show you how! Big kids warn us that she's coming if they can and there'll be a frantic rush for nail brushes, to be seen scrubbing ever so diligently at our necks. The sharp thwack of a hand on wet hair, the resonant sound of limbs banging the side of the bath and bottoms squeaking across the enamel are signals that Yatesie is showing someone how to scrub properly.

After we clean our teeth we go to bed to 'read' or talk. I'm no good at reading and I'm shy too so I don't want to talk. I either get a book and pretend to read while I listen to what's going on around me or I get a comic and work out the story from the pictures. We've got some Phantoms and Supermans as well as Donald Duck and other Disney ones.

'Lights out,' Yatesie announces and we close our comics and wait. When everyone is quiet she reads the Bible as we nod off to sleep. A couple of years later they decide that, instead of the staff doing the reading, one of the big girls should. One girl who hates reading discovers a Psalm that only has two or three verses. She reads the same verses over and over again, until she thinks it sounds like about enough and then pronounces 'Amen' in most holy tones. Twenty-nine girls smother giggles under their sheets. She does this every time it's her turn to read and doesn't get caught for ages.

Lights are turned out at the little kids' end of the dormitory first. Big kids make sure we don't make any noise because they don't want any staff coming in and catching them reading *True Confessions* under their sheets.

Nights are not as scary here. I fall asleep quickly and although I'm still woken up by the wolf sometimes, at least I'm fairly sure there aren't any monsters under the beds and I can't hear the cows.

But another kind of nightmare happens early in my stay when my reputation as a dirty thing is still fresh.

I'm being shaken from a deep sleep by the figure of a big girl who's under my mosquito net. A voice whispers close to my face, 'I've heard that you're a dirty thing. Come on. Do something to me.'

'No.' I'm not sure if I'm awake or asleep. I want to be asleep.

'Yes,' says the voice. 'Come on. Do something.'

I lie still.

'Come on. You know what to do.'

'No.' I hope I'm asleep.

She undoes her pyjama top and tells me to suck her breast. I know I'm awake and I'm scared.

The voice becomes more demanding, threatening. 'I'll get you tomorrow if you don't.'

'No.' I pretend I'm asleep. I'm very frightened. She might be a wolf too. A she-wolf.

Then she does something the wolf never does. She pleads with me. Through my confusion I realise that I have some control. If she has to beg then I must have a say in this.

'No. Go away.'

I roll over and pretend to be asleep. She gives up and leaves with a threat, 'You dirty little rat. I'll get you tomorrow.'

I lie there for ages worrying about tomorrow. I can't tell the others about this. They can't help me. I refused the she-wolf but she might hurt me. I don't want to do anything dirty. I've never wanted to be dirty. Never.

At last I go back to sleep.

In the morning I remember the night visit. Was it a dream?

When the she-wolf comes and threatens, 'You tell anyone about last night and I'll bash you up,' I know it was real. 'I'll say you started it, you little scab, an' they'll believe me.'

She's right. Of course they'll believe her, not me. I don't tell. No-one to tell. No-one to make her leave me alone. I don't realise that I have made her stop. I'm very lonely today.

Shame made me hide. Shame and fear. I was ashamed and afraid of anything to do with my body and of the need I felt to be near people. I longed for physical and emotional closeness but I was afraid of it too. I'd have to come out of hiding to get close, then people would see what I was like and send me away.

Thank goodness for school. School is a relief from Ivanhoe.

Here we're called 'homes kids'. That means we're not the same as the kids who come from families and from the migrant hostel at Dundas. It's easy to tell who's who. Homes kids always wear school uniforms that get ironed once a week and we all have the same hairdo—very short back and sides for boys and short bobs with side parts for girls. Hostel kids talk funny, they don't wear uniforms and don't stay long. Kids from families have all kinds of hairdos and their uniforms are usually neat and tidy though some-times they wear what must be party clothes. They speak more quietly and of different kinds of things from those we talk about.

Our school is a central school. Burnside Central it's called. We've got Infants, Primary and High School all in one place. That means our heroes, the high school kids, are always around. They're easy to pick. Jacko, Eric, Richard and Norm. They're loud and rough and their size makes them stand out from the rest. Being a homes kid is something to be proud of because those big kids are so tough. They're ours. We're theirs. They stick up for us. No-one dares pick on homes kids if our heroes are around.

I was rescued once by a hero. He was so awe inspiring I was actually frightened of him. Someone's picking on me. I don't understand. I'm frightened. A hero saunters up while I cringe under the bewildering attack. He puffs out his chest, grounds himself, feet apart, clenches his fists beside him.

'Whatcha think yer doin'?' he snarls.

Does he mean me or the awful other person? I hope he doesn't mean me.

Silence. Weighing things up.

'Well? Come on. Wanna make sumfin' of it. Wiv me?'

I'm frozen. I don't want to fight with him! Does he know me?

His voice explodes. 'Fuck off. Gorn. Leave 'er alone, yer mongrel or I'll see to ya!'

Then a soft fist in my arm, 'Don't worry. I'll stick up for ya.'

He forgets to stop shouting when he assures me I'll be all right. I don't feel all right until he goes and leaves me to recover from his help. I'm glad that he knows me though and that he'll stick up for me.

That's how it is. Homes kids look after homes kids. The rougher and tougher the big kids are, the more we admire them. I'm proud to be one of their lot but still I think it's best just to try to be invisible in the playground and not cross anyone.

At infants school, the differences between groups of kids didn't matter in the classroom. My first teacher was Miss Plumb. I loved her and I loved her name. It bounced along happily like its round, jolly owner. I'd stride along to school chanting 'Plumb bob. Plumb bob. Plumb bob.'

Miss Plumb didn't know that I was dirty so eventually I could forget about it too, at school. I was shy and inhibited but I drifted along, doing my best and I seemed to be being good without even trying. Miss Plumb thought so and I didn't want to let her down.

I was uncoordinated, clumsy and afraid of new things and new places but our Miss Plumb could get me to try anything. Going to the asphalt for folk dancing, I was so worried that I'd be hopeless at getting to the right place at the right time. It was like whirling around in a storm. Miss Plumb let me look in her book and I saw the pattern we were trying to dance. I translated it onto the ground and then imagined I was one of the happy little children in the picture in the book. At last I could get myself to do what Miss Plumb wanted. Now I loved dancing and I loved the music too. Lots of other kids grumbled about the heat but I was so caught up in my private joy at being able to dance a pattern from a book.

Today Miss Plumb has got a new surprise bag. She told us that children who are very, very good can choose a reward from it. She keeps us in suspense, convincing us that each prize is made of pure gold.

I'm chosen on the very first day! I tip-toe, disbelieving yet so proud, to the front of the room. I don't want to do anything to spoil this.

'Put your hand in and take one. Don't show anyone until all children have theirs,' Miss Plumb tells me solemnly.

A respectful hush falls over the class as I put my hand into the magical depths and pick up something lumpy and light. I don't recognise it. The lightness and smallness are a bit disappointing. I fish around for something bigger and harder but they're all the same sort of stuff.

'Only one,' Miss Plumb says quietly.

I pull one out and keep it hidden until all other very good children have theirs, then Miss Plumb declares that we can show what we have to the whole class. All hands open and on each sweaty palm lies one bit of popcorn.

'Oow,' exclaim the kids who are only good, not very good like us.

Some bits of popcorn have bright coloured stuff on them, but not mine. I've been tricked, conned. Just one little bit of popcorn with no sugary stuff for being so, so very good! I try not to let my disappointment show, for Miss Plumb's sake. She's so excited. When I get over the shock and finish my popcorn without choking, I remember why I got it. My spirit lifts a bit. At least I was the first one to show our class how to do surprise winning. I still love Miss Plumb for choosing me.

There was a cupboard called a press in our classroom. Out of it came all sorts of beautiful things. There were pictures that our teacher took out which we would make up stories around. They were not always bright cheerful pictures but they were always fascinating, especially if you could sit and listen to other people's stories and not have to tell your own. I was terrified of speaking in class. Those pictures were often of family scenes and us homes kids didn't have much to say about them.

Sometimes Miss Plumb brought lovely coloured paper squares out of the press and gave us one each to learn how to cut things out and make pictures. Plasticine, paint, slates, scissors, cards, wool, whole sets of sharp coloured pencils and games all came from the press. Each time something appeared, it was like getting a present. Sometimes I'd sit gripping my hands together tightly, watching the teacher make something that we weren't to make because there wasn't enough paper or enough time. Watch and envy.

My special friend is Evan Waley. He is a quiet, calm boy who I can boss around. He isn't a homes kid but he's often my partner when we line up at the door. Our names are usually close on the roll. Evan Waley has a particular flaw that will get him into serious trouble if I don't rescue him. He bites his fingernails. I'm very concerned. His nails are never, ever dirty but he shouldn't bite them. It's bad. He'll get belly aches. It must stop. I nag and lecture Evan Waley. It's good having someone more timid than I am to look after. Those little brown hands and the chewed finger-nails are my treasures.

His other great quality is that he's an excellent speller. We both are. Evan's a good speller because he's so brainy. I'm a good speller because I know that everything must be in exactly the right place all the time and I always remember where the right place for everything is. It's usually a competition to see which of us wins the weekly spelling test. Whoever isn't first is always second, except once when Ian Darwin snuck up on equal second with me then overtook me because I didn't write 'K' clearly. Now that I've got glasses I can see much better but I have some old habits to overcome. Messy work is not the least of them.

That's the way it stayed for a long time at school. I felt small but safe and I loved Miss Plumb. She didn't want me to be invisible. She drew me out into new worlds where warm currents floated in from times almost forgotten.

These currents came regularly at music time. I sat on the floor and waited eagerly to see the pianist open the music book. It wasn't finding out what song or dance we'd be doing that I couldn't wait for. It was the pictures that decorated the pages. I'd stare at them and make them move into hanky stories from long ago. If the song the teacher taught didn't match my picture, I stayed with my picture and ignored the song, mouthing words that didn't matter. There were fish, ducks, elephants, Dobbin horses, pixies and lots more.

When we took our shoes off and stood up to become the animals in the pictures, I was in heaven. We rode elephants, swam on ponds, galloped around farms and flew through the air. We swayed in the soft warm wind. We waved our branches and stretched them up to the sun and all was well in the world at school.

Miss Plumb could always be trusted. When she taught us new words, she told us what they meant and we all used them the same way. There was often only one right way to mean them and to write them but she told us clearly if there was more than one meaning. She also knew about jokes, when you could play with words and do tricks with them, like Daddy had shown us with the Mintie box cartoons. Miss Plumb fed my hunger to understand words. By her own example and by her enjoyment of us and our journey through infants school, she showed us that learning and creating were fun. At school I was good because Miss Plumb believed I was.

Soon I'll have to start primary school.

It's visiting day today and Nanna is here at the home with Daddy. Nanna has come especially to measure me up for my new blazer.

Other people are here too. There's Zelda. She calls Nanna 'Nan' and she calls my Dad 'Pop'. And there's Uncle Jack who brought everyone in his taxi. He calls Nanna 'Mum' and I think it's funny for a big man like him to call someone 'Mum'. I don't remember my mum now but sometimes things happen that make me wonder. Like when Uncle Jack calls Nanna that.

I like Uncle Jack. Look at him. He's always laughing and joking and no-one else can help laughing when he does. I wish I didn't feel frightened of him but he's so noisy and noisy people always scare me. Uncle Jack doesn't seem to mind if I stare at him from over here. I like watching him. Sometimes he smiles at me and gives me a wink. He knows I don't want him to come close to me and so, when it's time to go, he gives me a huge smile, leans over and gives me a little peck on the cheek. I like him.

Who's Zelda? I think I've seen her before but not here at Burnside. I remember her from long ago. Her face. I think I remember it, now that she's taken her pointy sunglasses off. Her face isn't warm but it's beautiful. Her glossy black hair curls and flows over her shoulders like Rose Red's. She watches us kids. Doesn't she know it's rude to stare?

When she's not staring at us I stare at Zelda. She lights a cigarette and I watch the smoke flow slowly up out of her nose, past her eyes that narrow to protect themselves, then it wafts around her hair and disappears. When she talks her voice is husky and cool. I do remember her. From somewhere in Daddy's world.

Could she be . . . She is from there. Could she be . . .

'Daddy, is that lady our mother?'

Daddy is flustered.

'What lady?'

'That one. Zelda.' I point straight at her so there's no confusion.

'No,' Daddy gasps and he sits down.

The others shift about looking uncomfortable too.

'Well. Who is she then?'

Daddy mumbles and then he's very quiet.

I want Zelda to be my mother because she is beautiful and she is someone, someone who could fill the gap.

Nanna gets out the tape measure and says it's time to measure us. She smiles gently as her arms go round me with the tape. There's nothing to worry about when Nanna is close like this.

She says a number after she's let go one end of the tape and everyone is surprised.

'My God!' says Zelda. 'She's nearly as big as me.' Then she says grown up words that I don't understand. Something about boys.

I can hear the others chuckling about what a big girl I am and I feel pleased because I think they are pleased. I look up at Zelda. I want to see her admiration. But she's not admiring. She's laughing! Laughing at me. She thinks I'm a joke, I'm silly because I'm big. I hate her. She's not my mother and I'm glad. She's horrible. A nasty, mean witch. She can't make our family whole.

Next time Nanna comes to visit she brings my new blazer. It fits perfectly and Nanna is pleased so I am too.

'Put your hand in your pocket,' she says with a twinkle in her eye.

I can feel something big and round. I pull out three big, round pennies. Nanna says it's bad luck to give someone a coat with empty pockets and that the pennies are mine to spend at the store. I don't have to hand them in to the matrons.

I skip off to the store feeling very rich. Pennies are so big! I take ages trying to work out what I can get the most of. I try to do the sums we're learning at school but I get mixed up with which numbers are for pennies and which are for lollies. Mr Duncan, the storeman, is impressed with what he thinks are my calculations but he guesses in the end and suggests a bag of mixed lollies.

'Will I get a rainbow ball?' Kerry, Kenny and I can have turns of sucking the colours off.

Mr Duncan assures me there'll be one in there as he screws the top of the bag. I skip back to Nanna and Daddy and share the lollies, but only because I know I should. Daddy says I should leave some for later and my new blazer pocket would be a good place to keep them. My blazer is hanging proudly in the tree near our table.

Later, when I go back for my lollies, Daddy says I should make sure none have fallen out of the bag. I find three more pennies in my pocket!

'How did they get there?'

'Must have been the fairies,' Daddy grins.

'Mm. Must have been,' says Nanna.

I skip back to the store but this time I don't waste time with sums.

'A bag of mixed lollies please.'

I try the fairies again later in my blazer pocket but Dad says there'll be no more today and I should be happy with what they've left already. Now I know who the fairies are and I'm cross with Dad for calling off the magic. Nanna says the fairies might come another day and to remember that I've got a blazer that was visited by fairies once.

INSIDE AND OUT

'You look after Kerry, Princess,' Dad always says when he's leaving. 'She's the youngest so you'll have to help her.'

I feel very grown up when he charges me with my sister's care and I try to do as he says. But it's hard. Ever since she came to Ivanhoe Kerry's been in trouble. The staff call the problem her stubborn streak. They're trying to break it, to break her. I try desperately to stay out of trouble but Kerry keeps hanging around me and getting us in it. I have to be her Analise, her big girl, so I get told off when she misbehaves. I'm told I should control her because she's my sister. Sometimes Kerry and I hate each other, or think we do. I learn lots of words at school but none of them help when we're trying to tell each other how much we hate each other. We don't learn words for that.

'You're just a scab.'

'You're worse.'

'I hate you, you scab.'

'I hate you more.'

'Well I hate you more than you can say.'

'Well I hate you more than that.'

'More than all the words in dictionaries.'

'More than all the words there are anywhere.'

'Well I just hate you.'

We go on like that until we realise how silly it is and we laugh. But sometimes it isn't fun and then the absolute frustration of not being able to find enough words boils over into violence. Sometimes Miss Yates breaks it up. She's always flabbergasted that girls can behave so badly, like louts, sheer monstrosities.

Sometimes I pick on Kerry and I don't know why. It's like when Yatesie picks on us. I feel so angry and take it out on Kerry. Arms lash out and I don't care where they land as long as they land hard and hurt. If I get a handful of hair, I hold tight and tug with all my might. Kerry fights me but I'm the biggest and her screams only make me angrier. If I knock her over I kick her as well as punch. Then her cringing and bashing my legs fuels my fury more.

When she's down and vulnerable, flashes of little Cherry and my love for her get through to me and force me to look at what I'm doing. I stop mindlessly bashing. Shame. Complete and utter shame.

I walk away, trembling, to find a private place to break my heart where no-one can see me. I hate myself. I don't think I really hate Kerry. I just get so frightened sometimes and angry. I'm terrified of violence, of being on the receiving end and of dishing it out myself. More when I'm dishing it out. I'm a horrible thing then. I don't want to be. I feel very protective of Kerry sometimes but how can I protect her from Yatesie and Ma Perro? I want to keep her safe. I want to stick up for her, to be heroic against those two.

It's dinner time and Kerry has been picked on by Ma Perro all afternoon. She's too upset to eat her tea. Tea is corned beef, boiled with the fat still on, and a sludge of lumpy white sauce and cabbage. It's Kerry's least favourite meal and she's got a big lump of fat. Ma Perro says she has to eat it all. She's shovelling in more and more. Her face reddens and Perro keeps screaming at her to

61

eat it. I want to make it stop. I want to shout, 'Leave my Kerry alone you fat pig. Eat it yourself if it's so good. I'll shove it down your rotten neck! Leave my sister alone.'

I scream it inside myself but outside I shut up. There's nothing I can do to protect my sister. I'm ashamed to stand by and watch.

Finally Kerry vomits. Ma Perro is furious. Kerry is filthy, she says. She can clean up this mess and get out of Ma Perro's sight before she gives her something to cry about. And she needn't think she's getting her pudding either!

I'm too frightened to stand up to staff. Kerry isn't. That's why she's always in trouble. She refuses to toe the line unless it suits her. Yatesie got so angry with her once she beat Kerry's head so hard that her eardrum burst. We didn't know that had happened but she kept saying she had a headache in her ear. She always complains about headaches in all sorts of places including her hand, her tummy and even her big toe. It always makes me laugh. This headache wasn't funny though. It wouldn't go away and Kerry had to go to Burnside's hospital. When she came home Yatesie left her alone for a while but Kerry couldn't hear properly after that.

Sometimes I admire Kerry's stubborn courage but most of the time I think it's stupid to keep arguing and refusing to do as you're told. It's much safer to give in. I want Kerry to do that, to protect herself but she won't. Or can't. She's always angry.

I try so hard to get things right. If I'm good I might get approval and approval feels a bit like they like me, those matrons. They might be kind to me and then it won't be so hard and lonely here. I don't want to be a crawler. I just want them not to pick on me or get angry with me.

Kerry and I are friends sometimes. Especially with jokes. We understand each other. It's like we speak the same language then. We're good at making jokes by using surprising meanings of words or dropping in rhyming words or slipping words in that don't really fit.

Our favourite board game is kept in an upstairs cupboard

where new toys are put to be given out for birthdays. We're hardly ever allowed to play this game so it never loses its appeal. There's a little book with a story that has some words left out. You read the story and when you come to a blank, you take a word card from the box and put it into your story.

'Mr McGregor was going on a holiday in . . . the bathroom. He packed his . . . dog and his . . . brother into his suitcase. He shut the door and got on the . . . mashed potato to begin his journey . . .' Kerry and I laugh our heads off. Some kids don't get it. We do and we nearly lose control of ourselves as tears stream down our faces and our sides ache. I want times like this to be the only kind of times I have with Kerry but they're rare. She fights on and on and the matrons keep on trying to break her by tormenting her, for nothing sometimes.

Dad taught us about laughing. Staff don't laugh. They think that if we're laughing they have lost control of us and they can't let that happen.

'Stop that racket. Stop it at once or I'll see to you.'

At school I leave all that behind. But dark shadow things follow me there sometimes and I find myself out of my depth.

It's a cold morning. We're in the playground when a frantic teacher comes rushing about blowing a whistle, piercingly, urgently.

'Children, pay attention! Go straight to the quad and stand still. Go! Quickly. Don't move off until you're told.'

The quad is a large rectangle of concrete slabs where we do PE, dancing, bean bag games, fun things. We can tell this is not one of those times. Something serious is happening and we'd better to do exactly as we're told.

Someone says, 'Blimey! Look at that. It's a mad dog.'

'Yeah. They bite ya.'

'Rip yer guts out, more like.'

'If we try to get inside it's gunna eat us.'

'Can't get in. The door's still locked.'

'Somebody's gunna shoot it.'

63

I peep through eyes that have been squeezed shut. There's a dog loping around, snarling. I know straightaway that it's the wolf! I know who it's coming for too. I push my way to the middle of the crowd determinedly but slowly, so no-one will notice me, especially not the wolf. I shut my eyes, freeze and wait.

Ages pass then someone says the dog has gone. I open my eyes slowly. Everyone's moving away. I stay in among the meandering crowd for as long as I can. You don't really know if that dog has gone and if he has, whether he'll stay gone.

I can't talk to anyone at school about wolves. Or any dark things. I'm no good at talking at all at school.

I would like to have talked that day at the swimming carnival. I wanted to yell and shout at them. Someone had drowned. We sat shocked as they pulled the lifeless body out of the pool. We sat in stunned silence, not understanding in our own ways of not understanding.

'What's happening?'

'He's drownded.'

'Drowned, you dope.'

They gave him artificial respiration; lay him down on his stomach, bent his arms and rested his head on his hands. Someone knelt astride his head.

What are you doing? Don't do that, I wanted to shout. I felt dark things in the air. I felt my stomach knot and it was hard to remember to breathe. The one that was kneeling over the boy lifted the lifeless elbows up, put them down then rocked forward, leaning on the boy's ribs, almost sitting on his head. Teachers just stood there watching! It went on and on, over and over again. Pushing, lifting, pushing, lifting. Pushing my mind into chaos.

Why are you all just watching? This is a bad, dark thing! Make it stop! I yelled inside myself.

But no-one did anything to stop the badness. They all just watched.

An ambulance came and took the boy away.

The carnival got going again and I wondered what was wrong

with me. I was full of energy and nerves. I don't know where it came from but I swam faster than ever and won some ribbons. That part was good because I had something to show in News.

'Oh Kate! Have you got something to tell us!'

'Hm.' I stand up and hold my ribbons. I can't think what to say though.

'You won those didn't you?'

'Hm.'

'Thank you, Kate. Sit down now.'

With Burnside kids I can find the words for everything but we don't talk about homes things with outsiders. We don't make jokes either, not in primary school, not when we're in 3rd class.

I hate composition too. Mine are always poor, 'lacking imagination'. Homes kids live in a different world to the others. There's nothing to write about. Outsiders carry on about all kinds of things, like what they did on the weekend, whose party they went to, where they went for holidays, new toys or clothes they've got. On and on they go. Skites! Hostel kids write about England or Scotland and what happened on their ships to Australia. Who'd want to know what the homes kids did on the weekend? We don't write or talk to outsiders about Burnside, especially if it's a criticism. It might get back to Burnside and then we'd be in for it. It's safer to keep our two worlds separate.

My teacher Miss Healey says I only pass composition because my spelling and grammar are so good. That's the easy bit. All you do is follow the rules and you're right with them. 'A verb is a doing word. A noun is a naming word. An adverb describes a verb . . .'

I've got a good idea. I'll pinch ideas for stories from library books to improve my compositions. No. I often don't understand what I read and it's becoming even harder. I can't tell what's going to happen next in the story so I can't guess what the word is when sounding it out doesn't work. Why can't the words all obey the rules? Every single one is a separate challenge. They don't flow into each other. I hate reading.

Choosing a book from the library is never a problem, though. Just grab anything, one with good pictures if possible, take it home and bring it back next week. No need to bother reading it. Until 5th class when our new teacher wants us to do book reviews! I find a temporary solution. A boy in our class has read and reviewed, *Across Texas*. He says that, although it's very long, it's very exciting. 'Very long' is very appealing. I gleefully take *Across Texas* to the librarian.

'Are you sure you want this one?'

'Yes.' More than ever.

'It's very long!'

'Mm.' Exactly right for me.

'It's more of a boy's book!'

'Mm.' I'll be a tomboy as well!

'It's quite hard too.'

'That's all right.'

'All right, if you're sure you can manage it.'

'I can read it.'

Stamp. Stamp. Stamp and I'm off with the fattest book she's got.

I bring it back next week and report that I'm still reading it and that it's so exciting I want to keep reading it. This works for a long time. I read bits of it and do short reports to prove I'm reading it.

'The hero fell into a rattlesnake pit but he got out all right.'

'It's wonderful that you are keeping on with this book, Kate.'

'Mm.' Good trick eh!

'Are you finding it too hard?'

'No.' Only when I read it.

'Good! Your reading must be improving. Keep it up!' Mrs Brack is so proud of my perseverance.

I might learn to read better if I let on that I'm struggling but it's too embarrassing to be that stupid. I might be a better reader if I wasn't so shy too. Sometimes we have to read to the whole of sixth class. There's no escape. I loathe being the centre of attention and I'm sure 6th class loathe my being there too. I stand out the front with my wretched book and mumble what I hope sounds like a sentence or two.

'For goodness sake girl, we need to hear you! Speak up,' Mr Hughs bellows from the back of the room.

Now I'm too intimidated to breathe, let alone read.

'Come on. Come on. We haven't got all day.'

I'm dreadful at anything that has to be neat too. The more pressure they put on me, the more nervous and messy I become. My hands always seem to be sweaty and dirty and my fingers won't relax. My handwriting is shocking.

One Friday in dictation a miracle happens. It's as if someone else, the supremely neat Shea Crumpton perhaps, gives me her hand to write three words perfectly. 'Boodle growled richly.' I'm so proud. I'm so stunned. Three perfect words! I can't repeat the performance but I get a merit certificate for 'Improved Writing'. My certificate, which I still have, gets smeared with vegemite at lunchtime, before I even get it home.

Boodle got me an award. I should like him. I think he's meant to be a playful family pup but I'm uneasy about him. I don't trust him. I don't understand why except that his name sounds wrong, threatening. There's no picture of him to confirm that he's not a wolf.

Primary school isn't as much fun as infants. The teachers don't seem to be having fun. They're not connected with us and our learning like Miss Plumb was. But there are exceptions.

We've just had a student teacher who was so enthusiastic about our learning. She was teaching us about germs. She didn't just rave on about hygiene and clean fingernails and that. Germs are interesting, not disgusting. She drew bacteria all over the blackboard. We had a board full of beautiful germs! She told us why they were or weren't dangerous. She told us how some of them move and said we'd learn about the others later.

''Scuse me Miss Healey but where's Miss Dixon?'

'Miss Dixon is unwell. She won't be back.'

I feel deserted, cheated and very sad.

'But she didn't tell us how the other ones move,' I blurt out.

'You can look it up in the library if you're interested,' Miss Healey suggests gently.

No. It won't be the same. I want to learn it from someone who wants me to know, someone who wants us to enjoy it like she does. There's no life or enjoyment in books.

School magazines have life in them though. They arrive in a bundle, all new and crisp, perfect white, all the staples in shiny rows up the spines. They're full of stories, poems, puzzles and best of all, wonderful pictures. How frustrating to be given yours and told, 'Do not open your magazines until everyone has one. Good. Now turn to page seven. We'll read the poem at the bottom.'

The poem is probably about war heroes or something.

They shall not grow old as we that are left grow old.
Age shall not weary them nor the years condemn.
At the going down of the sun and in the morning,
We will remember them.

How could they not get old? That's stupid. And all old people in stories get weary, so why aren't they going to? What about years condemn? Years are time. They can't do things. Our teacher explains and we have to memorise it. But why didn't people just write what they meant instead of making it so hard to understand them?

Meanwhile good things like colouring in, crosswords and anagrams are waiting in the school magazine. These are forbidden until we have struggled through stories and poems that don't make sense. If I don't understand a piece of writing I'd rather just colour in the picture or find something else to read.

One poem is an exception.

A stranger came one night to Joussef's tent saying,
'Behold one outcast and in dread,
Against whose life the bow of power is bent.

I come to thee for shelter and for food.
To Joussef. Known through all our tribes.
The Good.'

I didn't get it at first but Mrs Brack explained it and now I love it. I love the idea that someone is strong enough to be kind to a bad person who's really frightened. The part I love best is in Joussef's reply to the refugee,

Come in . . .
As one lamp lights another and grows not less,
So nobleness enkindles nobleness.

You don't lose your own kindness by being kind to someone else. I wish I had a Joussef of my own.

Poems that rhyme are easier to learn, especially if they're full of fun and excitement.

Hist! Hark! The night is very dark
And we've to go a mile or so
Across the possum park . . .
'Mopoke.' Who was that that spoke?
This is not a fitting spot to make a silly joke.
Dear me. A Mopoke in a tree . . .

This poem makes me feel as if the night might not be as scary as it feels sometimes. There are silly owls and people giggling in parks. I take the poem home and giggle at my dinner table version of Ma Perro.

Mopoke! Who was that that spoke?
Ma Perro's not a cow cream clot,
She's just a silly joke.

At home I can say my poems to kids and read some silly stories too. I only daydream about doing it at school, being brave enough to stand up and speak well, answer questions, tell news or read out loud. I want to be like kids who aren't shy.

Our school has a teacher who's very good at musicals. He's famous for most of the year for his insistence on the correct pronunciation of his name.

'Good morning Burnside Central,' says Mr Keplin at morning assembly.

'Good morning Mr Kepman' or 'Kepn', we reply.

'Listen,' he commands. 'Keplin. Keplin. Notice the teeth. Keplin. Keplin.'

He wants to see all our teeth to assure himself that his name really has an 'i' in it. Sometimes kids say 'Kepn' really loudly because he's bound to carry on and hold up school for a while. I like words to be pronounced properly too but his name isn't that important. He's got such a big head and us Burnsiders know that people with big heads are the enemy.

Mr Keplin is better known to parents for his annual operettas. These are big productions performed in full costume. The whole of Burnside Central School goes to Sargood Hall for them and lots of important people come too. Us Burnie kids feel a bit important because we're lending our church to the school. There's lots of excitement for months before, even in the least interested kids. Anyone who'd like a lead role gets auditioned. I feel very brainy because I know what audition means. Next, anyone who wants to be in the chorus auditions. Burnside kids never get roles so we never bother with auditions.

This year Mr Keplin announces, 'All children will be auditioned for parts in our operetta. There may be some among you who have undiscovered talent. We can find you and help you along. Perhaps to a lead role.'

'I'm not gunna be in it!' us Burnsiders grumble. 'He can't make me.'

I agree, but my daydreams start to see spotlights. I love singing in church with a few hundred other kids. What if I'm an undiscovered talent? I fantasise about how proud everyone will be of me if I get a lead role. I'll be famous. I might even get in *The Women's Weekly* wearing beautiful clothes, surrounded by adoring fans, including Tab Hunter, Jane Russell, Alan Ladd and Elizabeth Taylor.

The day comes for our class auditions. My fame on the stage in my mind is huge. My anxiety in the hall is huge too. I try to hide behind the pictures in my imaginary *Women's Weekly*.

'Next,' Mr Keplin calls. My *Women's Weekly* blows away.

'I don't want to be in it,' I hiss at my teacher.

'Just go up and try,' Mrs Brack urges. She sounds confident.

I walk onto the stage and stand alone in the silence; everyone waiting for my voice to show my worth. The pianist starts playing.

'And again,' Mr Keplin calls to the pianist when I miss the first beat.

My face reddens as I miss it again and again.

I wish I were brave enough to even try but I'm not.

'You see. You must listen to the music and come in on three. Ready? One, two, and . . .' Mr Keplin gives it a final try, waits with his mouth open. I stand with mine shut. I become angry with Mr Keplin for making me stay. Why can't you see I'm just too shy? I clench my teeth and stare at the floor. On the floor I see how stupid this is. I'm obviously not an undiscovered talent.

At last he lets me go. I'm very disappointed in myself.

'Good on yer, Shayley,' some Burnsiders say. They don't know about my *Women's Weekly* that is now in tatters.

As we go through primary school the differences between homes kids and outsiders become more obvious. Our manners and attitudes are coarse and, at the stage when we start caring about how we look, we know we are inferior. We seem unavoidably grubby and dishevelled. It's hard to keep the dirt out of our fingernails and skin. We never mix with outsiders but we got invited to a party once—Elizabeth Smedley's—and we went to her house at Carlingford. I'd been jealous of her sometimes. She always has interesting holidays and brings photos in to show us. She's been to a whaling station in Western Australia.

Then one day Elizabeth got off the school bus and was hit by a car. Her leg had to be amputated and she was away for a long time.

'Elizabeth will be coming back next week and I expect you all to help her. She may feel quite awkward at first so it's very important that we treat her normally. It will be hard but please do not stare,' said the teacher.

Treating her normally is easy. She's an outsider so we ignore her. Resisting the urge to stare is different. I've often stared at her thick, shiny plait hanging down almost to her waist. Now her hair is short, like Burnsiders' only shiny and tidy. I can't help staring at the gap where her leg used to be. I admire the way she manages but that gap is scary.

I'm apprehensive about going to her birthday party. We'll have to go somewhere new and we won't know what to do or say. We're told to remember good manners, remember we're representing Burnside and remember to say 'thank you for having us' when we leave. We chat all the way to Elizabeth's house, pretending we know what this party business is all about. But when we reach the front door we become quiet and stiff. It's time to stop pretending.

Elizabeth and her parents come to meet us. We're the first there. They're all friendly but awkward and posh. Hoity-toity. They don't seem to know what to do with a group of shabby girls who stand waiting to be told what to do. They show us to Elizabeth's room in case we want to put our purses on the bed.

'We haven't got our purses,' Val says and someone starts giggling.

'Oh. Well if you'd like to leave your cardigans there, please do,' says Elizabeth's mum. No-one says we haven't got our cardigans either, thank goodness.

We cop a sticky in Elizabeth's room. I'm stunned. The softness of it! The lacy bedspread, the dolls everywhere, the soft toys and the desk and books and games. I've never seen so many nice things in one place and they all belong to Elizabeth. To one person!

The parents usher us into the lounge room. They offer us drinks. We don't know what to say when they ask us what we'd like.

'Milk please.'

'Oh, er. I meant soft drink. Would you like a soft drink?'

No milk!

'Ah. I'm not thirsty. Are you?' I claim.

'No. Me neither,' says Maureen.

Then someone remembers Tarax. 'Oranges turn into Tarax' on the radio.

'Would you like Tarax too dear?' the mum asks red faced me.

'Um. Yes, please.'

The parents can't think of what else to do with us. They smile a lot, clear their throats as if they're about to give a sermon then they just look at each other. We smile at them and watch them look at each other.

'Do make yourselves at home.' They leave the lounge room to see to something in the kitchen. We whisper about whether we could sticky beak through the rest of the house. We'd better not. We wonder if we could eat the food the parents have brought in.

'Better not. They didn't tell us to.'

'Bad luck. They shouldna put it there if they don't want us to eat it,' and we all bog in.

Next we try to think of something else to do. We don't know if outside is out of bounds so we just sit and stare at the carpet. Our comfortable, familiar chatter becomes stilted and false. It's almost as if we don't know each other here.

Our not belonging becomes more obvious as outsiders start arriving. They're wearing party frocks, lipstick and fancy hairdos. They put their cardigans and purses in Elizabeth's room and give presents to the birthday girl. Everyone ohs and aahs and kisses are

73

exchanged with each gift. After 'Hello' we don't know what to say to the outsiders. They don't know what to say to us either so our separate groups ignore each other until the parents tell us all to come to the sunroom for the entertainment.

There's a clown who shouts a lot and does tricks and says things that are supposed to be funny. My reliable sense of humour fails. A magician comes next. He does more tricks. His most amazing trick appals me. He takes off his thumb! He says watch carefully and he'll do it again. I watch. He can! He can take off his thumb. It's the ugliest thing I've ever seen. It's wrong, with us all here to be nice to Elizabeth whose leg's been taken off. I'm so distressed I ask the father if the magician's thumb has really come off.

'No! It's just a trick!'

He teaches me how to do it. I practise it all the way home and teach the others too. We remember to say 'thank you for having us' as we leave but I don't mean it. I just want to get back to Burnside where I belong.

This adventure wasn't mentioned at school except that Elizabeth wrote a composition about her very nice party and all her friends who came along.

I knew I didn't fit in the mother and father family but, oh, how I wanted to have one now. And all those nice things in Elizabeth's room! Dad talks about when we are all together again so I imagine having all those things that Elizabeth and her parents have got. And parties that only Burnsiders will come to. Dad will have to get a new wife. That will speed things up.

NANNA

Nanna was a relief from everything. She stayed perfect as her visits became more regular. I felt her love and approval from the moment she arrived and said, 'Hello, darling Kate.'

She greeted each of us like that.

I liked knowing that my excitement at seeing her gave her so much pleasure. My appreciation of the presents she brought did too; the red sewing basket, the soft pink pyjamas, the solitaire game, the lolly pink socks and the silky soft gorgeous gussies that were more glamorous and colourful than anyone else's undies in Ivanhoe. Even the matrons', I bet. There was no-one else like Nanna in our lives then.

After a time we stop going to Dad's house on visiting days and we go to Nanna's house at Lakemba instead. Uncle Jack brings Dad in his taxi, picks us up and takes us all to Nanna's, if he isn't with another fare. If Uncle Jack is busy we go by train. Taxi rides are good. Our uncle can do magic. Sometimes we sit at a red light for so long and Uncle Jack gets fed up.

'We've been waiting too long, haven't we kids,' and he snaps his fingers. The lights change instantly to green and we're off.

I wish he had magic for car sickness. My head aches, my tummy lurches around, the taxi stinks of vinyl and I can't think of anything except how bad I feel.

'How are you kids in the back?'

'I feel sick.'

Uncle Jack stops the car and lets me get out. I don't vomit and he thinks I'm faking it.

'Must be time for an ice-cream, eh?'

'But I am sick.'

'All right. We'll stop up here.'

I feel so wretched I couldn't care less about ice-cream but Uncle Jack says it'll make me better. He sees lots of reasons to have ice-creams. They'll cool us off or settle us down or cheer us up or we'll just have them because they're nice. The best bit for me is that we get out of the taxi to eat them. I feel better, except for my resentment that he still thinks I tried to con him.

Going by train means no ice-cream but no sickness either. People on the train or in the street can be scary. If they're loud or drunk or dirty or unusual, I'm uneasy. But people are often interested in us kids because we look so alike. They stop to ask Dad, 'Oh. Look! Are your grandchildren triplets?'

Dad answers proudly, 'I'm their father. No they're not triplets. They're my three Ks.' He chuckles and introduces us.

'This is Kerry, the baby and this is Kate in the middle. This is Kenny, er Ken. He's the eldest.' Kenny's too big to be called Kenny, he says. He wants to be Ken now.

I like belonging to Dad like this, out here, where I'm safe with him. Out here on our way to Nanna's.

She lives on King Georges Road. After we get off the train, we walk up to her house, stopping at the grocery shop on the way to buy her present. She loves Columbines that you get in a long thin turquoise or pink box that has tiny ballerinas dancing up the sides. I want to carry the Columbines and give them to Nanna. Kerry does too. Ken's too big for that now.

An Italian man owns the shop. He knows who we are.

'Arah, da leetle kays. No mama!'

His strange way of speaking and his instant affection scare me at first but he knows the way to my heart.

'Put outa your hend.'

With a great flourish he takes the lid off a huge jar of pink sugar coated peanuts. He places some on each palm, making very sure we each get the same amount. Sometimes he lets us put our hands in and get some for ourselves. I stretch my hand so wide that I have to let go of some peanuts to get my hand out of the jar.

Good manners have been thrashed into us at Burnside and this papa is very impressed that we always smile and say 'thank you'. By the time we get to Nanna's house there are lots of pink stains on us but no more peanuts.

Nanna and Roger are waiting for us on the verandah or they appear in the doorway, Nanna wiping her hands on her pinny and Roger alert at her side, hackles ready to rise.

'Sit,' she tells Roger.

He sits, ears pricked, tail slowly wagging.

'Don't worry about him. He's a good boy,' she tells us. Roger is Nanna's Alsatian. He isn't just a dog. He's Nanna's friend and guard.

Nanna folds us gently one by one in her arms, names us, kisses our heads and tells each one how glad she is to see us.

'Are they all just for me?' she asks, delighted, as we hand over the sticky box of Columbines. Kerry has her hands on them too now. Nanna is always surprised to be getting her Columbines.

After Roger gets over our arrival on Nanna's territory, he's our friend and playmate too. He lets us stroke him, tumble with him and play ball with him. He's always smiling when we play ball. When he's had enough, he walks quietly away and lies down.

Nanna says that in summer she likes to sleep out on her porch on her cane bed. Dad says she shouldn't but she says she's safe with Roger sleeping across the top step to guard her and Dad agrees that no-one would get past him.

But Roger, despite all the fun we have with him, looks like a wolf. Lots of little bits of knowledge I have merge one day to make me afraid to be alone with him.

Roger sits down and Kerry kneels beside him.

'Beg,' she says.

Roger smiles, sits up and begs.

'Shake hands,' Kerry commands and Roger shakes hands. I watch Kerry hugging his neck then she tries to catch his tail.

'Hey. What's that sticking out down there?' I ask.

'It's his rude thing. You know, his doodle.'

Panic. He's a wolf!

It's over as quickly as it came, except for the uneasy feeling I'm left with about Roger. Then he does something that changes my uneasiness to terror.

Mostly we play in Nanna's back yard but the front yard is good too. There's a paling fence and you can just see the tops of people's heads as they walk by. Nanna and Dad sit on the porch watching us romp about with a tennis ball. Suddenly Roger leaps at the fence. He barks loud, deep threats. He bares his long white fangs. His hackles are up as he snarls all the way along the fence as someone hurries by. I scream, 'A wolf! It's a wolf!'

Inside I know. I'm terrified. Paralysed.

The next thing I know, I'm in Nanna's lap. She's holding me close and rocking me. She tells me it's all right. She croons that Roger's a bad boy to scare me like that. She tells me he's only having fun and he thinks he's protecting us.

I don't want to play with him by myself any more but I think I still love him. After a while. If Nanna does. I go back to playing with him as usual but I make sure the others are there, especially Nanna.

We got a letter from Nanna today. Miss Perryman always reads our letters before we get them. She waits beside me while I read this one. Roger is dead. Nanna is so sad. She misses him terribly.

Dead? We'll never see him again? This time I understand 'dead'. I sob and sob until at last I fall asleep exhausted. Before though, I hear another kid say, 'For goodness sake. What's she going on about? It was only a dog!'

No. I'm not breaking my heart over just a dog.

Nanna's place won't be the same without Roger but it's still Nanna's and there's still a lot to do. Near the back verandah there's a passionfruit vine that grows over a trellis. I like finding the tendrils that curl around things and won't let go. If you force one off, you can't make it straight. Tendrils are the ringlets of the plant princess.

Past the passionfruit vine there's an overgrown path that curves up the yard to an old lattice shed full of rubbish. Nanna calls it rubbish but it's not. We're allowed to play in there but we have to watch out for redbacks and the blue tongue lizard. They're the only colourful things in the shed. Everything else is old, faded and magic, packed so tightly on the shelves that I can't see the whole of anything much. I get my hands on an old doll with an arm missing and only one eye that opens and shuts. She's got a ragged lacy dress. I make her type on the typewriter until the letters all get stuck. Then she has to find the paint brush to flick them back to where they came from. When she's written to Burnside to tell them to be very kind to Kerry and me she can play tennis. The racquet with broken strings will do because we haven't even got a ball.

I like going to the shed by myself best. The others might spoil my games, take things I need and boss me about. I boss the doll about. I do it very quietly so no-one knows I'm here. If my dark father hears me he might come. If I hear him coming, 'Are you there Princess? What are you doing?' I sit very still, very quiet, not breathing, not moving, not answering.

If he keeps coming, 'Princess? Are you there?' I run out as fast as I can, push past him on the path and get to the house, to the safety of company.

Sometimes playing takes me too far away from listening

carefully and I don't hear the darkness coming. I get trapped in that shed. A shadow falls across the doorway and I know I'm trapped. I always hope someone will be with him or that he's just come for a chat. He always starts with a chat but his voice gets thicker and I know the dark father is here. I freeze. He pushes, pushes, crushes my breath away. Thick words fill the shed. And fear. All I can think of is the passionfruit vine. I must get to the vine. I run away as soon as I can, leaving the dark father in the shadows of the shed. I stay quiet with Nanna and the others. Nanna thinks I'm having one of my shy times. How can I tell her my truth?

Inside Nanna's house I'm safe. There are lots of intriguing things to look at but not touch. She lets us go into her bedroom if we ask her and if we promise not to touch anything. I try very hard to keep my promise so Nanna will keep loving me. It's hard to. Nanna's bed has a dull pink satin eiderdown and on it there's a doll whose dress makes a circle of lace all around her. Getting her dress all spread out again when I put her back is always quite a business. The wardrobe has mirrors in the doors and I like looking to see what I can see of the rest of the house through them. I can see who's coming too. Nanna's dressing table is beautiful. It's always the same. Neat, shiny and covered with heavy glass over lace doilies. Above each doily there's a cut crystal container. The two candle holders hold pink candles that aren't ever lit and the matching vase has roses from Nanna's garden. There's a dish, with a very heavy lid that's hard for a small hand to get a grip on. Nanna has brooches in there. This perfect room always smells of lavender.

Nanna discovers me in here and I hadn't asked to come in.

'Come out, Kate. You didn't ask,' she said softly, gently.

Nanna hasn't been angry with me before and I don't know what will happen. I think I do. I think she'll yell at me and hit and shake me, like they do at Burnside. I'm ashamed of myself and frightened. I hide from her. I keep waiting for her to find me and explode but Nanna just keeps being her lovely self, as if it's over. I have to let it be over too. Nanna is always safe.

Elsie's room is next to Nanna's. I'm not sure who Elsie is. She seems to live here sometimes and everyone is proud of her. We're not allowed in her room but I peep in. It's a mess. I don't want to go in.

Photos hang in the hall and I ask Dad who all the people are. He knows some and he says I'll have to ask Nanna about the others. There are lots of Elsie. There's even one of Dad with her and another little girl. Dad can't remember the little girl's name.

Nanna says Elsie is a good swimmer and wants to be in the Olympic Games. I'm a good swimmer too. Could I be in it? They laugh and say I'll have to practise very hard because only the best people in the whole world get to be in it. They don't say I can't though.

Elsie has lots of swimming trophies in the lounge room. They're not as interesting as the piano which we must never play. Elsie has learnt to play it so she can, but we can't. The way we do it is too noisy. I'm very jealous of this Elsie person. Who is she anyway? We met her one visiting day and she called Nanna, 'Nan' and Dad, 'Pop'. I tried calling him Pop too. I liked the Pop Goes the Weasel sound of it, but Dad got cranky and said I have to call him Daddy because that's who he is. He isn't my Pop. He didn't have to get cranky about it. I didn't get to ask him why Elsie's allowed to call him Pop. Then I forgot that I wanted to know.

Nanna always makes delicious baked dinners and if we eat them all up we can have ice-cream with Kiora passionfruit topping. I don't have to be bribed. First, I smell them then I look at them. All the peas exactly the same size, the pieces of potato that could fit together again to make a whole one and sometimes there are pictures in the squiggles of gravy on the plate. I don't spend too long on this examination. Eating is the best part. Then there's the ice-cream. Two perfectly rounded mountains exactly the same size with sunny yellow rivers flowing down them. We joke about passionfruit seeds being dead flies in the river but Nanna doesn't really like those jokes.

One day Nanna asks Kerry why she's not eating her potato.

'I'm saving that 'til last 'cause it's the best,' says Kerry, grinning with enthusiasm.

'If I did that I'd have to leave everything 'til last!' I say.

Nanna is so pleased with us both and Dad is proud. I'm embarrassed. Burnside kids don't judge anything adults do. They get into trouble for insolence, even if they say a nice thing sometimes. Kerry and I didn't mean to judge Nanna's cooking but she and Dad are so pleased with what we said! They don't get insulted. That's when I learnt that it's all right to say nice things to people, some people, even if they are adults. I wasn't game to try it at Ivanhoe though. Not yet.

Uncle Jack comes into Nanna's one day and invites us to go to his house to meet Aunty Lorna. They live next door. We walk down the boring side of Nanna's back fence, through a gate and here we are at Uncle Jack's house! Aunty Lorna comes out to say hello. She seems brittle but her invitation to come inside and have a drink and cake softens her, for a while.

As soon as we're in the house we start dashing about exploring. Aunty Lorna calls us back and says, sternly, that we were invited to sit down at the table and have a drink and a piece of cake. She says don't we know it's bad manners to run around sticky beaking at other people's things?

'Well Nanna lets us!'

'You're not at Nanna's now.'

It's no fun at Aunty Lorna's. We can't wait to get back to Nanna's. We don't ask to go next door again but we go sometimes when Nanna says it will be nice for us to go and visit there. She won't come with us but she'll be waiting for us to come back. She'll have a lie down while she waits.

Uncle Jack has another idea one day. His back yard wraps around Nanna's and his two sheep, Pinkie and Bluey, live there. We've seen them and patted them through the fence. Uncle Jack announces that he's taking Pinkie and Bluey for a haircut.

'Who wants to come?' he yells.

'Me. Me!'

Uncle Jack lifts Pinkie, struggling, into the boot and ties her legs together. I protest but he explains that he has to do it so she'll stay calm on her back in the car and not kick about. Sheep don't go in cars very often, not even for haircuts. Pinkie, looking very undignified, is transferred to the back seat. Next Bluey gets the rope treatment and he's put on the floor in the back of the car. I get in the back next to Pinkie's back end. I haven't seen a sheep from that angle before.

'What are those little black ball things coming out of Pinkie?' They're very neat, all the same size and shape, like peas only black, and they keep coming from somewhere among the wool. Uncle Jack explains what they are. Well, my feet aren't tied together and I'm not going with them.

Uncle Jack roars laughing. He says it's only because Pinkie is nervous and when she settles down it will be all right. No it won't and I'm staying with Nanna!

When they get back, Pinkie and Bluey look so silly. You wouldn't know they were the big, soft, spongy sheep we'd seen before their haircuts. I'm glad I stayed with Nanna. I feel a bit sad when we leave her today but I know she'll be glad to see us in two months time. She'll keep loving me, us, 'til we see her again.

I never imagined living with Nanna. We lived at Burnside and the only other person we might live with was Dad. Our mother wasn't coming back so Dad would have to get another wife or we'd stay at Burnside until we left school. Visits to Nanna would be oases in the waiting time.

In August, 1960, when I'd just turned ten, we got a letter saying that Nanna was dead.

No! She's not. She can't be. She's ours. She's there. She's always there. She must be. Just let me go and look. I'll find her.

I imagine hard, Nanna there at the door in her pinny, as if imagining will make her still be there. They say she's been ill for a long time and it's best that she's gone, not suffering any more. She's at rest now, in heaven. I cry a bit but it hurts so much. I make myself hard and I stop myself feeling. If I don't say the words or believe them they won't be true.

But I know they are.

I harden again and to my grief is added resentment that now I have to wear sugarbag petticoats that are very plain and bloomers whose elastic breaks at will, instead of frilly petticoats and gorgeous gussies from Nanna.

No more Nanna. Now it was hard to feel safe anywhere. We went back to our father's house on visiting days and I became more watchful. I hid away from the dark shadow again as best I could. Where did I belong? With my family on visiting days at Burnside? But was it real? Was the darkness still waiting, even there? I felt it probably was. Waiting for a chance. Any chance.

GETTING BIG

Our gang likes big tough girls. Allegiances can be so fickle but at least I feel I belong here in this gang. This week we like girls who think movie stars are stuck-up numbskulls and we don't like girls with curly hair.

'Crumbs, look at 'er stupid hair. Looks like she stuck 'er finger in the power point!'

'Yeah. Daft kids have got that sort of hair. She's not gunna be in our gang.'

We always like people with new toys.

'Geez. She's gettin' one of them hula hoops.'

'Yeah. She's nice. Let's have 'er in our gang.'

We never like crawlers.

'Hear her tellin' old Perro dinner was nice.'

Unless crawlers get something we want.

'She's allowed to get the record player but. I like her.'

We always like big, strong, tough girls. I'm definitely big and strong. My toughness is only a good impression but the others don't know that. I'm ten and growing fast. When we compare thighs and arms, we admire the biggest ones and I'm proud to show mine. I'm safe in my friends' ignorance about how bad I am inside my big, strong body.

Miss Perryman is in the sewing room where our upstairs lockers are. The sewing room is out of bounds and so we never see what is in our upstairs lockers except when the matrons decide to clean them out. They do this when the new clothes come in. These are second hand clothes that churches send to us. Miss Perryman is sitting at the machine, ready to adjust new clothes to fit whoever needs them and she'll throw out or hand down clothes that no longer fit. this gives us a rare chance to see what clothes we still own.

It's my turn. My locker is fuller than I expected it to be. I'm not allowed to fish around to see what I own so I strain to see as Miss Perryman spreads everything on the table. There are some favourite clothes Nanna gave me; I'm especially glad to see my turquoise shorts and top and my soft winter pyjamas. There's the sugarbag petticoats and bloomers, nice summer nighties, blouses . . .

Hold on. What's that left behind with the boxes of hankies? A shiny box all covered with flowers. It's with my things! It's so beautiful! Is it mine? Miss Perryman holds a dress against me. Who cares about the stupid dress!

'What's that?' I have to know.

'What's what?'

'That box. In my locker.'

'The set you got a while ago.'

She won't be distracted from shoving me and the dress about. If the mood is wrong she'll call me impertinent, whack me and snarl. The machine buzzes contentedly as it's fed the dress, distracting the matron. It's worth a try.

'Can I look at it?'

'Mm. All right,' she says.

I lift the box down. I'm in awe of it. I set it on the sewing table. I don't want to see inside until I've drunk in enough of the box itself but I have to open it quickly before Miss Perryman realises she's given in to me.

I don't know what the things inside are but I'm not disappointed. Two flower pictures inside pink plastic frames with pink plastic handles. They sit beside a big pink comb.

'What are they?' I whisper, almost to myself.

'A brush, comb and mirror,' Miss Perryman mutters as the machine gobbles in more dress.

Brush, comb and mirror. She named them so they're real and she said they're mine so they must really be mine. I lift them out one by one, slowly, inspecting every bristle, tooth and flower. Their perfection makes me frightened of them. Will I damage them so soon because I'm anxious and clumsy? I look hard as if more looking will make them more mine.

'Where did I get them from?' Things as good as this?

'From your Nanna. For your birthday, I think.'

Surely I'd remember this. I scan my memory. Dad always brings us cards and iced fruit cakes with our names on them for our birthdays. His friends from work, the Heatons, always send cards and hankies. Nanna always used to bring clothes that I loved and grew out of and toys that vanished. But I can't remember her bringing this wonderful thing at all.

'Can I have them?'

Perro will say I have no right to ask for things. Even if they're my things.

'No. We'll keep them here. They won't be ruined.'

But they're mine! Mine, not yours.

'When am I allowed to have them?' I want them now. They're mine.

'Leave them here 'til you're older.'

She goes back to feeding the machine without realising how important this is. It's too risky to argue with her.

How could I have forgotten getting this perfect set that's too precious for me to have? I own it even more because I love it so much. I love it so much because Nanna gave it to me. I love it

enough to risk, 'But I'll look after it, in my locker. I won't lose it.'
The machine stops. The keeper of my treasure shakes out the
dowdy dress.

'Try this on.'

I try the wretched thing on. I watch as the dress is put away.
On top of my set. Away. At the back. In the upstairs locker.

'Call Helen up now.'

Miss Perryman, old cat, just doesn't understand how well I'll
guard that set. Not just because it's beautiful. It's proof that
Nanna loved me. That's the meaning of the set, that she thought
I deserved the most lovely thing anyone ever had in the whole of
Burnside. I want it so badly but I have to admit that it's really
safer up here in the upstairs locker.

I'm growing out of my clothes so fast that there won't be many
reminders of Nanna left soon. It's getting colder. I want to cry.
Instead I tell my gang about the set. I grumble and say tough
things to show I'm not upset. I'm angry and one day I'll get her
for not letting me have it.

'Well. Stare off yer little scab,' I spit at Wendy bloody White
whose mother buys her everything, and if it gets nicked, she sulks
and pouts and her mummsie wummsie buys her another one.

Tough girls like us always talk like that when we're angry or
upset. We try to swagger about like the cowboys we've seen at the
pictures. Like Burnside boys. We say, 'shut up', 'fuck', 'shit' and
'up yer bum' as much and as loudly as we can, when the matrons
aren't about. We learn rude jokes so we'll be even more disgusting. Am I the only one who blurts them out despite my fear of
the dark things hidden behind them? I protect my secrets well by
being tough.

When I turned ten I got another secret to keep. I had my first
period. I didn't really know what was happening but I knew
enough to understand that it meant trouble. All that blood! From
down there!

One day I'd accidentally burst into a toilet where an older girl
sat. In the moment before I blustered out again, I saw blood and

bruises. Well, pubic hair that I mistook for bruises, not knowing there was such a thing as hair there. Blood and bruises! Crikey. Something dreadful's happened!

I told my friend Marl about it, to get it off my mind really, not to get answers.

'She's probably got her monthlies. Poor thing.'

Monthlies? What's that?

Marl made it sound ordinary but I didn't want to know about it. I turned away, as I did from all talk about body things, except rude jokes and big muscles.

Today I wake to find blood all over my sheets and pyjamas. I panic.

So much blood! What's happened? Can't let Yatesie find out. Don't want her to know anything about private things, dirty things. I can't help this. Whatever it is. What'll I do?

The bed-making ritual is in full swing. I'll hide it. Yeah. It's laundry day. I'll shove it in among the others. She'll never find it. Pyjamas too.

I bundle the offending things up and sneak them under the mountain of innocent ones to go anonymously to the laundry. There, I've dealt with all the blood.

I should know better than to think I can hide anything from Yatesie. Soon the search for the culprit is on and it doesn't take her long to find out it's me.

'Shayley! Yatesie wants you in the washroom. You're in for it!'

She'll make me talk about rude things then she'll beat me for being filthy. Scrubbing brushes are kept in the washroom and I've never forgotten her warning on my first day at Ivanhoe. There's no escape. I don't want to be dragged by the earlobe so I walk in, slowly, avoiding the old dragon's eyes.

'Is this yours?' She holds up the blood-stained sheet.

'No.'

'Is this yours?' She shakes her fist. The sheet trembles.

'No.' I tremble.

'By Jove! For once in your life tell the truth.' She drops the

89

sheet and throws up her hands. I flinch and wish I hadn't.

Silence. I'm really in for it now.

'It is yours! Don't lie to me.' She's solidly furious but she's holding back. What's going on? Why isn't she belting me? Keep looking down.

'Well. Isn't it?' she seethes.

'Yes.' What's the use? She knows. Wait for a flogging.

It doesn't happen. The coiled spring of her spins away on her black heel. She growls at Analise, 'Go and get her a bag.'

She's gone! I'm stupid. I'm a nuisance but I'm not a filthy thing who's getting belted. No hard, bristly lesson today. Get me a bag? What's that about?

Analise takes me upstairs to the sewing room. She walks straight in as if she does it every day! I've only been in here once before.

I take a quick peep into my locker to see if I can see my lovely set. Yes. There it is. I can just make out a corner of the box. I don't dare touch it. Seeing it there will have to do for now. I gaze around. There are mysterious cupboards and the shelves full of linen. Our mozzie nets are piled like giant ice-creams up to the ceiling. Analise gets a plump, floral bag down from somewhere.

'This is your bag. You keep it in your locker. When you need it, come in here and get it and when you've finished, put it back.'

I follow Analise to find out what on earth is in the bag that's now my own plump little companion, my excuse to visit my brush, comb and mirror set. We go to the upstairs washroom and Analise produces an elastic loop, two huge safety pins and a white towel. She hands them all to me.

'Go in and put this on.'

I go in and hold the things this way and that, trying to work out what the dickens they're all for. The white towel looks like a big flannel. It can't be though because the only water here is toilet water. What do I do? I'm too shy to ask.

'Do you need help?'

'Um. Yes please.'

Analise comes in. Once I know what to do it's obvious. Analise explains that once a month the girl 'on boiling' collects everyone's towels, boils them up in a kerosene tin on the stove and hangs them out to dry. Then she sorts them, by initials sewn into the corners and everyone puts hers back in her bag and back in her sewing room locker. Oh! The bleeding is going to go on for more than just one night, and more than just once! Every month!

Oh well. At least I'll get to see in my upstairs locker.

A couple of years later a lady with a hat, a Yatesie dress and a huge handbag came to talk to us about 'the reproductive organs'. After she's given us a talk and warns us about being close to boys, she shows us a film about very dark things. I shut it out. There are lots of sniggers and nudges that lighten the mood but I'm so confused. Why have they sent us to this bad, dark thing?

Other things the lady says are a relief though. Periods normally happen when you're between twelve and eighteen. I can't wait to be eighteen. They'll stop then.

Next outing day after my periods began my father comes too close. His thick, dark voice mumbles, 'They told me your troubles have started.'

Have I been in trouble? Well only . . . No! Yatesie has told him, him of all people, about my monthlies! How could she!

His hands are squeezing my breasts. His breath mumbles something about no more secret games. I shut down. I examine the hinge on the mirror very closely. I don't understand the words but a confusion of anger and relief fills me. I can't get away because adults have to be obeyed, my father is a good man, I'm lucky to have a father like him, he deserves respect and gratitude and I should . . .

No. No. I won't let you touch me or push me and crush or . . . or . . . or anything. I'm outraged at the violation of my whole being, my body, my private changes, my trust, my feelings. At last anger gives me strength. Strength to shove him back. Away. I hate him. I burst outside and cry. And cry and cry and cry. I want my body to be mine. My own. Private. Not everyone else's business. I want to be clean. Just me, clean and private. And good.

My father never trapped me in the bedroom again. I thought it was because I was so clever at hiding from him. It would be many years before I discovered the real reason.

Meanwhile at Ivanhoe, I diligently embroider my initials on my towels and the months roll on. I take to boiling the evidence of getting big with great enthusiasm. I enjoy the whiteness and symmetry of all those nice, clean towels hanging on the line and the lovely smell of sunshine baked into them.

One lovely day someone whispers, 'Tell you something if you promise not to spread it.'

'Yeah. Promise.'

'Yatesie's leaving.'

'Stringer!'

'No. She's really goin'. I got it from Marlene.'

I don't believe it. Girls leave when they're too old to stay. Analise left last week and I cried, secretly. Girls leave all the time and new ones replace them, but staff just don't leave.

It was true though. She's really gone! Miss Perryman is in charge now. Life becomes a bit more relaxed. Except for Kerry. She's reckless. She seems fearless. I wish she'd stop it.

I'm trying to stay out of trouble. But my first bad time over rude things with Miss Perryman is waiting just around the corner.

'You've gotta go up to the sewin' room. Ma Perro wants ya.'

We've started to relax with her so when I get to the sewing room I'm more curious than afraid. Until she starts talking about my breasts. I'm ashamed to stand here while she says my breasts are getting big, I have to wear a bra, so they won't flop about. I try to shut out chunks of what she's saying, to try to stay clean.

I don't want to know about bras or floppy breasts or what other girls do about theirs. I don't believe it anyway. None of my gang has to wear a bra. Why should I?

Miss Perryman gives me a white cotton thing and tells me to go and put it on. I haven't seen one of these before and I don't know anyone else who's got one. I want to be the same as everyone else. I don't want anything to do with this garbage. I hide the bra behind my toys and forget about it.

A few days later, 'Old Perro wants you in the washroom. You're in for it.'

What now? I creep to the washroom.

'Where's your bra?' Perro-bum demands, almost before I get in.

Oh no. Not this again. Don't look at her. Don't say anything. I shrug.

Angrily, 'Are you wearing it?'

Frightened. Why can't you leave me alone. I don't want to be in this dirty stuff. Leave me alone.

'Well. Are you?'

She moves closer. I don't understand the rage that springs up in me. I look her right in the eye and lie.

'Yes. I am.' This is my body not yours. I don't care what you do to me.

Suddenly she lunges at me, rips my blouse open screaming, 'Where! Where is it?'

I clutch my blouse around me. Furious. Humiliated. I want to belt her to kingdom come! I care very much what she does to me if it's this!

'Go and get it now,' she growls, 'and put it on.'

I do. I'm beaten. I try to work out which way the wretched thing goes, then how to do it up and how to tuck the strap ends in so they don't stick out like banners screaming, 'Big Breasts Hidden Here'.

My lie, my small defiance, has given me a tiny speck of courage. I decide to test it sometimes. I refuse to wear the bra.

No-one will be able to tell. And I'm just like everyone else in my gang. Weeks pass.

'Matron Rogers would like to see you at the hospital,' says Miss Perryman.

I feel rather important. I'm not sick. I don't need treatment for boils or paspalum sores or anything. No. I've been chosen to go and help with work at the hospital. At last I must be old enough. Big kids skite when they come back from work there. I stride proudly up the path, elbowing a few Tara School girls off on the path, testing my new power. Tara is a private school and those girls are such snobs. They think homes kids should walk in the dirt and mud so they can hog the footpath. Homes kids elbow them off and laugh as the snobs get bogged in puddles.

I ring the hospital doorbell. Matron Rogers, her veil all starched and white like angel's wings, lets me in. She doesn't smile. She takes me into the girls' ward. All the beds are empty. She turns to face me, looking very serious. All right. I'm ready to do whatever important jobs she wants done.

'Are you deaf Kate?'

'Huh?'

'Are you deaf? Miss Perryman has told you about wearing your bra. Are you deaf! Didn't you hear her?'

Stomach lurches. Heart sinks. I scream inside. Leave me alone you bloody dragon! It's none of your business. I'm silent, red, enraged.

'She tells me you haven't been wearing it. Why? Why won't you wear it? She's told you why you need to. Didn't you hear what she said?'

Look down. Not at her. I will not be part of this. Leave me alone.

'Come on. I'm waiting! Tell me. Why won't you wear your bra?'

'Because I hate it.' And I hate you. I hate everybody. I hate everything. I hate. I hate. I hate. Me.

I try to look insolent. To be insolent. To protect myself while I break up inside.

Suddenly she lunges at me, drags me into the bathroom where there's a mirror. Red puffy eyes, leaking in the mirror. She rips my blouse open, pushes my breasts about roughly, snarls, pushes me to more rage and humiliation, tells me why I have to wear the bra.

My anger goes inside, pushes out floods of tears to make enough room for itself in there.

'Now do you understand?'

I clutch my blouse around myself, Again. I keep quiet. Taste salt.

'Wash your face. Tidy yourself up. When you go home you're to put your bra on and keep it on. You'll feel much better. You'll look nicer too.' She says this bit softly, like perhaps she's sorry. Too bloody bad. I hate her.

She goes. I cry. I see myself in the mirror. I see ugliness. Everyone can see it, every adult.

I slouch out of the hospital. I want the ground or the air or something to dissolve me. I don't want anyone to see me.

Miss Perryman turns away when I get home. I hate her. I put the bra on. I don't feel better. I feel worthless. I hate everyone and most of all I hate myself and my bad, ugly body.

When I'm with the other kids none of this matters as much. It's adults' judgements, adults' darkness. There's always a kid around to boost me up when they see my red, swollen eyes.

'Don't take any notice. She doesn't know what she's talkin' about.'

'She's such a scab. What would she know anyway!'

'That's nothin'. Anyway, Elizabeth Taylor probably had a bra when she was nine or somethin'.'

Sometimes girls in other gangs eavesdrop and use our painful spots to get us. They do hurt a bit, but never the way adults do. Kids mean to hurt but they don't mean that they're telling you some awful truth about yourself. They're just using whatever they can think of to pick on you and win.

'Is that all you can think of to say! What about your warty bum?'

*

I keep growing, saying goodbye to favourite clothes from Nanna all the time. My favourite outfit is the turquoise shorts with the matching striped T-shirt. They're to be my play clothes for the week. After school I put them on ready to go to the laundry to pick up our linen. My clothes are a bit tight but I don't care. I'm in a hurry to get back for swimming.

We set off past Robertson, the boys' home next door. I can hear whistling but I ignore it. I'm not interested in that kind of thing. The whistling keeps up and we keep walking. The whistler is following us.

'Geez Mrs Shayler! Are they false?' the lousy cretin bellows.

I'm mortified. I know what the little creep means. We know jokes about falsies. Stinkin', dirty sod, shouting all over Burnside. I hate him. I feel naked. Humiliated. I hate this body. And these clothes that show it to boys.

Whoever he is, he must be on his way to work on the farm. He follows us across the road teasing me all the way. I hate him. I snatch the basket from my partner to hide myself. I wish we'd brought two. I walk faster.

When I get home and into my togs, I rip my T-shirt. I know it's awful that I can suddenly hate the outfit I loved so much half an hour ago. I say a quiet 'sorry' to Nanna. I tell Miss Perryman the tear was an accident. She gets me a horrible blouse that fits, that hides me better.

I slouch and hunch around trying to hide my shape, or the shame of it. Mustn't let my dirtiness show through my clothes. It's harder to keep this a secret. Boys can see it and it makes them shout rude things at me. They disgust me.

But knowing boys, the older ones anyway, means you're very sophisticated. It's different to having a boyfriend. It means you know important people, heroes.

Today I need to show off, to flaunt my tough connections. I seize a chance as we walk to school. Ken is standing at the gate talking with some other boys. I'll go up, slap him on the back and say, 'G'day Kenny.' No. 'G'day Block,' will be better. That's what his mates call him. Tough people do that backslap thing. It should look pretty good!

My heart's pounding. I'm glowing. I do what I hope looks like a kind of cowboy swagger over to the boys. One looks at me! I nearly give up. No. I've got to look tough. I keep going, hoping my friends hadn't noticed the falter in my swagger. At last I reach my brother's back. Without giving myself time to chicken out, I slap the back and yell, 'G'day Block!'

The back turns around. The front isn't Ken's! Where's his face gone? Who is this!

'Aw quit it, will ya!' The boy shrugs me off.

I take off. The others are so impressed that I've done it but how they laugh when I tell them who it wasn't. I laugh too. Later.

I keep pretending I'm tough and that I can take whatever comes my way. I usually need to do something tough after I've been in trouble, to prove to myself and my gang that I'm not really hurting. We all do, though we never talk about it. We just understand the need.

MUCKIN' AROUND

'This dump's a slave labour camp.'

'Yeah! And there's laws against that. Kids aren't supposed to be slaves.'

New kids always complain about working all day. Lazy things! All they want to do is muck around. I like playing too but I love work and who cares about the chilblains and warts. I'm really good at work even if old Ma Perro won't pass it when she's in a bad mood. I can polish every doorknob 'til it glows like a magic orb and clean out every skerrick of grease from a grease trap. I can polish the floors 'til they shine like still water and I can scrub a bath so clean that you can see your smiling face in it. The milkman puffs, 'G'day Cinderella', when he dashes through the scullery to the kitchen. He can see how well I clean out soot, sort ashes, chop wood and lift bags of coal into the coal bin. Everyone who walks past Ivanhoe, on the back road that I have swept perfectly clean, can see that I have picked up every single frosty leaf off the lawn, grabbing at them since five o'clock in the morning. Yes, I am very good at working and one day I'll be a really good housekeeper and mother.

The matrons reckon we should only be allowed to play if all the jobs are done. If they're cranky they keep telling you you haven't done it right and go and do it properly. Or they keep thinking of more and more jobs for us and we don't get to play at all.

When we work we try to have fun at the same time. But if the matrons are around we don't let them know that we're playing about like kids, taking each other for rides on our polishing rags or chucking the greasetrap slops at the cows. We rush to turn the radio down when we hear them coming and we stop singing too.

Learning the words to a new song before anyone else proves you're worth knowing because you're very modern and you're clever too—especially being able to do that American accent. Words to songs are like possessions except, of course, that they have to be shared.

There's a record player at the office and whoever gets there first from any of the homes can have it for the weekend. We live closest to the office so we have lots of turns. There aren't many records but we usually get the Anita Bryant. We love her wailing nasally songs. We choose Pat Boone, Dean Martin and Bing Crosby too. We sing along passionately, stopping only to laugh at ourselves or to matron's, 'Stop that ridiculous carry on or you can put that thing away.'

Later we choose Cliff Richard. His songs are easy to learn and interesting. They're about forbidden things like girlfriends and boyfriends.

We get other songs from school. I'm jealous of Kerry. Her teacher, Mr Dengate, knows so many good songs with choruses and excitement. Our class is learning,

Nymphs and shepherds come away,
Come away. Come away.
Nymphs and shepherds come away.
Come, come, come, come away.

Kerry's class is learning about brumbies, stockmen, gypsy rovers and convicts on ships. Our class's songs are not transportable. Kerry's are.

We all like rude rhymes that we whisper at the home but bellow out on the way to the pool or to school.

> *I'm in the army now*
> *I went to milk a cow*
> *The cow let off and I took off.*
> *I'm in the army now.*

Kerry and I make up songs by changing the words to dull ones. Our favourite is one we made up from a hymn.

> *Art thou weary, heavy laden?*
> *Art thou sore distressed?*
> *'Come to me,' saith One, 'and coming,*
> *I will give you rest.'*

One of us puts on her very best sympathetic pose and, almost rubbing noses while peering over the tops of our glasses, sings to the other,

> *Art thou weary of thy gravy?*
> *Art thou sad and dressed?*
> *Come to me you silly ding dong,*
> *Choc blanc mange is best.*

Then we change it to,

> *Art thou weary?*
> *Art thou sad?*
> *Art thou lonely?*

'Art thou mad!' shouts the other without missing a beat. Now we're in fits of laughter. We can cheer each other up like this sometimes.

Kerry and I couldn't be less alike if we tried when it comes to sporty things though. I'm clumsy and awkward, not comfortable in my body but Kerry can do anything. When we go to the playing field it shows. I used to think this place was called 'the playfizz' when I was smaller. It was a good name because we had to go there and get all fizzy inside, like sherbet. Kerry gets like that. She hurls herself at every ride there is. Monkey bars, trapeze, maypole, high slippery dip, lower one and swings. None of them slow her down.

If I play by myself on, say, the maypole, I enjoy the feeling of swinging out free, like I can fly. On the swings, with no-one else around, I can go as high as anyone. I can stand up and lean far, far back, almost upside down when I reach the top of the arc. I swing to the pleasure of the earth and sky, beautifully confused, taking turns at being above and below, above and below the grass! I rock myself into a trance. I could stay content for . . .

'Gissa go, Shayley. Come on. Get orf.'

The magic is lost. I become clumsy and nervous. I find the ground quickly, gracelessly. I can hardly balance much less fly.

We know all about movie stars too because on Saturday nights we go to the 'pichers' at Sargood Hall. Picture nights and what we scrape together from old magazines let us think we know all about these very important people who are like real life princesses and princes except that anyone can be one, as long as they're beautiful or handsome. We play movie stars games and keep scrapbooks. We use flour and water paste to stick the magazine pictures in and sometimes our movie stars go mouldy and stink worse than sour milk. If they survive the glue they're good currency for swaps or stealing.

'Swap ya a Tab Hunter for a cat's eye.'

Picture nights are quite an adventure. We get to go out in the dark and stay up late. Cartoons and The Three Stooges make us laugh and we can't wait for the lion to roar at the beginning of the films. The films are usually noisy ones about war or cowboys and Indians. We cheer for the cowboys to kill all the Indians who are automatically bad. The only way to deal with conflict is to kill those Indians who should let the cowboys have whatever they want or need. Indians never shed blood when they're shot. They just fall off their horses and stay still and clean while the goodies ride off into the sunset.

If it isn't cowboys we're cheering for it's men in planes with English accents. Grown ups at home and at school always talk about things as happening before or after the war. World War II is the main event on their mental calendars. We're often told that Burnside made a proud contribution to the war by evacuating all the children and letting the armed forces stay in the homes instead.

Every year soldiers come to look at Burnside and, because they're almost the only men we see here, we inspect them too. When I first heard that the soldiers were coming, I was caught up in the excitement.

'The soldiers are comin' this arvo!'

'They might bring lollies!'

'They will. They always do.'

The men stood looking at us and we stood looking at them.

'Do you like lollies?' they shouted at last, after all the boring 'Hello's and 'How are you's were over.

Our eager smiles and shouts of, 'Yeah' confirmed what they already knew. They threw handfuls of lollies on the ground and we dashed at them to get more than anyone else. I quickly ripped the wrapper off mine and greedily shoved my prize into my mouth. Ugh! Disgusting! I'm gunna vomit.

Someone said it was because they were rum flavoured but that they weren't all like that. I didn't scramble for lollies again and when I watched the others do it, I got a funny feeling of it being awful to make us grovel about in the dirt for lollies anyway. I was very disappointed with the army but there was still a reason to look forward to their coming.

They were heroes. We'd been taught that war was a necessary and glorious thing whose purpose was to make heroes. I didn't separate dead ones from living ones, young ones from old. Men were heroes if they were in uniform. We were proud that some boys who'd left Burnside had gone to the war and given their lives for their country. Later I realised that 'given their lives' meant that someone had killed them, mangled their bodies and spilled their blood while they screamed in agony, but for now it was as if they just faded gloriously, tidily and painlessly away. We read books about war and teachers talked about their fathers, husbands or brothers who'd gone to fight. The names of ex-Burnside war heroes were inscribed on a memorial outside Sargood Hall.

'What did you do in the war, Dad?' I ask my father.

I want him to be a hero that everyone admires. He becomes uncomfortable. He doesn't want to talk about it. But I want a hero, so I persist.

'I tried to be a soldier,' he says apologetically, 'but I couldn't pass the medical. Because of my eye.'

'What eye?'

'This one. The glass eye.'

I hadn't known it was glass but I was very disappointed that my Dad wasn't a war hero.

Then he told me a story and I didn't know if it was true. I wondered if he made it up so I would have my hero. I wanted to believe him. He said he'd been a spy in World War I and had been very good at it. He said he got Germans drunk at parties and tricked them into telling him secrets, then he told the secrets to England because they were the goodies. He hated Japs and Germans.

I didn't hate the Japs like he did. I didn't even know any.

I didn't know who Germans were either except that we had a cook who was German and she didn't seem like a bad person.

103

Mrs Keller was just strange, a strange little lady with a very stern face, big round glasses, wiry hair and a deep mumbling voice. I think it was mumbling. Her accent made her hard to understand.

Tonight Miss Perryman is off duty. Mrs Keller announces, 'Girls, for you tonight I haff speshull ting. Ven you are bathed, you come to me and vee begin. Yah?'

'Yeah!'

We imagine cakes in bed or the radio turned up really loud or staying up late.

We all get bathed quickly and gather around Mrs Keller who sits like a queen on a chair near Fiona's bed. She has her guitar with her and it has lots of coloured, nylon ribbons hanging from the fretboard. She says she is a famous singer in her country and she wants to sing for us now. We're used to the dormitory having to be quiet so it's very exciting to have the sub-matron telling us to be noisy. No-one will scold and shout and send us back to bed with lights out early.

Mrs Keller places her guitar correctly, pouts sternly and begins strumming. She groans. Thirty girls look on befuddled. Is she serious? We can't tell. She groans and mumbles on, then she adds some swaying to her act. Some resourceful girls get very tired suddenly and just have to go to bed and pull their blankets up over their faces. Those of us who had enthusiastically rushed to be at the front are stuck.

'Now, I teach you. Yah? You learn zeez tings. Listen.'

Mrs Keller tries so hard to teach us some German songs but we're finding breathing hard enough without risking strange guttural sounds that have no meaning as well. We try to be tactful when we say we're very tired. At last our star lets us go to bed. Bible reading and lights out are such a relief.

Special events are organised for us at other times too. Cracker night is definitely the most exciting night of the year. In the weeks leading up to Empire night, a small pile of rubbish becomes a large pile of rubbish and that becomes a mountain. That's how it seems as old mattresses, logs, car tyres and other mysterious things are added. When the mountain is enormous we put on coats and beanies and off we go, all full of anticipation and excitement. We're going out in the dark! More and more kids arrive from the other homes until the mountain is ringed with a buzz of excited chatter. Staff relax and it feels as if they're about to have fun too.

But first comes Mr Ross.

'Oh no, here he goes.'

'Boys and girls, this is a very special night and we are privileged to be able to have it. It's a celebration of the Empire that we are so proud to be a part of. The Empire that our armed forces have lost their lives defending. However, before we begin the celebration here tonight, there are some things you must remember.'

'Yeah. Yeah. Push off will ya. Get the crackers goin',' impatient rebels whisper.

Staff turn deaf ears for once.

Mr Ross reminds us that we're not to get too close to the fire, that we're to stay still while crackers are being set off, that we're not to try to catch any and that any boy or girl caught leaving the fire will be in severe trouble. Tension builds. Can't he be quiet and get the crackers. Why would big kids want to go away from the fire anyway? They'd miss all the fireworks!

At last the big boys light the fire and soft 'ohs' and 'ahs' begin, punctuated by, 'Geez. What a stink!' Complaints like that aren't real complaints. They're just a safety valve that stops excitement boiling over. As the mountain is licked by flames, tension mounts. The crackers. Get the crackers!

Crackers left by parents are put in with those donated by church people. Kerry, Ken and I get to keep the sparklers Dad gave us and share them with friends. I hate choosing who to give them to. Some people will have to miss out and they'll be cranky. This isn't the kind of night when you want people to be cranky with you and threaten to get you later. I don't want anyone to miss out anyway, especially not me.

From the big box of crackers come bungers, double bungers and jumping jacks, all meant to scare the wits out of you. Some kids scream, some laugh and some little kids cry. Most kids glance around at the staff to watch them jump out of their skins. We laugh 'til our sides ache.

We have rests from the noisy crackers when the beautiful ones are lit. There are cartwheels that spin around leaving a trail of stars as they whirl and there are Roman candles like fairy volcanoes. My favourites are sky rockets that whoosh above us, exploding in a burst of stars that I hope will fall near me so I can catch them. We start singing,

Catch a fallin' star and put it in your pocket.
Never let it fade away.
Catch a fallin' star and put it in your pocket.
Save it for a rainy day.
For love may come and tap you on the shoulder
One starless night . . .

After the crackers we wander home exhausted. Bleary eyed little kids dawdle to bed thinking only of sleep but big kids are too excited to sleep. They have plans for tomorrow.

The boys who get up really early to go to the dairy always detour after cracker night. They collect all the fizzers and all the crackers that were accidentally dropped. They glean most of the worthwhile remains. They know how to take out the gun powder and make new crackers that they can let off whenever they like or sell to other kids. Us girls try, usually in vain, to find something worthwhile because we can use them in swaps or give them, with embarrassed smiles, to our boy heroes. They could be thank-you presents for protection in the playground.

I'm grateful to the big boys for something else too. Burnside has lots of Scottish things, like the names of the homes and the things they arrange for us to learn outside school. Boys can join the pipe band and girls can learn highland dancing. I love both.

The boys practise playing drums and bagpipes in Sargood Hall on Saturday afternoon. They practise marching up and down our back road. Mr McLatchey is the band master and he's very impressive roaring out orders to the boys as he swings a shiny stick around without dropping it or hitting anyone.

I like it best when they practise in uniform. Then they are magnificent. They wear kilts with sporrans, coats with shiny buttons and lanyards, long socks with little ribbons near the top and black shiny shoes. Best of all are the big fluffy black hats with chin straps that seem to squash their mouths shut, unless they're pipers, of course. I feel so proud of our boys as their kilts swing in time to the music as they march up and down the road. It's amazing to see them all so neat, clean and orderly. They look so grown up and tame. I wish we didn't have to make fun of their knobbly knees and hairy legs.

Us girls do highland dancing. It's hard but I love it. We learn lots of steps and whole dances too, the Sailor's Hornpipe, the Highland Fling and best of all the Sword Dance. 'Real' swords are reserved for those who learn all the steps well, so we practise and practise with wooden swords and learn that dance more quickly than any other. The real swords are kept in scabbards in a dark cupboard under the stage. Oh, the excitement when the sword box is dragged out. You grip the handle of your chosen weapon firmly and pull the blade out through the glug of Vaseline. The handles have lovely lacy guards so if it's used for fighting, your hand is protected.

We'd really like to play sword fights but if we do, Mrs Trenary will ban us from using steel swords and then it's back to wooden ones. As with folk dances at school I'm intrigued by the patterns we dance, looping at corners and crossing diagonals with loops in the middle and so on.

Anyone who shows talent can stay back for extra lessons and go in competitions wearing a kilt and frilly blouse, a velvet jacket, long socks and pumps. I'm so jealous of Heather. She's lithe and graceful and points her toe perfectly. Her movements are tight and tidy but they flow to just the right beat. She never loses her place or her timing. Us clumsy girls giggle so much when Mrs Trenary is watching us dance, we can only just make it from corner to corner without thinking about steps and beats as well. Tripping on the steel swords is so much noisier than tripping on the wooden ones.

People visit us more often these days to do good works and then they go. Even though we might have liked them, we try not to get too attached because they never stay long. If they promise to come back you shouldn't believe them because they probably didn't mean it. They just didn't know how to say they wouldn't be back. It was easier for them to leave us waiting for their return than to simply say they wouldn't be back. They didn't have to see our hopes fade to disappointment as we waited for them in vain. Mrs Perrin is different. She tells us she's visiting from Canada so she'll come for eight weeks and then she'll be going home. She wants to teach us how to march and twirl a baton. She gives us a demonstration.

'Geez. Look at that! She must be a movie star.'

'Talks like one and she's got lippy and nail polish and that.'

'I'm gunna do it.'

'Oh yeah. You're gunna be a movie star too are ya?'

'Yeah and get those really tight slacks and frilly blouse.'

'Come on. She's calling us.'

The baton thing is hilarious. When we try to do it as well as practise being glamorous we're hopeless. Chucking sticks around while we're trying to march in lines in our imaginary sleek slacks and long painted fingernails is beyond us. Girls get clobbered by sticks falling from the air or coming at them sideways. Girls who aren't even in it are blowing up when they're assaulted by batons that try to escape from us marchers. We manage to really upset the lady from Canada by having too much fun.

'Mrs Perrin has very generously given up her precious time

for you. You should be grateful. What an opportunity! But are you grateful? No. All you can do is behave like a pack of lunatics! Like ungrateful wretches!' . . . blah, blah, blah. 'Those girls who don't want to learn can just stay out of the way and let those who do have some appreciation of what a privilege . . .' blah, blah, blah.

Next week when Mrs Perrin comes to try again, hardly anyone goes for lessons. We'll have a better time playing together or watching the girls who decided to keep going with the marching. Miss Perryman just about begs us to go. She's so desperate that some of us say we'll do it. As long as we don't have to march as well as do those twirly things we're right. When Mrs Perrin says goodbye and returns to Canada, we feel sad. She was nice and we knew that she meant us to have fun and be more refined than we normally were. We don't want to be drum majorettes but some of us definitely want to be more refined—like her.

Mucking around with other kids was much better fun than being with adults. The expressions of the childhood we craved often clashed with adults' sense of what was right for us. They couldn't just let things flow. They had to organise and supervise and interfere. They had to judge everything and they usually found us wanting. They didn't know how to just muck around.

OUT TO WORK

When we were older, about twelve, we were sent out to work at the office, the hospital or the little kids' homes. The best thing about this work was that it got us away from Miss Perryman, whose temper could still explode at any moment. While I was out working I was exposed to new ways of thinking that showed me that I had some rights that had to be respected. I learnt to see that there might be some goodness in me too, although I wasn't always a great success at this kind of work.

The office next door to Ivanhoe wasn't far but in some ways it was a world away. Here were the people who gave permission for parents to visit, who The Church People went to before they inspected the homes and to whom really bad kids were sent to be punished. Very important people worked in the office. Into their world I took my nervous clumsiness and my painful shyness. I was thoroughly intimidated by their greatness.

My first job is to get their afternoon tea. Miss Brogan shows me how to boil the jug, how to make a pot of tea and where the big red Arnotts biscuit tin is kept.

'Mr Ross likes white tea with one sugar and give him a Scotch

Finger and a Nice. Mr Hardie has black tea with one sugar and two Morning Coffees. They're the thin, plain ones and Mrs Simpson has coffee . . .'

Uh. What comes after Mr Ross likes . . . ?

'Carry them carefully, won't you. No-one likes soggy biscuits,' Miss Brogan smiles then she leaves me to it.

Soggy biscuits. That's all I remember. No-one likes soggy biscuits. I make a nice cup of tea for everyone. I give sugar to some. Oh, I'd better make a cup of coffee and give that to someone. They're all getting two of whatever kind of biscuits my hand lands on. Perhaps they won't notice.

I carry the tray to each desk. I deliver the tea and what might still be recognisable as biscuits if they grab them quickly. Everyone says a cheery 'thank you' but they don't repeat it when I collect their cups and their saucers full of soggy brown stuff later. The cups rattle their way back to the kitchen where I wash them and pack them away never to see them again. I don't get many office duties.

Everyone likes hospital work. Most people don't mind Matron Rogers but it's better when she's not there looking over your shoulder. At last I'm old enough to be the hospital girl and I wander up the path on Mason's Drive, silently arguing with Tara School girls coming the other way. I don't push them any more. Not often. Tara girls are pimps. They can get you into trouble. Anyway some of them look nice too and you can't be sure if you're shoving a nice one or a snob.

The walk to hospital takes a while. Over the bridge across the creek, past the farmer's cottage and past Ross Home where the big boys live. Sometimes we see them and they wave to us. This part of Burnside is surrounded by bush. It's so quiet. The only sounds are the wind in the gums and the wonderful song of a million magpies.

Matron Rogers meets me in the clinic, looks me up and down then tells me what to do. I don't like her but working for her is easy. After she gives her instructions she goes away and leaves me to it. Sometimes when she comes back to check your work, she says, 'Good.'

I like the clinic. Everything smells clean and is neat and organised. All those shiny silver dishes on the trolley, piles of perfect white gauze squares, big paddle pop sticks for ointment, scissors and tweezers, jars of ointment, bandages and dressings. All so clean and in place. The dirty, bloody, pussy things have a special place too, away from the rest. Matron Rogers always reminds me to wash my hands. That's good. I get to muck around with her taps that you turn on with your elbow so your hands can't dirty anything.

It's better when Nurse Elly is on duty and Matron Rogers is off. We all love Elly. We don't have to call her Nurse Elly. Just Elly. I'm too shy to talk to her but I watch and listen, fascinated. She's young, cheerful and so alive. She tells us jokes, sings top forty songs, chews chewy or bubble gum which she offers to us.

'We're not allowed to have chewy.'

'I'm not gunna tell, am I? Spit it out on your way home. Anyway, what's the matter with it?'

'Yeah, what's the matter? Thank you.'

Elly teases her hair up and wears combs to hold the frizzy mountain in place. She talks about bodgie boyfriends, dates, Holdens, rock n' roll, milkbars, romantic movies, bobby socks, rope petticoats and so on. Rumours spread about boys pretending to be sick or purposely hurting themselves so they can go to the clinic and flirt with Elly. Matron Rogers is always cranky with her and that makes her even more popular.

If I don't have to roll bandages and tidy up in the clinic, I have to go to the wards to make the beds, with proper hospital corners, and finish them so there isn't a single crease or lump to be seen. The steel cabinet beside each bed gets dusted and a towel gets put exactly in place.

After I finish at the hospital I wander back home too late for any Tara girls to challenge on the footpath. Usually there's time to skite about what Elly said that day and then the dinner bell rings.

Sometimes I go back to Reid Home to work. When I first go

back I remember what the staff thought of me when I lived there. I haven't thought of the words or events for a while but now impressions all come creeping back. Mrs Henderson's betrayal, Mrs Grable's certainty that I was filth and Miss Thurland's hatred. I'm filled with dread as I walk back there with Maureen. She's a scab who no-one likes.

'You go in first,' Maureen whispers.

'Why? You go first. You're the eldest.'

'But she hates me.'

'She hates me too.'

'Does not.'

'Does so.'

'Come on. We'll just go together then.'

Maureen knocks timidly.

'Well. Don't just stand around out there. Get in here and get on with your work.' The familiar snarl brings back an old churning in my stomach.

'Arfnoon Miss Thurland.'

That's all Maureen gets out as she bolts through the kitchen, through the dining room and away. I try to follow, stunned that anyone would dare run in Miss Thurland's presence.

'You get back here, whatever your name is.'

Maureen's nowhere in sight so she must mean me. She inspects my face and recognises it.

'Oh, so you're back, are you, whatever your name is? How dare you run off like that? You stay right here.'

Oh no! A whole afternoon alone with her. I wait for instructions.

'You're not here to stand around, you bludger. Get your apron on and get busy.'

'Where are they?' my trembling small voice squeaks.

She snatches an apron from a hook behind the door, throws it at me and turns her back. I stand waiting.

'What are you standing there for? Get to work!'

'What do I have to do?'

With a mighty huff that could have knocked the pumpkin off the table, she asks me what I think the pumpkin is sitting there for. I shrug and then the pennies drop.

'Where are the knives?' I mumble.

'Oh, get out to the scullery and see if you know how to stoke the heater, you dolt.' She's had enough of me for a while I suppose.

'Where is it?'

Another mighty huff and she screeches, 'You've just walked past it, you fool!'

Out the door. What a relief! I prod the warmth, slowly.

'Get back in here. I didn't tell you to watch it burn.'

She tells me to peel the vegetables that she's laid out on the table. She's angry when I still don't know where the knives are kept.

Later she presents the pumpkin.

'Do you think you could cut this up in time for dinner? Or is that too much bother for you?' She thrusts a huge knife at me. 'And look out if you cut yourself.'

I start cutting the pumpkin. I can't really see. I'm clumsy anyway but my tears and my shaking hands make things worse. Next time I come here, I'll bolt through the kitchen like Maureen did. I don't care what the other jobs are or who they're with, I'll do them, as long as they're not near Miss Thurland.

Sure enough I cut myself. I have to hide the blood and keep cutting. I work slowly, turning the pieces with blood on them so it won't show. Miss Thurland jeers about my being so slow but I just plod on. When the pumpkin is all cut she barks at me to wash it. What a relief! I get the pumpkin into the water before the dragon can see how badly it needs washing.

Next she tells me to go to the dining room to set the tables. I'm so relieved to be getting out of her dungeon, but I'm not prepared for the shock of being in this room again. In the stillness, away from Miss Thurland, I stand and look around. The same deep loneliness that I'd nearly drowned in on my first day here sweeps over me. I stand with a full tray of spoons and forks and I sob.

'Now what's the matter with you?'

Fear of the dragon gets me moving, drives away the loneliness. I know how to set tables. There's comfort in the regular slow dropping of spoon and fork, spoon and fork. Each place is set perfectly to mirror the one opposite. Each table exactly the same. I know I've done this job well but now I have to return to the dragon.

The afternoon passes in misery. I'd rather face Mrs Henderson and Mrs Grable with my past shame than work for Miss Thurland again, ever.

The next day Maureen and I walk back to Reid.

'I'm not doing the kitchen today. You can.'

'You sap! I'm not doin' it!'

'I did it yesterday so you have to today.'

We argue all the way to the scullery door. When the dragon roars, Maureen rushes in, dashes through the kitchen and escapes again. So, it comes down to who gets through the door first, does it? Through the afternoon misery I make my plans.

I'm ready for Maureen the next day. I don't let on. I knock, wait, look calm. When the dragon roars I shove Maureen out of the way and escape upstairs to the bathroom. Ha ha. Made it!

There's a new woman working here who doesn't know me and Mrs Henderson doesn't seem to recognise me. I keep my head down. In the bathroom I gaze at the fish on the walls and something warm stirs in my memory. I don't quite recognise it, then it's gone. The mermaids, the treasure chest and the starfish are still here and I smile about them and about my anonymity. I'm buoyant, peaceful, nearly floating. I wash the nameless little body of a girl in the bath and she smiles at me.

'I have to do that,' Maureen announces beside me.

'What?'

'That. Bath 'em.'

'Do that one. I'm doing this one.' I'm content and in charge.

'You have to do the kitchen,' Maureen sounds triumphant.

'What?'

'You have to go down.'

'No. I'm not doing it!'

'She said you have to. It's not my fault. She doesn't want me. I told you.'

My heart sinks and my stomach lurches. There's no arguing with the dragon. I want to poke Maureen's eyes out and box her stupid ears. I go back to the dungeon.

'How dare you go running off like that. Think you can leave that useless idiot here. You're no better. Get out there and get your apron on,' the dragon roars.

Everything I do is wrong. She roars about my hair, my clothes and especially about my thongs and how their flip-flopping about the place drives her mad. I'm an idiot, a wretch, a dolt, a tramp, a bludger. I'm sloppy, slovenly, filthy, useless, lazy and stupid.

None of my faults put her off making me work with her though. Whoever goes with me to Reid Home, Miss Thurland always makes me stay in the kitchen while the other girl goes up to the bathroom.

There's just one exception. One morning I go to work at Reid and Miss Thurland doesn't need any dolts to help. My work is changing the beds in the dormitory and bundling up the linen ready for washing at the laundry. By now each home has a washing machine so that emergency washing can be done there rather than waiting for the laundry to do it.

'Take the wet sheets downstairs to the laundry. We'll put them through the washing machine,' says Mrs Henderson. She's fed up that she still has to deal with little bed wetters.

This washing machine isn't like anything at the big laundry. It's a nice tidy white box whose top opens up. I cram the sheets in and read the words around the dials. Geez, what's all this? Which one do I do something with?

'What are you doing?' demands Mrs Henderson.

'Putting the sheets in the machine.'

I keep my head down.

'What are you doing that for? You can't put wet sheets in the washing machine! They're to be rinsed first, in the tub. Don't you ever listen to what you're told!'

'I thought you said we had to wash them in the washing machine.'

Still with my head down, wondering what a washing machine is for if it isn't for washing.

'You thought! You thought! That's the trouble with you, Kate Shayler. You always think too much. You always have.'

That's how Mrs Henderson lets on that she knows me.

I'm hurt at first by her criticism but as I rinse the sheets I realise that I don't care much that it was a criticism. I'm intrigued by who I am and was. I am a person who thinks a lot. I like that. I think a lot. They tell us at school that thinking is good and I've been doing it since I was a little kid. Without even knowing it! Mrs Henderson had raised a speck of confidence in me, even though she hadn't meant to.

My next challenge comes from working at Troup, the other little kids' home. I'm very anxious about going there. It's a new place. I'll be disoriented. I'll meet new people. I'll have to learn new rules and do new jobs. New things always scare me. I'm so painfully shy of adults. I don't trust them to be fair or predictable. I'm sure that whoever the staff are they'll make the same judgement of me as Miss Thurland has.

I'm even worried about these little kids at first but they don't care who I am. They seem to like me so I start to like them too. Except for Larry Hindmarsh. He makes me anxious. Larry Hindmarsh talks about rude things all the time. Tits and doodles and bums. He bashes and bullies the other kids and he's always in trouble. He pretends to cry when he gets scolded but as soon as the matron has gone, he's back to his old tricks.

Larry is being really bad today. I'm helping kids get undressed for their baths. Suddenly Larry grabs my breast and pinches it really hard. I'm stunned. It hurts. I whack him to make him let go. I'm shaking, sore, embarrassed, confused, wondering what to do. I feel violated but it seems ridiculous that a four-year-old, a little kid, can do that. I'm a big kid! I'm thirteen!

I don't want to tell on him. Pimping seems so cowardly and anyway, how can I talk to the matron about it? She probably won't believe me. She'll think I'm dirty. Perhaps Larry won't do it again. But the little wretch has found a weakness so he pinches and punches me as often as he can. I'm always furious but I feel powerless. Apart from the occasional whack I give him to make him let go.

All this ends when another little kid, who can't believe her eyes, tells on Larry.

'Kate, is it true?' Lindsay's matron asks.

I have to tell her now.

'How long has this been going on?' she asks gently. Gently!

'He always does it.'

'Oh Kate. Why didn't you tell me?'

What can I say? I shrug.

'Heavens! Having your breasts pinched! You don't have to put up with that. Not from Larry, not from anyone. You must always report things like that. Don't just accept it. It's not good enough. It's not right, is it?'

Isn't it? Must I? Should I? How? I'm so confused but she was forceful.

No. It isn't all right, is it! But how do I say it? Would you believe me if I found the words? You might just say I'm being dirty. But you don't think it's dirty talking about breasts like that. Breasts, not tits. You think I should be treated well! I should expect to be treated properly. I have the right to control who does what to my body. Do I? I don't know.

My head is so full of new ideas but I'd better get back to work. I can't just sit and think. It's another speck of confidence for me though and it's soon followed by another.

We've just got home from Reid and we're talking about what happened there today. I'm telling the others about all the names

Miss Thurland called me and how horrible she was. Miss Perryman walks by. I stop talking. Mustn't let her catch me criticising staff.

'What did you say?' she asks.

'Nothin'.' I'm not saying it when you're here.

'It was about Miss Thurland, wasn't it?'

'It's nothing.'

Mind your own business. I wasn't talking to you.

'You said Miss Thurland called you something. What was it?'

'Nothing.'

You're not trapping me. I'm not telling.

Miss Perryman is getting irritated too.

'If she called you something, I want to know about it. I won't stand for it.'

Won't stand for it! What's it to you?

'By Jove Kate! Tell me what she said.' 'By Jove' means she's about to blow up. 'You don't have to put up with it.'

Since when? Better tell. I choose one word, still not trusting.

'Bludger,' I mumble.

'A bludger! Ye gods and little fishes! How long's this been going on?'

'Ages,' I mumble, and shrug in case it's not that bad.

'The hide. How dare she! Bludger indeed! We'll soon see about that.'

Now she's volcanic. She's furious, but not with me! Could she be angry with Miss Thurland?

'What is it? A bludger?' I risk the question. I'm confused and I need to understand.

She tells me it means you're lazy. You always take things you don't deserve. You expect other people to pay your way. I still don't get it.

'But I don't pay.'

'No. But your father does. There isn't a finer, harder working man. Oh, he always pays his way, all right. He's not one to go asking for charity.'

Now I get it. To call the daughter of a hard working father a bludger is an insult to him. I feel very proud of my Dad and I'm amazed that Miss Perryman is so passionately against the insult. She's genuinely offended. She says she won't tolerate anyone speaking like that about him. She says she'll report it to the office and she storms across the lawn.

She comes back and says she doesn't think we'll have to go to work at Reid Home for much longer. I'm relieved but I'm anxious too. We don't trust things that go our way. There's always a cost to wait for. Will we be called liars after a while and have to go back to that dragon and cop more insults?

We wait but there's no cost. It's real. We never go back to Miss Thurland's dungeon.

So specks assemble that make me feel better about who I am and what I deserve. Perhaps I'm not entirely bad any more.

HAPPY FAMILIES

Kids are coming and going constantly now. They come from broken families then leave with step-fathers or mothers to make new families. Family is what everyone else wants and I want one too, one where I can live happily ever after, like Elizabeth from school. I'll have a lovely room like hers with all those beautiful things. That's what families are. Yes, I want one too.

Whenever girls leave we go through a ritual of wishing each other luck, promising to write regularly and the one who's leaving promises to visit as often as she can. I cry when some girls go, secretly, and I hold on to their promises. Some write or visit but most don't, probably because they're having so much fun. I wish I could get out. Only Kerry and I and a few others seem stuck here.

New girls ask, 'What are you here for?'

''Cause my mother's dead,' I reply.

I say it without feeling anything and they seem surprised. Well, why should I be sad? It was ages ago and it's like we never knew each other, my mother and I. I don't remember her and I don't try to. She just doesn't matter any more.

I hope my Dad gets married again though, like other fathers do. He doesn't seem to have any lady friends, except Miss Perryman. Yeah, Miss Perryman! She's in love with him. Everyone knows it. We've seen it in the love comics we read under our blankets.

Sometimes my father touches Miss Perryman on the arm when he talks to her and she looks up and smiles. That means they're in love. Sometimes he kisses her on the cheek. How embarrassing! He even greets her with a hug and a kiss! In front of everyone! She beams smiles for him that she never has for any of us! When Dad drops us off after visits, they stay chatting on the doorstep for ages. When we stay at Ivanhoe on visiting days she gives him cups of tea. No-one else's parents get that. And she's always saying that he's a real gentleman with such fine English manners. I'm very proud of him but why does she have to draw attention to the two of them carrying on like that. It feels sort of dark.

It's so embarrassing and confusing! It makes me friends with the enemy. My gang doesn't like Miss Perryman but I'm beginning to. Dad says she's nice and good.

'Ma Perro's gunna be the Shayler's mother. Ah chunder! You'll hafta be such a pimp then!'

'Mr Shayler loves Ma Perro! Let's write it on the wall!'

I want them to be in love so they'll get married and we can have a family. Dad talks to us all the time now about when his three Ks come home to live and be a family.

Everything will be perfect then. Is Miss Perryman our chance for that? But what if she's mean all the time and what if I lose all my friends.

There are worries in secret places of me too that I don't want her or anyone to know about. I can't remember details of the dark thing there but it's about Dad and being alone with him. It hasn't happened for a few years now and it feels like it might have been a bad dream I had, not a real thing that happened. It feels like it was a long, long time ago. When a memory starts to surface, I get scared and panic. I bury it away and divert the energy with other busy thoughts, practising spelling lists or reciting birth dates of everyone I know. Memories come less often. I think I used to have nightmares about my father being very bad and dark. About a dog or something.

What if Miss Perryman marries Dad? What will that mean? I don't understand where the boundaries of light and darkness are in the muddle of relationships. That love stuff is something to do with people marrying and setting up families, so something about it must be all right. So many questions wander about in my mind.

'Dad, are you going to marry Miss Perryman?'

After he gets his breath back he says, 'What made you say that!'

'You always kiss her an' cuddle her an' that.'

'Ah no, Princess. Your Dad is just so grateful to Miss Perryman for looking after my precious girls. That makes us friends.' He pauses to chuckle. 'No, we'd never get married.'

He sits quietly for a while then adds, 'There was only one . . .'

Then he stops. He realises that I'm still listening.

That settles it then. There won't be family for us with Miss Perryman. The others can tease all they like. What do they know about love anyway? At least I've learned something about the difference between love and friendship.

Soon there's another possibility for getting a family. A rumour starts spreading that the reason for The Church People coming is to let them look us over before they decide who they'd like to buy. If they like the look of you, they pay for you at the office and take you to live with them. The official name for this is 'adoption'. It's in the dictionary, so it must be true. The Church People adopt kids like I buy lollies from Mr Duncan's store.

The Church People are coming today. Those of us who want to be adopted try to look angelic and nice and pretty so they'll adopt us. I'm not very confident but I try my best to be tidy, tuck in my bra straps properly and smile nicely. The buyers smile back but they leave without plans for anyone. I'm disappointed.

I tell Dad about my hopes for adoption. I don't understand

why he's so upset, angry almost. He says it makes him so very sad to hear me saying that I want to be in a different family. His eyes glaze over and he goes on and on.

'We are a family. My three Ks and me. I'll never, ever let anyone split us up. That's how Norma would have wanted it.'

I remember that Norma was my mother but she isn't now so what's it got to do with her?

'But we don't live together like families do.'

'One day we will. When you all finish school we'll be home again, together. We're still a family while we wait. You mustn't ever, ever wish you could be adopted. You've got a family. You're Daddy's Princess. You're one of my three Ks and that's how it will stay.'

I like to hear him say I belong but as he hugs me, too tight, I don't feel safe. His hands are trembling. I know he loves us and doesn't want anyone else to have us but family seems so far away. And our family doesn't feel like the sort everyone else is getting.

Shirley from Dunkeld Home was adopted and she's gone to live at Villawood. They called hers 'fostered' but it seems the same as adoption. Her mother is going to visit her at Villawood. Why can't we have that and Dad could still visit but at a different place? I don't talk with Dad about this any more.

We discuss adoption openly at Ivanhoe. Miss Perryman hears us and tries to sort us out. She can't. We can see what's going on. After a while they get a social worker to explain adoption and fostering to us. She assures us that we're not for sale and that we'll only go to another family if Burnside and our parents think it's best for us. My hopes are dashed. Our father will never let us go.

My father's happiness is my responsibility. Kerry and I are told constantly that we are the reason for our father keeping on working into his seventies when most men have retired. We give him his will to live, they say. So I try to think of ways to keep him happy.

I tell him I can't wait 'til I'm sixteen so I can go and live at Marrickville. When our visits to his house are over I tell him I wish we could stay. This is a lie though. The mistrust of the dark side of my father is intensified at the house. I have to work hard to chase off the memories when I am there. But for now it's safe to tell those lies. I'm still at school and I'm trying to keep my father happy.

Zelda is at Dad's house today. I remember her vaguely and wish she'd go away. I still don't know how she fits into our family. She and my father speak to each other with a brittleness that I have never heard in my father's voice. I react to harsh voices in my usual way. I stay outside. If I get too close to the window I hear Zelda shouting. She's still there when the taxi comes to take us back to Burnside. She's there when Dad comes out with us to say goodbye. I'm glad she will see how I show Dad how much I miss him and how I make him happy.

'Dad, I don't want to go back. I want to stay with you.'

Zelda's slap across my face stings!

'Don't talk to your father like that,' she snaps.

I'm stunned. No-one has ever slapped my face. Not even Yatesie or Miss Thurland. Now a witch who I hardly know has stung me deeply. I'm furious and confused. The red smarting spreads across my face and down into my clenched fist. I want to beat her up more than I've ever wanted to beat anyone up before. To beat and beat and never stop beating her.

Who is she anyway? Nobody. Yes she is. I hate her. I want to rip her guts out and . . .

My father steps in and gently but firmly tells me, 'Goodbye, Princess. It's time to go.' A gentle kiss and he guides me to the back door of the taxi. 'I'll see you in a month.' A gentle push towards the seat. 'Be good 'til then. It won't be long.'

The taxi drives off filled with my hatred for the witch-woman who turns up sometimes, hurts people, then disappears. What's she doing there arguing with my father and upsetting him anyway? She doesn't live there and she's got no right to hit me.

Miss Perryman tells me that my father has collapsed and can't come next visiting day. She doesn't look in my eyes for long, but

I see the red in hers and the tears. I'm anxious.

He always comes. She never cries. What's happening?

I follow her up the front stairs, where we're not allowed to go. I need to understand, need to hear her say that I didn't hear her properly, that my father will be coming.

'He's collapsed,' she gulps.

'Why didn't he get up again? Did he hurt himself? Why can't he come?'

Miss Perryman turns around to face me.

'Your father has been working much too hard for a man his age. It's not just a matter of getting up. He's too sick to get up.' The red in her eyes intensifies as she explains, 'He's completely exhausted, Kate. He's an old man and the doctor says he needs a long rest. That's why he can't come.'

He's not old! He's my father! He can come. He has to. My fear turns to anger. He's just too lazy and selfish to get up and come and see us. He's just going to leave us here without him so he can have a sleep!

Cold fear drifting around. I'm about to be nobody. A nobody who doesn't belong to anyone. Visiting day comes but Dad doesn't. Why am I so frightened? This isn't how it will always be. He'll be here next time.

Miss Perryman is very kind and gives me and Kerry special jobs to do to keep us busy. But she has her own work and, anyway, she can't replace our Dad. I take my anger, or is it my fear, out on Kerry. Why does she have to hang around me all the time? Every time I tell her to shove off, she comes back again and hangs around. I wish she'd just piss right off and let me be . . . be . . . alone. She keeps forcing my emptiness out in the open. I keep trying to be alone where I can push it down, pretend it isn't there, stop it obliterating me.

We're all very glad to see Dad next visiting day. When he arrives he kisses Miss Perryman and thanks her for looking after his precious girls again. They talk about grown up things for a long time while Kerry and I stand around waiting to tell him we

126

missed him and we hope he's all better.

Since his collapse, Miss Perryman has been doing more favours for Dad. One in particular makes me more uncomfortable than all the others. She asks if he can have special permission, because of his frailty, to use our toilets instead of walking all the way to the school. I pray that they'll say no. I'm worried about the dark thing that I can't quite see any more, the dark thing that might come here too and scare my friends. Besides he's not frail. I don't see why he needs that privilege. The office people don't give permission. I'm relieved.

Miss Perryman suggests that I take my father to the school to make sure he's all right. I refuse. She won't make a scene in front of Dad. I can't tell her why I'm being so mean. I study my father as he goes off alone. He doesn't exactly walk. He shuffles along, slowly. His back is bent over so far he seems to be looking for something he's dropped. He does look frail. I ache with the guilt of not being willing to help him. I'm ashamed of my fear of him. I try to fix things.

'Why do you walk with your back bent over, Dad?'

'Oh. I can't get it straight any more, Princess.'

'Why not? Can't you just stand up, real straight?'

'Well now, let's see.'

He stands up and with his hands on his hips, he stretches his shoulders back such a tiny little bit.

'How's that?'

'It's not very straight.'

'It's the best I can do, love. Unless you think you could stretch me out straighter.'

How can there be a back so bent, so unable to get straight? I stand behind Dad, hold his shoulders and gently try to force his back straight.

'Aah. That feels good,' he sighs and pats my hand. 'But I don't think we can get me any straighter. My old back's got some bad bones in it, you see.'

'Does it hurt?'

'Only sometimes,' he grins. 'I'm all right. Don't worry about your Dad. You just worry about getting through school and coming home so we can be a family again.'

But I do worry about him. I'm afraid of his bad back that can't straighten and I'm afraid of his frailty. I need him to be strong, like he's always been. I bury the fear inside and hold on to that part of my father's strength that I feel will always be safe and sure. His love, the love that makes me somebody.

I ask him later on if he's old. He laughs and asks me what old is. I don't know.

'Tell me what an old man—old codger, they say don't they—tell me what an old codger looks like.'

I describe a white haired person with a beard, who can't hear or see very well and has a walking stick. Dad laughs again and assures me that he's getting a bit old but he can still hear, his good eye can still see and, although his hair is white, he doesn't have a beard. I say I like beards and I wish he had one. I don't know why I like beards except that old people with beards might be kind, like Santa Claus was when I believed in him.

Next visiting day Miss Perryman calls me to the front door. She says I've got a visitor who she doesn't recognise. I'm scared at first. New people always worry me. At the door there's a very old man with a white beard that reaches down to his waist.

Who is it? A swaggie? Why does he want me? What should I do? Why is Miss Perryman telling me to come and talk to a stranger?

Just as I recognise the familiar string bag, my father rips the beard off, chuckling at his joke, bewildered by my fear. He thought I would have guessed it was him straightaway and that I would know, as soon as I saw it, that the beard was made of string. He shows me how he put it on and teases me for a while before he puts the beard away in his string bag and we go to the seats in the shelter for his visit.

'Mr Shayler has permission to take the girls out next Saturday.'
'Mr Shayler has permission to visit the girls on Saturday.' These

memos come from the office every month. They have for years. I'm so proud of my Dad. He always comes. I don't mind that I'm not a princess any other time because I am when he's here.

Miss Perryman reads out the memos after tea. I listen intently. I always do even though I know ours will be there. She gets to the end. She hasn't read ours! My father has suddenly vanished. In a flash I know he's dead. He was old and frail and I can't deny it any more because now he's dead.

Panic. Pounding heart. Trembling chin. Sobbing voice. Mine. Blurting out, 'What about us?'

I can't help it. I don't want to be nobody.

Miss Perryman is stunned. 'You know your father always comes. Do I have to read it every time?'

Inside I scream, Yes. Yes. Yes. You bloody well do have to read it! Every time. Every single time. Read it. Go on. Read it.

Outwardly I try to look composed. All I can sob is, 'Oh.'

I keep crying with relief, with anger. Relief that I still belong. Anger that she could play such a cruel trick, even if she hadn't meant to. She should know I need to hear my memo. I'm embarrassed that I let them all see me cry. I feel foolish. I feel all of this but most of all I feel incredible relief that Dad is coming. He isn't dead and I'm still somebody. My Dad is indestructible.

To save my father having to come and get us, Kerry and I go by taxi to his house on outing days now. Although I enjoy going away from Burnside, being at the house is getting boring. There are lots of things I want to look at but Dad watches over them and says that we can't have them until we're older.

He's not looking now so I take a little grey book out of the sideboard. 'Treasured Memories' it says on the cover. I open it up and find a yellowing piece of paper folded between the pages. I leave it 'til later and begin to read the first page in the book.

'So Dear Mrs Iyfod and Harily, Mishing you she . . .'

The running writing is too hard to read. I turn over to the next page and find a poem.

Oh. It's grand to have a pal like you,
One who kind a'knows a fellow through and through;
When days are dull and gloomy,
And I'm feeling sort a'mooney
I just pause awhile,
Reflect awhile,
Then smile awhile,
Cos' I know I've got a pal like you!

It sounds goofy but it's friendly so I keep flipping through the book. Every month has a page, every page has a poem and dates with names written in. 'Pop Manson, Jean Iylord, Zelda, Kate . . .' and so on. Some of the handwriting is Dad's, recognisable from the letters he sends between visiting days. Some is different. A stranger's hand.

I go back to the folded paper. I start reading, 'A few weeks after Norma died, Kate said to me one day: Daddy, is Mumm . . .'

'Give me that,' my father says. He takes the book and paper away. 'You're too young. You won't understand.' His shaking hand replaces the paper and he locks the little book away.

'But it was about Kate. Is that me? I just wanted to read . . .'

'You wouldn't understand, Princess. You can look at it when you're older.'

I'm offended. I want to look now. I'm really very mature. I don't want to upset Dad so I'll leave it for now but I'll remember where that book is. I'll find it and understand it another time.

Dad has forbidden us to look behind the doors of the dresser in the dining room but now we're getting more daring. He can't hold back the tide of our curiosity. He tells us the things we find belonged to our mother. We can tell he doesn't like talking about her. I don't mind. I just want to look at the jewellery because it's beautiful not because it was hers. There are no emotional connections. Dad says when Kerry and I get bigger we can have it all. I can't wait, so I take a piece every now and then. Kerry does too. I want to own beautiful things now but whatever I take to Burnside gets pinched. I finally stop taking things when I realise that if I keep it up, there'll be nothing left for me to own later.

There are only three people in the Sydney phone book with our surname. Two are listed under C. Shayler. Dad and someone else. Dad doesn't like us to play with the phone but we do anyway. It's the only one we can muck around with. He doesn't like us answering it either. But we do.

'Hello.'

'Hello. Can I speak to Mrs Shayler please.'

'Mrs Shayler? She's dead.'

'Oh no. When?'

'A few years ago.'

'Who are you?'

'I'm Mrs Shayler's daughter.'

'Is this Cecil's house? Is this the Tempe house?'

'No. It's Charley's.'

'Oh. Please get Mr Shayler.'

My father rescues the person on the end of the line. He's always distressed and he muddles about and tells them about the other people in the phone book who have the same name and initials as his.

'Are they our relations?' I ask after he hangs up.

'No. We haven't got any relations.'

'Why not?'

'All my brothers and sisters stayed in England.' My father tells me he lost touch with them all when he came to Australia. There had been about twelve children and he could remember most of their names; Annie who died, Bill, David, another Annie. They lived on Lord Derby's estate outside Liverpool where his father had been a gamekeeper. He keeps calling England home and he says that's why he talks funny. I've never thought to ask if our mother had any relations. Mother was a word, not a person.

*

131

I still hope Dad will marry someone one day. My hopes are boosted when Mrs Fitzpatrick, who lives down the road, starts coming to visit when we're there. I like her. She's small and she's got a deep gravelly voice and a rich Scottish accent, like the people on Dad's records. She tells us what some of the words mean and she likes that music too. Sometimes Mrs Fitzpatrick gets snappy but most of the time she's cheerful, matter of fact and she likes jokes.

She tells us to call her by her first name, Alice, but we tell her we're not allowed. We're not even allowed to know adults' first names! She says Fitzpatrick is her husband's name and she doesn't like him any more so she doesn't want to be called by his name. This is incredible! Mothers and fathers always live happily ever after don't they? In love comics they always love each other forever. The idea that they might stop loving each other is unbelievable. Anyway we know we shouldn't call Mrs Fitzpatrick Alice, so we compromise and call her Mrs Fitz instead.

I wish Kerry would get it right. It's not Mrs Fritz. She makes me blow up the way she gets it wrong all the time. You have to get words right, especially names. If Dad is going to marry her we should call her by the right name.

Mrs Fitz always cooks frankfurts for lunch. We love them and the best part is the Fountain Tomato Sauce. We only get it about once a year at Burnside so here at the house we let the fountain spurt oceans onto our frankfurts to make up for the drought. Years later, Kerry and I joked that you could tell a person who'd grown up in Burnside by the amount of tomato sauce they put on everything.

Dad and Mrs Fitz didn't marry but she came to the house for a few years. When she stopped coming I missed her. My father said she was too old now to walk up the hill. I asked him why he didn't marry her and, again, he was stunned.

There was never another Mrs Shayler so Kerry and I would stay at Burnside until we finished school.

When Ken didn't appear one visiting day in 1964 I asked Dad where he was. Dad told me Ken was at home. He'd been expelled because there'd been 'some trouble' and so Dad felt lucky to have one of his k's at home early.

I knew I didn't know my brother very well any more but I was sure he wouldn't have done anything bad enough to be expelled. It must be a joke. The next time we saw Ken was at Dad's house and he was happy and free. He said he'd kicked the house master's dog and refused to apologise and that was the cause of the trouble that got him expelled.

Ken was back in our family. But he felt like a stranger, this brother of ours.

HIGH SCHOOL

'Katherine Shayler,' the voice droned through the microphone.

No-one answered. We stood waiting for our names to be called so we'd know which roll class we were in for our first year of high school in Carlingford. There were homes kids, posh Carlingford kids and the lot in between who were from family houses and the migrant hostel. To us homes kids, they were all called 'outsiders'.

'Katherine Shayler. From Burnside Central. Does anyone know where she is?'

'Hey Shayler! It must be you. Go on. It must be.'

'Nah. They said "Katherine". It's not me.'

Oh heck. The surname's mine. Might be me. Better go in case it is.

'Shayley doesn't even know her name,' someone teased.

'Yeah. And she's s'posed to be brainy too!'

'Oh well. See ya.'

Try to swagger. Look tough. Talk about embarrassing! Fancy not knowing my right name. Katherine? Where'd they get that from? Geez. What if it's not me? What if they call me later?

This morning we'd done our work quickly, washed and dressed in our new school uniforms for the first time. We'd grumbled about the stupid panama hats that were like nothing on earth and the scabby green and white striped dresses. And what about the bommy gloves, awful brown ones that made your hands sweat and made you drop your school case. I secretly liked my crisp new uniform but I didn't tell. I needed the security of group grumbles.

We set off to the bus stop meeting other homes kids on the way. We each had our exact bus fare in our pocket and we knew what to say. 'A weekly, please.'

The driver didn't say much, not to anyone. As we got rowdier, his silence let us think we could do or say whatever we liked. There were no staff watching to judge or punish. Our driver was bald and his head seemed to be just an extension of his neck except for the shiny dome at the top and the ears that stuck a long way out to warn you that the top was coming. We christened him 'Pin 'ead'.

'Eh Pin 'ead, don't stop for that lot! Ah, go orn, keep goin' ya sucker!'

Tough kids like us weren't nervous about the new school. We'd always thought we were going to do high school at Burnside Central but the high school department had been closed. We now had to go to Cumberland High, a new school at Carlingford.

Inside I felt abandoned, frightened of the high school, of the strangers I'd meet and all the new teachers. I was frightened of the bus trip, where to get on, where to get off. I worried about what subjects to do and about all the things I didn't know how to worry about properly yet, but that would come up for certain.

On the bus our differences as homes kids screamed louder as more and more outsiders got on with immaculate uniforms, perfect plaits or long, curly ponytails adorned with pretty, satin ribbons. They have shiny new school cases and they take their bus fares from wallets into which they put their change, ready to spend at the canteen. They're calmer, more quiet. We'll be outnumbered at high school and we'll be the smallest.

Waiting in the school playground for the first bell takes forever. Outsiders meet up with old friends, skite about Christmas presents, boyfriends and holidays, plan outings and sports club memberships, whisper behind their hands and point at more lowly beings who are alone.

At last the bell goes. Everyone gathers in the quadrangle. We spot a few teachers who've transferred from Burnside. I hope they see us and wave. That will mean we belong here as much as they do. No-one waves. Their friendly smiles and chats with new teachers are betrayals.

'Roll classes will be formed now, so wait quietly until your name is called. You will then line up with your roll class teacher.'

1A names are called. None of us are in with that brainy lot. We whisper insults about them. I had been brainy at primary school. Although I'd been among the last to be chosen for sports teams, I'd always been near the top in brainy things. Not now. None of us are in 1B or 1C either.

I must be somewhere up here. Have they forgotten to put us on their lists? Are we at the wrong school? Nah. Homes kids'll probably get called out separately, after everyone else.

'Suzanne Smith.' Suzanne walks to 1D's line. I don't know her.

'Marion Thomas.' Another stranger joins 1D.

Then Katherine Shayler. What if it isn't me? I strain to hear which other Burnsiders will be in 1D. No-one. I'm alone. Better listen to see if they call me, Kate, for 1E or 1F or worse. They don't so I stay in the 1D line. I hope none of the strangers in my class noticed that I hadn't known my name.

As we're taken to our roll call room, I note every landmark so I won't get lost. Us Burnsiders didn't think to plan a meeting place for recess. I don't want to miss them and be alone then as well. I'm the brainiest Burnsider. I don't know my name. I'm lonely.

'Welcome to 1D,' Mr Dillon says. Everyone stops chatting.

'First I'll mark the roll and we'll check your details, then we'll talk about being at high school.'

Our teacher reads out names, addresses and dates of birth. Those for Katherine Shayler match mine so I settle on being her. Mr Dillon peers over his glasses for too long when he reads my name. He's thinking, 'Ah yes. The dunce who doesn't know her name.'

This day is a blur of anxiety. We have to choose what subjects we want to take. I want to take whatever my friends want to take but they're not here. Will I do Art? I'm good at drawing the horse that I've copied hundreds of times from the *Girls' Crystal Annual*. I might get to be in Miss Morgan's class. No, Mrs Dengate now. She was at Burnside and she teaches us Life Saving. I like her, so I choose Art. That's the only subject I'm sure about. I choose the rest using less than academic means too. Home economics? That's just cookin' so I'll be able to do that. We have to do Maths and English and either history or geography. History's just tryin' to remember a whole lot of dates and names so I choose geography.

I can remember very little of what teachers tried to teach that year. I would learn a more enduring lesson from a new friend, Karen McGuire.

I keep looking for Burnsiders in the playground but it's hard to find them among all the strangers. Because I like learning, I don't really fit with Burnsiders when they skite about muckin' up in class. I don't want to be in it. I don't want to be in trouble at school. So, as far as friends are concerned, it's as if I live in a different world at school.

I'm isolated. I need a friend to tide me over 'til home time when my Burnside friends will be there, laughing and showing off as usual, and I won't mind. I won't be alone.

At last a new Carlingford girl makes friends with me. Karen doesn't know about the stigma of being a homes kid but she knows about the stigma of having a stutter. It makes her very shy. It's our failings that let us become friends.

We look for each other at recess and lunch. We talk solidly, often with no hint of the classroom stutter or shyness. We talk about anything that comes into our heads, except Burnside stuff. I tell Karen bits of it but then I feel ashamed and I stop. We talk about school, what Karen did on the weekend and she updates me on the latest episodes of TV series. She can't believe there's a person on earth who doesn't watch TV. I can't stop pretending I want to know about everything she watches. It's better than sitting by myself.

I'm happy when it's just the two of us but Karen starts taking us to groups of outsiders. She hangs around at the edge, sometimes stuttering her way into conversations, because she wants to make friends with them and be accepted into weekend sports teams. I hang around because I don't want to be alone. Lonely.

After school every day, I wait at the bus stop checking a hundred times that I've got my ticket, then that I'm at the right bus stop and that the kids I'm with are all the right kids for my bus. As the bus pulls in, I check a hundred times that we're getting on the right one. At last, inside the bus, I can stop worrying and I enjoy the safety of my friends.

We accept each other as we are. The boys don't tease me as much now. Mostly they leave me alone, but I know they'll be there to stick up for me, or any of us, if we need them. Losing your bus ticket can be catastrophic. We don't get pocket money so buying another ticket is out of the question. You just have to walk, be late and be in trouble at each end of the day.

'Come on, Shayler. Get on!' the boys shout through the back window. They always push on to the bus first so they can sit at the back and shout insults at the driver. They tell him how to drive, how he looks, who to let on and off and where to stop or not. They skite about the trouble they've been in, which teachers they've told off and how they've gotten out of doing homework or detention. When the teacher on bus duty insists that girls be allowed on the bus first, we know to leave the back seat for the boys.

Now they're keen to get going and I'm holding them up. Can't they see me frantically searching through my pockets and my case while the last few people get on?

'What's up?' Stonehouse asks through the window.

'I can't find my ticket,' I hiss.

'Here y'ar. Quick. Take it!'

A hand appears out the window offering a ticket. I snatch it and get on, my face glowing like a stop light. I'm terrified of getting caught. I can't wait to give the ticket back.

'Nah. Not yet. Wait 'til we get off.' Now it's Stonehouse's turn to hiss. 'Pin 'ead might see.'

On the way home I find my ticket in my school bag.

Kids lose their tickets every now and then and it gives the more enterprising ones an idea. If only a few people buy tickets and pass them through the window to the rest, we can spend the rest of the bus fares at the canteen. Those who want to be in it can take turns. I don't want to and that's all right, if I don't mind a bit of teasing. They reckon I'm becoming a goody-goody anyway. I don't want to admit to them that it's because I'm too scared of getting into trouble.

I don't want to tell them that I steal money either. That's my secret and, although they'd be proud of me if they knew, I don't want them to know. I'm ashamed. On outing days I steal money from my father's work coat that he always leaves hanging on a hook behind his door. I always leave some for him, copper pennies and halfpennies mostly and the threepences and sixpences too. I take the shillings and two bobs. If I asked him, Dad would probably give me some but we're not allowed to ask him for things. I'm ashamed of stealing from him, especially after he told me that one day whoever took the money hadn't left him enough for his fare to work. But the lure of having canteen money is too much. I keep taking it if I get the chance.

A few kids try the bus fare scheme in the first week and they don't get caught. Soon after though, the bus company introduces different coloured tickets for boys and girls. This is a minor setback and the scheme picks up again with girls and boys syndicates. A bus inspector appears one afternoon and calls for all tickets to be shown at once. There's so much fumbling and passing of tickets behind the inspector's back, under seats, in left-over lunches and through the air. So many kids say they've lost their tickets. He knows something's going on. The game is up. The bus company refuses to take Burnside kids on its buses.

Now Mr Hardie has to drive us to and from school every day in Burnside's mini-bus. Our first few trips are very quiet. We know why we're here and we're expecting to be in more trouble than the telling off we'd got in our various homes. Those of us who weren't in it should have pimped on those who were they said. No we shouldn't! There's much less mucking about on the mini-bus because Mr Hardie is second in charge at Burnside and he won't stand for any nonsense. He has the knack of calmly telling anyone, before they get too bad, to stop behaving like a lout and they do. He's lighter, so the louts are lighter too. Mr Hardie is a busy man who leaves in the mini-bus at eight-twenty sharp and if you're not ready, you walk.

Miss Perryman is in a really nasty mood this morning and I'm copping it. She refuses over and over again to pass my work. I do it over and over again, perfectly, but it's never good enough. I don't know why she hates me so much today. At last she snarls, 'Get ready for school. It'll all be waiting this afternoon.'

I rush to get changed but it's impossible. I can't see through my rage and tears that Mr Hardie's waiting. The others are all on the bus.

'Get the rest of your things and get. Gorn, move yourself. Mr Hardie's waiting.'

I don't have time to wash. I grab my shoes, stockings, tie and case. I run for the bus in bare feet. Mr Hardie shuts the door as soon as I'm in and drives off. I try to pull up my stockings and hook them to my suspender belt without anyone, especially the boys, seeing. Girls are sympathetic.

'You done it good an' she knows it. She's just pickin' on ya.'

'She'll probbly do it to me tomorra.'

Danny Barber, who has as much tact as a thirsty blowfly, laughs, 'Hey! What's Shayler up to?'

'Shut up, Barber. She's in for it.'

'Oh. Poor sheila.'

Even Danny the Dope shuts up.

I watch out the corner of my eye to make sure the boys aren't looking. No, they're not. They're looking thoughtfully out the windows. I like them just now. They aren't often that sensitive. I'm loaded with emotion. I cry a bit. It lets some of the anger and hatred out. I hate Miss Perryman fiercely. Next time she does it I'll make sure I miss the bus completely. I'll walk.

Apart from the case full of textbooks and the panic about being late, I like walking to school. It's a long way but it's nice to be alone with a purpose, to walk along thinking my own thoughts and being who I want to be. Walkers are likely to meet King's School boys on their way to school. They look like mini soldiers with their slouch hats and heavy blazers with red epaulettes and braid. Some kids reckon they're worse snobs than Tara girls, so they're fair game to be nudged off the path. They don't seem to mind where they walk though, so I don't bother testing them. I feel sorry for the tiny, little boy soldiers. They look lost inside their great heavy coats, their baggy shorts and their big shiny shoes. They look as if you could fold them up and put them inside their own school satchels.

I look in people's yards if they're not around and I listen to the magpies in the high gums. I peer into cars to see what sort of people are in them and I pretend I'm bushwalking and sing softly to myself the songs we whisper when the matrons can't hear.

Ask your mother for sixpence,
to see the new giraffe,
With pimples on his whiskers,
And whiskers on his
Ask your mother for sixpence.

I swing my case along and make up silly rhymes too.

When I get to school, Karen is often practising on the basket-ball court. Sometimes I watch, fascinated by one girl in particular. We all are. Mary Zen is the first Asian person I've seen. Her whole face smiles when her heart does and that seems to be all the time. Mary is a genius with a basketball. She can toss goals from anywhere on the court. She spins the ball on her hand and lofts it skyward with an effortless flick. The ball goes exactly where she wants it to. Every aspiring basketball player is jealous of Mary's magic. My friend Karen is but she never says so.

'Um. I c-c-can't meet you at l-l-lunch today.'

'Oh. Why?'

'I'm t-t-trying out for the b-b-baasketball team.'

'Oh.' Try to hide the disappointment.

Karen makes it into the school basketball team and that means we can't meet on practice days. I sit by myself then, unless I find a Burnsider.

After a few weeks Karen says, 'I c-c-can't meet you for l-l-lunch any m-m-more.'

Any more? What do you mean any more? You can't mean any more! At all!

'How come?' Try not to sound desperate. Disguise it with a very modern TV phrase.

'Well, I w-want to be in the Saturday team so I haave to be friends with them.'

'But we can still be friends at school.' I hate the squeak in my voice.

'But if I'm f-f-friends with you, I c-c-can't be friends w-w-with them.'

'What?'

'I have to h-h-hang round with them so they'll l-l-let me on their team.'

I know what she's saying: 'Carlingford people don't make friends with homes kids. You're not as good as us. You might contaminate us.' But she can't say the words.

I turn away. I go away. By myself. I hurt. I cry. I hurt more and cry more. I can't stop. I pull myself together to get into class but I can't hold it. There's another flood of hurting and crying. I'm sent out to see my class tutor who's supposed to give us advice about personal problems. I've never talked about personal problems before. I didn't know I had any. Until now. Now I'm desperate. The only thing I can think about is that Karen has rejected me. I'm alone because I'm not good enough. I've got to find someone who can make this right, who can stop it hurting. I can't stop it myself, no matter how hard I try.

At the staff room door, I take a deep breath and knock, not loudly enough, but wanting someone to hear.

'Can I see Mrs McAlpine?' My good manners are gulped down with sobbing.

'She's very busy right now. Can you come back at three?'

'No. I . . . I can't wait that . . .' Words disappear in great sobbing gulps.

'Oh! You'd better come in and sit down,' Mrs McAlpine's voice says from the other end of the room.

I bluster past teachers who'll be able to hear what I'm saying. I don't care.

'What's the matter?' Mrs McAlpine asks softly.

'Karen McGuire won't be my friend.'

It sounds so small as the magnitude of it overflows into the tissues my tutor hands me.

'These things happen at your age you know. You'll meet other friends.'

She doesn't understand how serious this is.

Mrs McAlpine waits.

Is that all? Am I meant to feel better now? To be comforted, ready to leave?

'But I . . .' I have to stop. I blow my nose, noisily.

'Don't worry. You seem like a nice person. You're not an axe murderer are you? You don't have two heads do you?'

'No.'

It's not funny! It hurts. You've got to make it stop.

'Then is there any reason why you won't find other friends?'

Yes there is. I'm shy and I'm ugly and . . . and anyway I don't want other friends. I just want things to be like they were. Karen and me.

'But she was my friend and now she says she can't be.' I struggle to find a way to ask how I can make myself good enough. Mrs McAlpine struggles to see why I'm so upset. There's a gaping chasm between my hurt and her understanding. I try to fill it.

'She won't be my friend 'cause she wants to be in the basket-ball team . . . 'cause I'm a Burnsider . . . 'cause they can't be friends with us . . . 'cause we're homes kids.'

'Oh dear. I see. You're from the homes and this friend of yours isn't.'

The chasm starts to fill.

'Yeah.' At last. Now, tell me what to do.

'Well you can't do anything about being from the homes can you?'

'No.' Oh please, hurry up and say something to make the hurting stop. Tell me what to do. Don't say there's nothing.

'Well!'

Well what? I just look at her, waiting for the answer.

'Well. It sounds as if she isn't worth worrying about. Do you think she is, if she suddenly stops being your friend because you're from the homes?'

I shrug. I don't know how to think like that. It sounds right. Karen isn't worth getting this upset over if that's how she is. But it doesn't take the hurt away. There must be more to it. It still hurts!

Mrs McAlpine thinks she's solved the problem. The evidence is that I've stopped sobbing. I'm busy thinking, while I sniffle, about how to process what she's said.

'Now, you'd better go and wash your face and go back to class. You can come and see me again if you want to. And don't worry. You'll meet other friends.'

The idea that someone isn't worthy of my friendship is so very new. It's different to proving your worth in a gang. It's not how we do it at Burnside. Something tells me that what Mrs McAlpine said is right but the hurt makes me keep doubting. I feel so lonely and worthless. I had a friend and a space where I belonged and now I don't. I'm a nothing, a nobody at school.

I feel as if everyone's watching and thinking, 'There's that scabby homes kid. Look at her. No-one wants to be her friend. Always by herself. Hope she doesn't sit near me.'

The rest of the year is awful. I get through some classes because of mutual dislikes and mutual humour that helps us cope. Music is like that. We're all there because we had to pick an elective. We thought music would be easy, a bit of a sing then go. It isn't. Most of us have no understanding or interest in analysing pieces. To compensate for our lack of talent we rewrite meaningless silly songs:

> Down yonder green valley,
> Where streamlets meander,
> I first met that dear one,
> The joy of my heart.

to rich and thoughtful pieces, not much appreciated by our teacher.

> Mrs Chalmerson's a bunion,
> She looks like a pickled onion,
> Her legs are like clothes pegs,
> As straight as can be.

I'm in my element here. The art of picking out distinct physical features is the basis of teasing at Burnside and my love of words and rhymes helps too. Kids like my playing with words that help express our frustration and those with similar interests band together. Laughter is the common language that joins us, at least for a while, at least in class.

As soon as the recess and lunch bells ring, I'm lonely again. If only someone would say, 'Come and sit with us' or 'Want to come to the canteen?'

Sometimes I meet up with other homes kids and get relief but most of the time I'm alone. The others have set up their own routines and assume I'm still hanging around with Karen. Instead I'm hiding on the seats around the back of Building 2 where less active, more quiet groups sit. This is a good place to be alone. It turns out to be a good place to find just the right friend too, but not until the next year of school. This one stays lonely except at home.

At home I think I might be becoming happy.

CHANGES

We're putting new stores away in the pantry.

'Good morning, girls. How are you?' a posh voice says gaily from the window above.

Don't answer. It's a grown up. Some church tart probably. All stuck up and posh. We giggle and swallow the sultana's we've pinched. She'll think we can't hear down here and she'll go away and leave us to try our luck with raisins or jelly crystals or . . .

'Good morning, girls,' the voice tries again.

Pretend not to hear. Who is she anyway?

'Good morning, girls. I'm talking to you down there.' Louder and more pushy.

Better answer. She's just gunna stand there all day saying it.

'Morning.' Now go away and let us get on with what we're doing.

'How are you?'

Hasn't she got anything to do? What's she want?

'Girls! I asked you how you are?'

Oh la de dah! Yeah well. What's it to you? Might as well answer or she'll just say it again.

'Good.'

'That's good. Now, would you tell Miss Perryman that I'm here, please.'

As if we've got a choice! I tell Miss Perryman there's a lady on the porch who wants her. I don't know who she is.

A few minutes later Miss Perryman does a very strange thing. She brings Miss Tarlton, the lady from the porch, to introduce her! To us! She's just come to work at Burnside, we're told, and she wants to meet us and get to know us.

I don't get it. Is it a joke? It doesn't seem to be. What does she want to meet us for? What do you have to say to her?

Miss Tarlton asks us what we were doing when she interrupted us and what we like to do in our spare time and what we like best at school. Staff just don't talk to kids like that!

What do you say? What are the right answers? Will there be punishment later if we don't get them right, if we disgrace Burnside?

Miss Tarlton keeps smiling and looking at us when we speak. Looking, she is, right into our eyes!

Soon after that, a group of university people come with folders and lots of questions. They choose some girls and not others to answer their questions. The chosen ones are told to tell the truth when they're asked questions by the folder lot. The folder people promise that whatever kids say will not be repeated to anyone. We don't trust them. Whenever we complain about anything, it gets back to Miss Perryman and we're always punished.

I want to be among the chosen so I can find out what the questions are and what it's like trying to answer them but I'm not chosen. I'm so curious that I put myself in the way of the folder people sometimes, hoping they'll decide to ask me something anyway. One day I succeed. A lady is waiting for someone else to come and she starts chatting with me.

'Hello. What's your name?'

Aha, easy.

'Kate. Katherine really.'

'How long have you been here, Kate?'

Yes. I know that one too.

'About ten years.'

'My! That's a long time. Do you like it here?'

Uh oh. What do I say now! I don't know the answer. Not the true one. I know 'yes' is the right one. But what's the truth? Sometimes I like it and sometimes I don't. It doesn't matter. This is where I live. Anyway I haven't got time to stand around chatting. I have to go.

'It's all right,' I mumble.

Then I'm off. I'm so jealous of girls who know how to sit with strangers and answer their questions truthfully.

The chosen kids tell us afterwards what the questions were. Do you like living here? What do you like about it? What don't you like? What things do you get into trouble for? Do you think it's fair? What do you wish you could change? Very dangerous questions these.

Some kids reckon they told the people what they really think about being a slave and coppin' it every day and eatin' slops. They expect to get into trouble for what they said. They wait but no-one gets punished. It seems that those folder people have kept their promise. They must have liked us.

Miss Tarlton seems to enjoy talking with us, or trying to. It takes a while for us to trust her and stop worrying about her friendly, personal approach and all her questions. Whenever we bump into her she has a cheery word to say or another question. She never just ignores us. We think she might be a bit loopy.

One night Miss Perryman says she's going out to a meeting of all the matrons. We have to behave ourselves for the new sub-matron. She never goes out at night. I try to imagine what the matrons would have to talk about. Nothing comes to mind. Miss Perryman says that some experts are coming to talk about how to make changes so that living here will be better.

Make it better? How? What are they changing it for? I don't like changes. What if the experts say everything's wrong? What if

149

they make us change everything and we don't know how to do it?

I want to stay close to this. If I watch it happen I won't get lost in it. Miss Perryman says she might be able to tell us more when she gets back. She doesn't seem to want changes either.

When she comes back she talks to us about what they wanted her to try. They want her to be more like a mother so we can be more like a family! To start with, instead of calling her Miss Perryman, we have to call her something else.

What else? We call her lots of things behind her back but what else is there to call her to her face. She's Miss Perryman. No-one else.

'Have you got another name?' I'm too unsettled to hold my questions back. I want answers about how to do this changing thing.

'No. Well, yes. My first name.' Oh yeah, as if we'd be allowed to call you that. Wonder what it is though.

'What is it?'

'It's Valerie,' she says a bit shyly.

Aha, now we know your secret. But why did you tell us! It's not our business. Is it?

'But we're not allowed to call you that!' Make sure she knows I'm not being insolent.

'No. That's not what they meant. They just want us to think of something else instead of Miss Perryman.'

'But that's your name.'

She explains that in families people don't use names like that and that's what we're trying to be like. A family. Miss Perryman and some of the other kids come up with possibilities. There's Miss Perry, that's more friendly. Or there's Mum Perry. That means she's sort of instead of our mothers. If we want to, we can call her Mum. No-one says anything about that. I don't think she really wants us to call her Mum. Or there's Aunty Valerie.

Choosing the right name is such a challenge. We have to think who she is to us, who we are to her and how we all fit together. It causes a lot of discussion behind her back.

'Aunty Valerie sounds like goin' to the dunny!' someone whispers. We say we're going to visit Aunty Val when we're going to the toilet sometimes.

'Yeah. Let's call her that well.'

We decide Aunty Valerie isn't a safe name. We might giggle too much at it. I'm glad we reject it.

Girls who don't like her say they'll call her Old Ma Perro. Or Ma Perroscab.

Some of us think that Miss Perry is just shorter and so it's really just the same. Some girls choose to call her that anyway.

I think about the name for ages. I want to get it right, to find a name that shows the relationship properly, now that the question has come up. Miss Perryman isn't going to be my mother. I don't need one but I want a mother so I'll be like other people, people in families. The five years I've spent with her at Ivanhoe are beginning to mellow the relationship I have with Miss Perryman. I don't hate her as much and sometimes I even like her. I want a name that means all that. If she's going to try to be more like a mother, then she should have a name that means that.

I choose Mum Perry. The self-consciousness of giving a name to all my secret hopes takes a while to get over. So does the teasing but after a while this becomes the most commonly used name.

In an effort to be more motherly, Mum Perry invites us into her room. Now she's in the one Yatesie had, and it feels like going into a new country, with a stranger.

It's a nice, tidy room but it isn't warm and rich like Nanna's or like I thought all old ladies rooms would be. I don't dare look too carefully because it's bad manners to sticky beak in adults' things. I might get into trouble and be sent out.

Mum Perry show us a picture of a young woman walking down the street. She's wearing a suit with a long tight skirt, high heeled shoes and a hat with a long feather in it. She says it's Valerie Perryman. Her! We don't believe it but we've got sense enough not to say so. The woman in the photo is young and lovely and her arms are thin, without those long floppy parts at the top.

151

Next Mum Perry shows us a photo of a very old lady. It's her mother who lives in Yerrinbool but who'll soon be moving to Cronulla. Yerrinbool is the place Mum Perry always says she's going to on her days off but I never imagined that old ladies like her had mothers!

If she's got a mother, she might have other family people too. A husband? Or sisters and brothers? I ask her, very politely, of course. She had a brother but he died and there's no-one else except her mother. The war took the young men away, she says. I think I know about war. I think I understand. She had someone but he faded away in the war.

Mum Perry seems to like telling us things. She says that although she hasn't got children of her own, she has friends whose children are like hers. That doesn't count. You have to be their real mother for it to matter. She's got one daughter-like person who she's very proud of. She reckons we might hear her on the radio one day. It's hard to imagine Mum Perry knowing a singer. Only bad or morally suspect people do that. That's why we're not allowed to listen to the radio much.

We're allowed to have a look in the staff sitting room too. This is a beautiful little room that enfolds you in its soft warmth. The floor is covered with a plush cream rug with flowers on it and a blue ribbon pattern for a border. Big deep lounge chairs and shiny little tables wait around the edge of the rug for the little fireplace to be set aglow. You can go out onto a balcony from the sitting room and see the other homes. It's like being in a castle, looking out over your estate: there's Troup, Lincluden, Dunkeld, Cumbrae, Eskdale, Blair Athol and Airlee.

The staff rooms are still out of bounds but now we're allowed to go and knock on the door if we need something. In Miss Yates' time we'd never have gone to get her, even if we thought we were dying. We don't choose to be in Mum Perry's company either but being allowed to seek her out if we need to feels like a warmer breeze is blowing around us.

Outings change now too. We usually only go to the pictures

in the hall, the playing fields, the pool or bushwalking to Lake Parramatta to pick up sticks for the fire. Mum Perry starts thinking of other things to do with us. One day she says we're all going to Cronulla. Her mother will be there and we can meet her. Most girls are excited about going to the beach and some of them whisper about meeting surfers and getting boyfriends. None of that interests me. I'm intrigued by the mother. She is why I'm going to Cronulla.

We pack piles of sandwiches and fruit and divide them between the big kids to carry.

We get a bus and then two trains to Cronulla. Sunshine pours over us when we get off the train. Mum Perry takes us to a park where there are lots of busy, bustling people. Some stare at us. I suppose they don't know how one woman could have so many children.

I'm nervous around so many strangers. I stick by Mum Perry or, if I can't, I keep her in sight. She sends us off to play on slippery dips and swings and us big kids have to watch the little ones while she waits for her mother. I can't wait for her to get here. She's a real mother. She might invite us all to her place. It would just be us and her there. And what if she liked me so much she asks to adopt me? I could go and be in a family at Yerrinbool, wherever that is, and then here at Cronulla. Dad knows where Cronulla is and he knows how to get there so he could visit me when I get adopted by a real mother. Or he could marry her.

At last Mum Perry waves to someone and beckons a very old lady over to her. She hugs her mother. They sit on the bench and chat, as if they don't know I've been waiting for the mother too. Eventually Mum Perry calls us all over and introduces us. The old woman smiles and says it's nice to meet us and she's sorry she has to go so soon. Most kids go back to play but some of us hang around to get a better look. The two women talk for a while, ignoring our stares. Mum Perry calls her mother 'Hearts' and her mother calls her 'Vally'.

Hearts leaves soon after. She melts into the crowd of strangers.

We hardly know any more about her now than we did before. I don't mind that I won't be adopted by Hearts. I want a beautiful young mother, like a movie star.

Another day we're off to Prince Alfred Park for ice-skating. Everyone is excited, especially the girls who know how to do it. They give us instructions on the train. I suppose I'm excited but secretly I'm more terrified than excited. I get so nervous at new things, especially sports. Failure is guaranteed.

At the ice-rink we swap our shoes for skates. Some kids, including Kerry who learnt skating at school sport, dash to the middle of the ice. Others of us creep and sway to the edge. I get my first step over with very quickly. After a few more tries at standing up on the ice I give up. I'm nothing but a black and blue mop for thawed ice. I clutch the fence and totter around in monotonous wobbly circles. Clever people whiz by and sometimes crash to the side for a rest.

'G'day, sis. How's the skatin'?' Kerry glides in beside me, glowing with confidence and pleasure. I glare with the indignity of my failure and my wet clothes.

'Can't you do it?'

I hate the way she uses words so accurately sometimes.

'Come out with me. I'll show ya. It's easy. Hold on to me arm.'

She sounds so confident. She almost has me convinced that I'll be able to do it.

Out we go, not looking much like the twins we're often taken for, one standing straight and confident, the other bent, stiff, grasping the arm of the confident one. The confident one laughingly telling the bent one to stand up straight and relax, telling the bent one how to move her feet and how to keep her legs right. Perhaps the bent one is deaf. She wobbles and lurches then her feet slide out from under her and she pulls them both crashing onto the ice.

We laugh so much we can't get up. Other skaters fall in a heap on top of us. From the bottom of the pile we finally stagger up, still giggling, to try again. The result is the same. The bent, wet and bruised sister creeps back to the refuge of the fence. Kerry does a powerful pirouette, defying the ice to drag her down again.

Mum Perry wants to take us to the pictures at Parramatta but it costs too much for thirty-one tickets. She's trying to get them to let us in for free. Each day she tells us how it's going and our disappointment mounts. Eventually they give us a discount, so we can go if we walk to the pictures to save our bus fares. People stare at us as we walk along but we feel safe in our group and some girls pull faces at the spectators.

We say 'thank you' as we file in and sit down. The film is *Witness for the Prosecution*. I don't understand any of it except that there's a beautiful lady who looks like she's a liar one minute and an angel the next. I remember the name of the picture because it means that Mum Perry stood up for us and won us a new kind of outing.

She seems to enjoy the challenge of haggling for free entry for thirty children. She's loath to accept a discount unless free entry is absolutely out of the question. She gets us into the circus for free. I love it but wish they'd just have one thing happening at once so that you don't miss out on anything. Best of all is the walking around looking at the animals, though I'm disappointed that the elephant's skin is so rough and dull. The ones in story books were always smooth, shiny and magnificent. And what about the tiger? Had he ever been fierce? And the lion? Was he king of anything? They only came to life and roared when the ring master cracked his whip.

We've been to the Parramatta Show too. Mum Perry entered things we cooked in an exhibition and I won first prize for a plate of patty cakes and third prize for a damper. I didn't believe it until I got my ribbons and certificates. I felt very important when I read 'Mrs Shayler' on the certificates. I laughed at the thought that I'd competed with mothers and won. That proved that I'd be a good mother one day.

Changes keep happening at Burnside now. If you watch from the outside you might not see anything, but things are slowly changing inside. If you stop and look every now and then, there it is, the same Burnside but a different colour or texture, like dough baking in a slow oven. We're changing inside too.

The best physical changes happen in other homes before ours. We never visit each other so we're not sure if the rumours are just that or whether bathrooms are different now and dormitories are really vanishing. We just have to wait our turn.

We go to Huskisson for holidays while the Ivanhoe renovations are done. Burnside owns a big holiday house near the lagoon at the beach. All the homes have turns of going there so we don't get a turn very often, but now we're going.

We get up even earlier than usual but no-one minds. The sunrise sends golden light across the shelter where our thirty kit bags are waiting. Mum Perry has already organised clothes and linen for us to pack into our bags. We have to check that none of that is missing before we put some toys in. We're too sleepily excited to care. We wait for the bus to take us to the station where the long train ride will begin. On and on rattles the train until sleepy eyes force themselves open as someone squeals, 'Hey look the river!' The wide, glistening Shoalhaven that separates Nowra and Bomaderry tells us we're nearly there.

The house is called Murdoch Holiday Home. It's a wonderful place. It smells of mosquito repellent, noisy fun and rules that are made to be broken. Gangs and being tough don't matter now. Everyone likes everyone and Mum Perry relaxes even more than she does on bushwalks at home. Arriving at 'Hukko' means the rules of Ivanhoe are about to dissolve into the sand. The only rules are, 'Don't walk sand inside' and 'Don't go in the staff rooms or in the kitchen, unless on duty'.

At Hukko we go in through the front door. We never do that at Ivanhoe. We're allowed to go just about anywhere else in the whole house after we've bagsed beds and put our kit bags away. We've got a lounge room where we can go whenever we want to. We sink into the old chairs to talk loudly or softly, play board games, read or listen to records or the radio. This place is ours.

There's a back yard that's mostly sooty sand through which a few brave bits of grass try to grow and where families of ants have regular, orderly outings. The yard is bordered with bracken ferns that separate us from the mangrove swamp. There's no fence to hold us in, almost nothing to say, 'Do not go there'. The warmth of our freedom keeps us close to the house.

Something else does too though. A mysterious man lives somewhere in the swamp. Some kids reckon the old rotting tent we've seen him hanging around is where he lives. He's like the swaggie at home but he's mean rather than mysterious. He talks nearly all the time and his tone is nasty and threatening. We're really scared of him so he keeps us from going out of bounds. When he appears near the house, board games inside become instantly popular and even reading gains unheard of appeal.

We spend most of our days on the beach where we have picnic lunches, build castles and moats and dungeons or play shuttlecock. Big kids take little kids for rides in the big wooden canoes, the Burnie and the Arunta. I love the beach but I'm so allergic to sandfly bites that my fun is often curtailed by my arms and legs being completely bandaged to try to keep the sandflies off. The black tar that we smother all over ourselves before we head off each day doesn't seem to work on me.

Walks to the village can be boring but Mum Perry sometimes makes up for it by buying a huge bag of lollies that gets passed around as we wander about the streets and park. We like Choo Choo bars best because they last the longest but Rainbow Balls, snakes and musk sticks are popular too. We're not allowed to have cigarette lollies. They make us look common.

Mum Perry can never pass by the bakery when the air is full of the temptation of fresh baked bread. She tells us to wait and she disappears inside to ask for bread, whether or not she's brought money. She buys or cadges, we're always told which, lovely golden round tank loaves. We all wave and smile at the baker if we get free bread and sometimes we do it for the paid stuff too, because we love the bread. Then we wander along like ducklings, ready to snatch the bits of spongy, warm stuff Mum Perry rips off the loaves. She's laughing and enjoying herself as much as we are.

One day as we walk home from the village a man on a bike comes careering around the corner heading straight for us. We don't see him until he's almost on top of us.

'Quick! Off the road. Over to the side!' Mum Perry commands. Half go to one side and half to the other. I'm in the middle, still deciding where to dash. The man has to swerve to miss me. He falls off and lies groaning for ages. Then he gets up, mumbles something and limps away, pushing his bike beside him. We spread back across the road and walk home. I'm embarrassed that I didn't get out of his way in time.

Next day we're in the park and a hand shoves me. Nothing goes wrong with our tempers at Huskisson so I turn around to see who's teasing me.

'You idiot. You bloody fat slob! You've spoilt our holiday and now we have to go home,' a girl, a stranger, screeches.

What's she talking about?

'You broke my father's arm, now we have to go home. I hate you, you stupid idiot . . .'

A woman comes and takes the girl away as Mum Perry charges over, fuming. The girl's still screaming. I watch, shaking. Friends gather around while Mum Perry growls, 'Well, the hide of some people! Can't take responsibility for their own silly mistakes.'

Then she watches to make sure the family goes away.

'Must be that bloke with the bike. You know. Yesterday.'

'Yeah. The one that fell off.'

'Never mind, Katie. It's not your fault. He was going too fast anyway.'

They must be right but I stay quiet, hurt. I'm so ashamed that I spoilt her holiday. She's spoilt mine now but only for a while. I just hope it isn't true, what she said, that I'm a fat slob. I care about that kind of thing now.

We walk out through the mangrove swamp sometimes. We sing all the way. The swamp man keeps us together, no stragglers, nobody rushing off ahead. We turn back if the water gets too deep or the fine, black sand gets too sloppy. Otherwise we walk and walk and walk. We don't have to keep everything spotlessly clean at Hukko. When we get home we just take our shoes off outside, wash the sand off our feet, brush it off our clothes and go inside whenever we want to.

We have to be spotless on Sundays though. We go to church. It's a little wooden building that seems to be on holidays too. The best thing about the service is the singing but not for the songs. They're either ones we don't know or ones we sing at Sunday school. It's the organist, Mrs McKetridge, who makes singing so much fun.

Mrs McKetridge is very large and ancient. The little organ she plays sounds ancient too. We always jump when she starts to play. The boom in the tiny church blasts anyone who's nodded off back to consciousness as if Christian soldiers are marching across their eyelids. When we get control of our giggles we join in the singing while Mrs McKetridge gets busy swaying, pulling out the organ stops or whacking them back in. When she plays the piano accordion instead, we've got no hope of singing. Mrs McKetridge hoists her accordion onto her lap that's already full of belly and breasts. She arranges the straps on her shoulders, gives a huge smile and begins playing. As she plays, her knees pump open and shut in time with the music. The hem of her frock creeps slowly but surely up to her knees, then slowly but surely up and over them onto her swaying thighs. The big pink bloomers, anchored with elastic just below her knees, are displayed for all the world to see. Chubby pink cherubs sway to the song while Mrs McKetridge pumps on, singing joyfully to the Lord. We nudge each other and giggle and pass the message on.

'Cop the bloomers!'

It's better to pretend you don't know the song in the first place than to start singing and stop when you burst into fits of giggling. Miss Perryman gets very cross if no-one sings but she gets even more cross if we stop. She's very embarrassed by the bloomers. She

159

frowns at us to stop giggling but we can't until the bloomers are out of sight. After a while. Until the next hymn.

Our fun-filled, carefree days at Hukko are interrupted by Beach Mission. Everyone wants to save our souls. In the Christmas holidays people from churches all over the state come to beaches like Huskisson to preach the Gospel and entertain holiday makers.

The team erects a huge marquee and puts banners and bunting everywhere to entice children to come on the promise of more fun than they're already having. Teams of happy Christians march around camping grounds and sand dunes singing and calling kids to come. Grateful adults shove the kids in their direction and go back to sleep in the sun or play cards or read.

We go because we have to but most of us don't mind for the first few days. Beach Mission leaders are cheerful and enthusiastic. The games are good and so are the stories and songs. We're divided into juniors and seniors and taken to various places in and out of the marquee for activities that are meant to teach us about God and Jesus. It's like a bigger Sunday school. A few days of Sunday school is enough though and then us homes kids would rather go back to doing what we'd done before Beach Mission arrived. At the end of Beach Mission, all the parents are invited along and we have to put on a concert. We hate that. We're so shy of outsiders and we don't make friends with them, even here. They're not keen on us either. We're together because we have to be.

During the year you get a nice birthday card from your Beach Mission leader. It says, 'I was so glad when you gave your heart to Jesus at Beach Mission. I'm sure you are now living in His grace. I pray for His blessing for you in the year to come.'

Getting a card in the mail is special.

When it's time to pack our kit bags, clean Murdoch Holiday Home and pile into the train back to Parramatta, it feels like we're leaving a magical place, sandfly bites aside, to go back to life inside a rule book. It feels sad.

But not this time. This time will be different.

We don't see the difference at Ivanhoe until bath time. We're disappointed that we still have a dormitory but our bathroom is wonderful. Instead of three baths in one room, there's a wall that makes two rooms. One has two baths and one has a bath and a new shower. I've never seen a shower in a house before. Mum Perry says all this is so we can have privacy.

I know this includes me but why do I need privacy all of a sudden? It's only girls here. I've heard new girls whingeing about having no privacy. They always try to cover themselves up. I thought they were just trying to act like they were very grown up. When we get changed for bed, they put their nighties over everything first then take their clothes off underneath it. I practise pulling my jumper, blouse, singlet and bra out through the armhole of my nightie like they do, but it's for seeing if I can, for being a magician or doing a puzzle to get all the bits through in the right order. It's not for privacy.

Still, privacy is here now so I start to want it as much as anyone else. A better name for what I want is probably solitude but privacy is what we're given. We argue and argue about who should bathe where and when. Mum Perry is dumbfounded by the complications privacy creates.

'Lord love a duck! You've been sharing the bathroom with her for years. What on earth is the matter with you? Get in now or miss out.'

Each of us comes to the conclusion that privacy means we can get away with longer baths and more hot water if we're in the room with the door. The shower is in that room so you can try both if you're quick and no-one catches you. My first shower isn't like the ones at the pool. This one is bliss. Standing alone, clothes in a pile nearby, gentle, warm water sprinkling lightly on my face and shoulders, steam curling about the world that only has me in it, feeling like I could easily drift up with stea . . .

'Come on you in there. Get out. It's my turn.'

I like privacy. I can ignore what I can't see. I'll just float away.

'Come on you. Get out or I'll pimp.'

Lots of showers end that way.

Showers are more popular than baths at first so I decide to go back to the tub. Privacy has to be sacrificed then since there's no curtain across the bath. At least it's only one person who might burst in here instead of a free for all in the old part. Privacy is terribly important now.

It means being able to be alone more often. Not lonely. Just choosing to be alone and to be, in the aloneness, whoever I want to be. There isn't a lot of time for that after our holiday at Huskisson. Soon we have to go back to school. Lonely school.

JENNY AND ME

The usual choosing of subjects, stealing glances to see if anyone I knew was in my class and sitting alone on the seats behind Building 2 for recess and lunch filled my first day in second year. I'd done well in first year and I'd been moved up in Geography, English and Maths, so there were no familiar faces in any of those classes. I settled into the routine of being lonely at school and comfortable when I got in the mini-bus to go home.

When it's hot at school, lots of interlopers take the usual seats that us lonely people use. We have to rush to get any place at all.

'Hot isn't it?' says the plump, round faced girl who I've seen in geography recently. Her family is new in Carlingford and she doesn't have any friends yet. That why she's here on the lonely people's seat.

'Yeah, isn't it!' The only thing I can think of to say.

'You're in Mr Smith's geography aren't you?'

'Yeah. You too.' We both smile recognition.

'What's he like? I mean is there much homework?'

'He's nice. We get a project or something every week and some reading.'

'Does he give you good marks or is he mean?'

'Oh. He's all right I think. Better than Mr Previn.'

I can't believe I'm having a conversation with a stranger. It isn't too hard either. Jenny and I start sitting together in the classes we share and in our space behind Building 2. We relax into the friendship that creeps up on us and stays with us throughout high school. Despite our differences.

School lunch on Monday. On our usual seats. Jenny arrives, stands beside me with two paper bags and her purse. She places the bags carefully on the seat, unzips her pocket, places her purse neatly inside and does up the zip. She presses her dress to make sure the pocket is sitting neatly then she sits down.

She opens one bag. Steam rises, drifts across to dampen my nose.

'How come you have a pie every Monday?' and a chocolate paddle pop too.

'Mum hasn't got any fresh bread so I have to get a pie.'

I crunch into my sandwich to reach the congealed spaghetti and tired lettuce inside.

'Have you got a paddle pop too?' Did you get me one?

'Uh huh.' Warm gravy dribbles down her chin. She wipes it away with a neat white hanky.

My paper lunch wrap crackles to a ball in my hand. Chuck it in the bin. Damn, missed. Better get it before a prefect cops me.

Jenny takes the paddle pop from its wrapper. She folds the wrapper in half then half again and puts it in the pie bag.

The chocolate paddle pop. The Monday treat. My Monday torture. It stands there all smooth and shiny with a perfectly round top. Jenny's red lips approach slowly and wrap around the top. They move slowly up taking with them the thinnest layer of just melted chocolate. Here they come again, pushing a little ripple of melted chocolate down the sides. There's still a lot to go. She hardly ever bites her paddle pop. It always takes her so long with that slow deliberate licking.

'Is it nice?'

'Mmm. Nop bad.'

'Chocolate again eh?' Can I've a bite?

'Uh huh.'

She never gives me a bite. I never ask.

'Have you tried any other kind?'

'Nuh.'

Now the top's getting thinner, shinier. The sun threatens to bow it over. Quick Jenny! Get it before it falls in the dirt. Once I saw the puddle of her paddle pop sacrificed to hot, dry asphalt. Don't let it happen again!

The lips work quickly down and up and she might let the teeth help now. Talk won't distract her.

I lick my lips. They seem to be drying out again.

Jenny catches every bit of paddle pop. Not one single drop falls.

She places the clean stick into the pie bag and folds the top neatly over. She stands, brushes imaginary pie crumbs from her uniform and walks comfortably to the bin. I sit licking my lips. They're parched. Jenny is my best friend. She comes back and we sit together chatting and laughing. Feeling like we're melting in the heat.

Jenny and I are different in many ways but our friendship strengthens because of a common outstanding feature. We're both chubby. We don't discuss it much but we both have buttons that strain across our breasts and bellies and we know that no-one envies us this.

Tutorial classes are introduced at school so we can discuss social issues relevant to people our age. The first topic our group chooses, well some of our group, is, 'Should girls wear bikinis?' Bikinis are probably very rude, like getting about in your undies, but I listen to the arguments of my more enlightened and worldly classmates. Girls say things like, 'Only tarts wear bikinis. What more could you expect from that kind of girl!'

'Yes. No modesty. And they don't leave anything to the imagination.'

'What about that Barbara Parker! She looked so cheap in that bikini on the weekend. You should have seen it. It was even smaller than a two-piece!'

Boys snigger and say, 'Yeah! We should've seen it!'

'If you've got what Barbara Parker's got, you should do the world a favour.'

The discussion moves on.

'If you've got a good figure maybe it isn't too bad. But maybe a two-piece is more, you know, more ladylike or something.'

'But you can only see a little bit more in a bikini. I mean the worst bits are still covered.'

'The best bits you mean!'

From discussing the best figure for wearing a bikini, the discussion moves on to what shape girls should be at all. Jenny and I know that we're not that shape. I don't think we're too big but I'm learning that 'big' at high school is different to 'big' at home. I'm really disappointed because I love swimming. I still daydream about having coaching and being famous, like Dawn Fraser or being a movie star like Esther Williams. A girl my size has to let those dreams go according to our tutorial class.

We know boys are less interested in us than they are in other girls. A nice face and lovely eyes aren't enough for them. That's a relief in some ways. I only know Burnside boys who are very rough and outspoken about very private things. They force me too close to things that I need to keep forgotten. But it would be wonderful to have a boy think I'm really special and treat me kindly and show everyone that I'm worth his attention. Oh well. I don't mind that they don't. Not really. Neither does Jenny.

But then there's Warren Garland! The coolest blue eyes smiling out from behind the shiny sweep of jet-black fringe. The soft deep voice and the walk as smooth as any movie star. Comfortable with anyone and comfortable alone. Known to be the strong silent type who doesn't like bitches or loud girls. A boy who everyone wants to know but who is very choosey. The boy who got in my way when I was trying not to bump into him.

'Kate isn't it?'

'Yeah.' Oh crikey! He spoke to me. He knows my name.

'How do you like our commerce teacher?'

'He's all right.' Let me get away. Don't you know I'm shy!

'There's gunna be lots of homework.'

'Yeah.'

'Maybe we could help each other with it on the . . .'

'Gotta go. Jenny's waiting.'

I escape, hating my shyness and fear, confused about how I felt and what he seemed to be thinking.

'Wow! What were you talking to him about?' Jenny's green eyes are greener.

'Nothin'. Just commerce.' I don't think I know what it was about. Do I?

'What did he say?'

'That we could help each other with homework.'

'Oooh! Are you going to?'

'Nuh.' Jenny thinks I could manage it!

'Why not?' She's incredulous. Homework with Warren Garland!

'Can't. We're not allowed to have visitors.' Thank goodness. What would I do with Warren Garland at Ivanhoe?

'Go to his place then.'

What! Me in a boy's place? Warren Garland's place! I'd faint.

'Not allowed out.'

Warren smiles at me often but I manage to avoid talking to him again. That's a sort of relief but how I wish I was beautiful and modern, worthy of the wonderful Warren Garland. His invitation hasn't made me drop the commonly held belief that boys prefer slimmer girls and they don't make passes at girls who wear glasses. It does make me hope that maybe one day, when I stop being shy and when someone very special . . .

But there's a dark shadow that haunts me and makes me afraid of boys. Only I know about that shadow, know in the sense of being aware of something deep inside myself that I must never confront. The form whose presence created the shadow is now completely obscured. All I know is that it's dangerous being alone with and close to boys and to my father. It's just like the lady who talked about the reproductive organs said. She warned us, didn't she!

There are lots of girls at high school who I want to be like. Jenny and I talk about them sometimes. Jenny talks admiringly but not as if she's unhappy being Jenny. I want to be good at sports, not just swimming. The discussions about bikinis mean I shouldn't even be seen in a one-piece costume let alone draw attention to myself by being good at swimming. Asking at Burnside's office for money for carnivals is always difficult too so competition swimming is out. I deliberately lose races that I could easily win now.

I want to be like Mary Zen but I'm nowhere near that clever. Anyway I don't like the basketball girls. Then there's Lois Connolly, a tall blonde powerhouse on the cricket field. She dances up the wicket and belts almost every ball out of the grounds. She bowls stumps down and catches as if her hands are magnets. She's absolutely fearless. That's what I want most. To be fearless, instead of shutting my eyes and swinging the bat, hoping it'll connect, knowing it probably won't. Moving cricket balls are so hard! They hurt too.

Or there's Yana Bergstrom who's short with thick straight red hair that swings like a kilt when she walks. Yana is a softball genius. She can slog a ball wherever she wants it to go, catch from anywhere and, like Lois, she's fearless.

Normally Jenny and I are among the last to be chosen on teams in sport but for a little while I'm chosen in the middle lot for softball. This doesn't last long and it's a fluke that got me here in the first place.

I'd been standing way out in the field daydreaming while my team played on. I looked up and saw something hurtling down at me from outer space. Instinctively I put my hands up to protect myself, not to catch the meteor. I miscalculated the speed and seemed to be standing waiting for ages for it to land on the ground in front of me or behind me or anywhere but in my hands. Miraculously the ball thunked right into my hands. I held it hard. I was shocked.

'Chuck it, Kate. Third base,' someone shouted.

I chucked it to what I hoped was third base and Yana Bergstrom was out. Yana Bergstrom! Another girl too, but Yana Bergstrom!

'Didn't know you were such a good fielder!' Yana congratulated me after the round. I wanted so much to be thought well of that I didn't tell her it was a fluke. Jenny was very admiring of the way I'd positioned myself exactly right and waited so surely for the ball to drop into my hands.

I could laugh with Jenny and tell her the truth.

We aren't good at sport but we excel at talking in class. Not answering questions or joining in discussions. No. We excel in private debates and chatter. Especially in geography. Mr Jones is our teacher and we love him dearly. We don't want to make him cranky with us but he's just so nice and comfortable and we can't stop talking. We're always genuinely sorry when he turns around and catches us again but he has to get really angry, not just cross, for us to be jolted out of our chatting.

When Jenny is with me in class, I think I appear to be normal but when I'm alone, I'm still extremely shy. After I decide to accept that this is me and I can't change it, I find high school much easier. I concentrate on listening and learning. I get moved to higher classes each year and my confidence improves. Confidence in my ability to learn, but not in my social abilities.

The confidence that's beginning in me at school is fragile. My friendship with Jenny is strong. It's essential for my survival at school.

THE PURPLE ROOM

We have another holiday at Huskisson and this time there's no Beach Mission to interrupt us. Just lazy days playing at the beach and more active ones walking through the village or the swamp. The sadness of leaving is again tempered by the changes we knew were happening at home.

We come home to find that our dormitory has really gone! Walls have been built to make private little bedrooms with two beds and two wardrobes in each. The beds have colourful matching bedspreads. There's the blue room, the purple room, the orange room and so on. It looks as if upstairs has been swept with a rainbow! The shutters and wire mesh have been replaced with glass windows that open and shut behind matching curtains.

The colour of the place makes us run around like mad things. We dash about looking in the rooms, bagsing the ones we want, bumping into people around corners that replace aisles and pretending to be lost in the corridors.

Mum Perry says who will be in which bedroom. Some girls grumble about who they get so Mum Perry changes them but she gets fed up with trying to please everyone.

'Ye gods! That's enough. You only have to sleep in your rooms. It's not as if you have to spend the rest of your life in them.'

My room mate is Christine. We share the purple room nearest the staff rooms because we're the eldest and we stay up the latest. Christine's mother is a widow from Tibooburra. She put her two daughters in Burnside a few years ago. Christine says it took all day and night in the train to get to Sydney. I don't really understand how big this country is. My world is so small, so compact.

Christine says that everybody knew everybody back home and there was no privacy. 'Why isn't there any privacy?' Surely they have bathrooms and bedrooms in Tibooburra.

'Ah, it's just that everybody knows everyone else's business. It's just a small town, yer know.'

I don't know but I don't tell. It's obviously a different world.

We're rather keen on getting suntans at this stage and when Christine describes Tibooburra I say, 'Gee, it must be easy to get a suntan there.'

'Nah. Yer tried not to.'

'Why?'

'Yer don't wanna look like an Abo!'

'A what?'

'Abo. You know Aborigine.'

She means the poor blackfellas we pray for at Sunday school. I hadn't thought of their skin as being nicely tanned before or of their having anything I could possibly want. I hadn't realised that black people live in towns in houses either. There's a lot to learn in the purple room.

'I reckon it'd be great to be an Abo. You wouldn't have to lie out in the boiling hot sun to get a tan.'

It's uncomfortable saying 'Abo' but you can try different things here. As long as Christine doesn't pimp.

The best thing about being in the purple room is that I'm allowed to have my most prized treasure in it. I've asked Mum Perry if I can have my brush, comb and mirror set and she's let me. I have to keep it upstairs in my bedroom. My bedroom! My brush, comb and mirror set in my bedroom! The words make me smile. There's so much to smile about. I've arranged my treasures on the dressing table part of the wardrobe and I put their box away carefully in one of my drawers.

I can't wait to get back to school to tell Jenny what's happened.

'We've got bedrooms now with . . .'

'Where have you been sleeping?'

'Eh?'

'Where were you sleeping before you got a bedroom?'

'In the dormitory.' Neither of us can believe the other's confusion.

'An' we've got windows and our own wardrobes . . .'

'What have you got?'

'Wardrobes.'

'No. Before that. Windows did you say?'

'Oh yeah. Windows. And I've got this purple bedspread that matches the curtains and . . .'

Jenny's celebration of my new life at Burnside is always preceded by this kind of confusion that has to be sorted out. She's made assumptions, that are often challenged, about what we Burnsiders are changing from. Still, she thinks my purple room sounds nice, with all its new things and with my brush, comb and mirror set displayed on the dressing table.

In the privacy of our bedrooms we can talk with just one other person, we can read comics uninterrupted or we can sew or knit or sleep. It's rather lonely at first and we don't know how to be with just one person. We watch each other closely and wonder if we can trust each other not to spoil our privacy. We do visit other rooms and kids visit us too, to make sure that we're still who we were before. Mum Perry puts a stop to that because we're supposed to be settling down ready to sleep, not careering around the dormi . . . the rooms.

Christine and I get used to each other's company. We both have little sisters and we both like getting away from them at bedtime, to reassure ourselves that we're more mature.

Whether it's because we have privacy now and more personal space, or whether it's a coincidence of my age, it's now that I become more interested in my appearance. People have told me that I'm tall for my age. So tall that if I keep growing at this rate I could be an air hostess, if I could manage without my glasses. I'm as blind as a bat without the specs but I like that people mean that I look nice enough to become something glamorous.

We've only had one mirror at Ivanhoe until now. It's in the shelter, at head height. We use it for quick glances to make sure our hair is tidy before meals, not to see whether or not we're glamorous. Lately I've been using it to monitor my lack of progress in getting rid of pimples. Air hostesses don't have them.

Matron Rogers is trying to help get rid of the acne. I go to see her at the clinic every week. She shines her too bright light in my face and begins the ritual.

'Mm. Not much better. You must wash your face properly. Have you been doing that?'

'Yes, Matron.' 'Course I have. I don't actually like having pimples you know.

'Have you been using the special soap?'

'Yes, Matron.'

I like having my own special face soap that no-one else is allowed to touch. The soap means that I'm very, very clean. And I am myself, special, because I need things that are different to anyone else's things. I'm not just one of the crowd.

I usually leave the clinic feeling fed up with being told that I've got pimples because I don't do this, that and the other. Still, Matron Rogers is trying to get rid of them so, although it's annoying, I let her keep trying and I try not to let her worry me. One day she gives me a nice surprise.

'I want you to try this cream as well as the soap. It's skin-coloured so no-one will notice but you'll have to wear it every day. Put it on after you wash your face,' she says as she rubs some on the offending face. She shows me in the mirror.

'But I can't wear it to school!' Wow she's giving me make-up.

Just wait 'til the others see this. They'll be so jealous.

'Why can't you wear it to school?' she demands.

''Cause we're not allowed to wear make-up.'

Outsiders have been in lots of trouble lately for wearing it and that new stuff, mass-something or other, on their eyelashes.

Matron Rogers huffs and sets me straight.

'This is not make-up. It's medicated cream to treat a problem!'

Today I leave the clinic elated. I've got make-up and I have to, Have To, wear it to school. I'll have to remember to call it 'medicated cream' when the teachers ask me.

'Hey Christine, don't faint but Matron Rogers gave me make-up!'

'Bull.'

I show her and she's impressed.

'You look nice today,' says Jenny.

'Oh! Do I?' Wanting, but not quite daring to believe it.

'Have you got make-up on?'

'Yeah,' I grin, enjoying my daring and the fact that I've got an excuse ready for teachers who are bound to challenge me.

'They'll only tell you to wash it off.'

'They can't,' I say smugly.

'They tell everyone else to.'

'Yeah, but this is medicated cream.' There see. I'm safe. Thanks for the practice.

'Oh. So it's not make-up.' Jenny disappoints me for a second.

'Not really. Looks like it though, doesn't it?'

'Yeah. It looks really nice. Hope they let you keep it on. It's nice.'

The teachers let me keep my make-up on after I tell them what it is. Some other kids tell me how nice I look too. Outsiders! Yana Bergstrom even comes up and tells me that her mother said what a lovely face I have after she'd looked at our class photo. I'm very pleased. I wish I didn't blush so easily though. Maybe people can't tell through the make-up. I don't know what to say when I get compliments from outsiders.

*

We're told that we're going to Parramatta to have our hair cut. Up until now it's been cut at Burnside and we all have the same bob cut just below the ears and parted at the side. Bobby pins, clips or elastic bands with ribbons are allowed, to keep our hair off our faces. New girls always hate that they have to get their long tresses and curls cut off. They have to be told that it will stop them getting nits and that it will be easier to look after.

Now we're off to Gastoni Brothers where real hairdressers are going to cut our hair into 'styles'. We're quite excited and some girls say they'll look like girls at last.

I'm curious and because a group of us is going together, I let excitement overrule my worry about going to an unknown place. Girls talk about how glamorous we'll be after we get proper hairstyles. I secretly hope I'll look beautiful too. For so long I've thought I was ugly to everyone but my father but lately it's been different. I haven't been told I'm bad for quite a while now either.

I start to feel uneasy at Gastoni Brothers. They are men. I wait for my turn but I always move to the back and avoid the eyes of the man who comes every now and then to say, 'And which of the lovely ladies will be next?'

He's so handsome and I'm so . . . so . . . it must be shy. But what if there's a dark place back there! No there won't be. The others come back grinning and happy.

What if they cut my hair and what if I'm ugly? The longer it takes, the longer I can hope I'm not.

We watch our friends come back from the cutting chairs, all smiles and giggles and we tell them how nice they look, in unison with the Gastoni brothers. They do look nice too, with their pretty styles and their smiles stretched wider by the forthright compliments we so rarely give each other.

At last there's no-one left for me to hide behind.

I sit in the hairdresser's chair not daring to look in the mirror. The man's hand touches my chin and I stiffen. Now I'm embarrassed by my anxiety. My face glows.

'We'll take the glasses off first. There. Now put your head up so I can see your face. Oh what beautiful big eyes! No. Keep your chin up. You must not hide those eyes. Such a lovely face. Please. Keep your head, yes, up.'

I'm so confused. He said my eyes are beautiful and my face is lovely. It means I'm not ugly but I'm scared of something. I want to go back to the others. He said what I want to hear. Why don't I feel good, like I thought I would? Why am I upset by his closeness, his hand brushing lightly on my cheek, my neck, my jaw, breathing onto my neck, my ear, my face. Words, soft words close to my ear. I want to run away. Gentle snipping, going on forever and I want to run away and scream. Every nerve screams for it to stop. Light sprays of water cool my face. I try to listen to his compliments.

'Yes. We must let your eyes show. Head up please. And not too much around your jaw. Yes?'

'Mm.'

'No, you see, you must keep your chin up. Yes, that's better.'

At least my glasses are off, I can look in the mirror without seeing. I don't want the others to think I'm being vain, peering for too long to see myself. They know about my eyesight, or lack of it.

Finally it's finished.

'Ah beautiful! Now you put your glasses back on and look.'

I put them on quickly and sneak a look in the mirror before dashing away from the hairdresser who told me I'm not ugly. And who I was so afraid of without understanding why.

I'm still blushing when I get back to my friends. They give me the same compliments I gave them. 'Very nice' and 'Wow, that looks good' and 'Geez! You could be a movie star when you grow up'.

We climb demurely into the bus but it doesn't last. We are still us.

'Oh. So beautiful! I love you, my darling,' Dawn pouts as she imitates the hairdresser.

'Oh. Your hair is so lovely! I will cut it all off and take it home,' Christine grabs Maureen's hairstyle.

'Let go, you bum. You'll spoil it!'

'See Daisy blushin'. She's in love with that Ricardo one, aren't ya!'

This goes on all the way home until we've forgotten that we were demure and lovely not long ago.

Do I really have a lovely face and beautiful eyes or did they just say that to all of us. I've never used the mirror to study my whole face before but now I'm curious. I'll have a look and decide for myself what I think about my face.

A quick glance around to make sure no-one's looking. A quick glance in the mirror to make sure a long look isn't going to disappoint. No. It's all right. Pimples all covered, hairstyle tidy, overall impression—all right.

Next I look slowly. I'm surprised. I like the face I see. I'm surprised at how little I know this face that I've . . .

'Hi Shayley Eyes! Whatcha doin'? You'll cop it if you pop 'em ya know.'

'Yeah. Yeah. I know.'

I don't care about Matron Rogers just now. I want some privacy to finish my inspection. I need the mirror in the purple room, the privacy mirror. I have to wait until after tea when we're allowed upstairs. I wait until Christine goes to have her shower. I look straight at the face in mirror in the privacy of the purple room. The face I see is a nice face, not a bad person's face. I've got a face that I like. Yes, big eyes. The face is kind of balanced. I hope other people meant what they said about it but whatever they think, I have a face that I like.

Changes keep happening. We're allowed to have pocket money too now, if our parents can afford it. They leave it with Mum Perry and she keeps record of it and gives us advice about what to spend it on. Sometimes it's forceful advice but, amazingly, it's truly just advice.

Dad leaves money for us, though he tells us he doesn't have much spare cash so we have to be careful what we spend our money on. We shouldn't buy rubbish and we shouldn't buy anything that he might be able to get cheaper if he shops around. Kerry and I agree.

I imagine all sorts of glamorous purchases, like some angora twin sets the same as the one Miss McCredie wears to Sunday school with her pearls and nice pleated skirt. Then I'll get some fabulous jewellery like the things the movie stars wear in the magazines. Then every colour of nail polish there is and lippies too.

I tell Mum Perry about the angora twin set idea but she seems alarmed or shocked or something. She says I'd better think of smaller things and keep that idea for when I go to work when I am older.

Christine and I have noticed that Denise has been looking rather glamorous at school lately so Christine asks her what she's done to her hair. She says her Mum bought her some rollers and that's the difference. She'd been curling and teasing her hair.

Christine and I buy some rollers too. We read the instructions inside the bag of funny looking plastic cylinders with little spiky bits in rows up and down the sides. Then we get to work, feeling very worldly and sophisticated. After all the hair we can catch is tangled in, we sit in our beds and read magazines. Gradually the plastic pins start digging deeper into our skulls. We have to make adjustments so many times before lights out! We have to sleep in our rollers and we're certainly ready for sleep. Neither of us has thought about how you actually do sleep with little hedgehogs tangled up in your scalp. As soon as we lie down the problem is obvious. Where do you put your head? There's absolutely no way you can be comfortable, except face down into the pillow but then you can't breathe. We want to survive this, not be glamorous in our coffins, so for the sake of beauty we toss and turn all night.

When we get up next morning we have to find half our rollers among our sheets. My hairstyle looks like it's ready to light a bonfire and Christine's looks like an eagle's nest. We have to stick our heads under the tap and damp the hair down before we go to school.

Christine gives up rollers pretty quickly but I persist through a few months of tortured nights because I want to be beautiful and sophisticated. I'm making progress.

Our next purchase is nail polish. Bright pink, foul smelling nail polish that someone knows how to put on because her mother's got some. We need emery boards to make our nails the right shape and someone shares hers around. We don't know what shape to file our nails into so we go for a pointy sort of arrangement. We didn't know you needed nail polish remover either to get the stuff off and nail polish is banned at school so we spend Sunday night chewing it off and do the last bits in the bus on Monday morning. I decide nail polish is better for putting my initials on my toys so no-one will pinch them any more.

So the changes that are imposed upon us begin to change the way we see ourselves and each other. We no longer play in gangs of tough, nasty girls whose lives are full of anger, fear and resentment and whose competitive energies are devoted to hurting others or getting them into trouble.

Now we're being treated as individuals and so we're able to consider each other more gently, as people. We've got more energy for caring. We compete to make each other laugh not cry.

SOCIAL CREATURES

The effects of the changes existed only within the world of Burnside and, to a lesser extent, with my friendship with Jenny. They now had to be tested in the outside world. We were pushed by degrees into that world and each journey proved that we didn't fit in there. Coming home to laugh or cry was such a relief.

'Mum wants to know if you could come over on Saturday,' says Jenny.

'What for?' I remember Elizabeth's party.

'Just so they can meet you, I s'pose. 'Cause we're friends.'

Yeah but what if they don't like me? And what if you decide you don't either? I won't fit. And there's your father. What about him?

'Don't think I'd be allowed.' Thank goodness.

'Couldn't you ask? Mum really wants to meet you. And I want you to come too.'

'All right. I'll ask.' You might forget about it.

I don't ask but Jenny doesn't forget.

'Did you ask?'

'Nuh. Didn't get a chance.'

'Mum said she'll write a letter if you like.'

'That'd be good.' It'll take longer and she might forget.

Jenny's persistent mother writes a friendly note on pretty paper. Mum Perry is pleased for me!

'Yes. That will be all right. I'll check with the office, of course, but I think it's a good idea.'

'Why?' We've never had to go out to people's places before. Except once. Why do I have to now?

'I have to check. You can't go without Mr Ross's permission.'

'No, I meant why is it a good idea for me to go?'

Mum Perry looks surprised.

'Don't you want to go?'

'No.'

'Why ever not? Jenny's your friend, isn't she?'

'Yeah but . . . It's just that . . .'

I don't know how to tell her I'm scared, that I won't know what to do or say, that I'm afraid they won't like me, that I'll be so lonely at school again.

'I think it would be good for you to meet your friend's family. That's what other children at school do, don't they? They visit each other's places.'

'Yeah. But what if they don't . . . you know . . . what if I can't . . . what if they don't like me?'

Mum Perry looks as if I've spoken in a foreign language.

'For Pete's sake, Kate! The girl's your friend. How long have you known her? Years. Why would she suddenly not like you? And why wouldn't her family like you?'

I can't explain about it being the wrong context for Jenny to like me. We're friends at school, in our uniforms, behind Building 2 and in geography. It'll be different at her house with her parents there and everything. I'll be clumsy, awkward, tongue-tied. What'll I wear? Bommy Burnside clothes. Jenny will see me in old-fashioned bommy clothes. I'll be so shy and they'll think I'm dumb. And what about the father?

Mum Perry gets permission for me to go. I have no choice. I

put on a skirt and blouse, knowing Jenny will hate them. I'd rather wear the uniform that defines our friendship. I get a bus, by myself, to Carlingford, chanting Jenny's directions to myself all the way. Jenny lives in a brick house with a garden along the path to the door. I ring the doorbell, hoping no-one will hear it, then I can go home. But the wretched thing chimes so loudly I'm sure even my father can hear it at Marrickville.

'Come in,' smiles Jenny, dressed in slacks and a nice blouse.

I'm shaking all over but Jenny is just Jenny.

'You must be Kate,' says a smiling voice whose face appears from around a corner.

'I'm Jenny's mum. I'm very pleased to meet you.'

'I'm pleased to meet you too,' I lie through dried up lips. Mrs Franklin's welcome is warm and I relax a little though I'm still as brittle as toffee.

'Would you like a drink?' Jenny asks.

'Yes, please.' And could we have it away from your mother so she won't see me.

'Yes, love. What would you girls like? I'll get it.'

How do I know what they've got?

'Kate?'

'Um. Is there any Coke?' Elizabeth's party to the rescue.

'Um. I don't think so but we've got lemonade or Fanta.'

'Fanta, please.'

Mrs Franklin goes to get our drinks. Jenny and I sit down.

'Wow! You're really shy of Mum, aren't you!'

'Yeah. Sorry.' Already disappointed, aren't you! Wait 'til your father comes!

'It's OK. But she's just my Mum.'

'Yeah OK. But I can't help it. I don't know what to say.' I don't know what to say to you either, here.

Jenny looks confused as I wonder what to say next.

'Here we are, girls.'

Mrs Franklin puts three drinks on the table.

Three drinks! Oh no. She's staying.

'Dad will be home soon and then we'll have some lunch. I hope you like casserole, Kate.'

'I've never had it,' or a face this red either.

'They have to eat whatever they get,' Jenny informs her mum.

'Well, if you don't like casserole we won't make you eat it.'

Jenny's mother likes her joke. I do too, though I'm not sure if it's meant to be one until I see her smiling.

'Oh. Hello. You must be Kate,' a towel says from above a dressing gown that moves through the room.

'Oh. Pamela! Go and get dressed then say hello.'

'Oh, all right! I'm just passing through. Didn't hear the doorbell.'

Crikey! She's giving cheek to her mother!

'All right, Pam. Now you know Kate's here, go and get dressed!'

Her Mum didn't yell at her! She took it as fun.

The familiarity and the laughingly cross tone of the mother surprises me, makes me relax. They're still comfortable even though I'm here. I feel more like I'll be able to get it right if I be like I am with the girls at Burnside. I feel myself bend with the company.

'That's my sister. You know, Pam.'

'She had a very late night last night. In fact she's just got engaged so she's had a bit of a sleep in.'

I'm just not used to being spoken to like . . . like . . . like that by an adult. It's friendly and I don't know how to respond.

'Oh,' is as deep as I can go.

'Yeah. I'm going to be a bridesmaid.' Jenny's so proud.

They chat cheerfully on about the boy and the wedding plans and how Chester and Pam met. They're so comfortable with each other and so proud of Pam. I want to fit but I know there isn't a place for me among all this. My part is to hear it all at school. Still, I like being included for now and I like watching it all unfold.

The front door opens. Jenny's dad comes in, kisses Jenny and his wife. I become brittle instantly.

'And this is Kate, Jen's friend from school.'

Mr Franklin smiles.

'Yes. Nice to meet you, Kate. Sorry I wasn't here earlier. Had to earn the daily bread.'

I'm surprised that he speaks quietly, kindly and that he's sorry for not being here earlier. I almost feel safe. As long as it isn't going to be just him and me . . . I like what I think was a joke about the daily bread in 'Our Father'. I don't know if it's all right with God and Burnside to laugh but I do anyway. They won't know. Jenny said once that her Dad doesn't believe in God so I'd assumed he would be awful. He isn't.

The afternoon passes slowly. I watch and listen as they talk with each other and smile a lot. Pam and Jenny give cheek and the parents chuckle about it. Sometimes they ask me questions and my monosyllables give the conversation nowhere to go. Jenny's family stays warm and friendly.

'I'm so glad you came to visit us. Now we know who Jenny's friend is,' says Mrs Franklin as I leave. 'Now that you know where we are, you must come again. Do you think they'd let you?'

'I don't know.'

I'm exhausted but not too exhausted to realise that I'll never voluntarily come here again. Friendship at school with Jenny is enough. The rest is too hard.

Jenny is quiet as we walk to the bus stop.

'See you at school,' she smiles as I get on the bus.

'Yeah. See ya.'

I worry that Jenny has seen me at my worst and won't want me for a friend any more.

At school on Monday everything is as it has always been. Jenny is still my friend.

'Mum said you're sweet,' she says casually, unaware of how much anxiety I've generated over this judgement.

'Sweet?' That means I'm all right. Tell me again.

'Yeah. She said you've got nice manners. And you're a bit shy too.'

'Oh. Yeah. Shy.'

'Let's check our homework.'

Jenny sees no need to reassess our friendship. No new elements that matter have popped in as far as she's concerned. I stop worrying.

My visit to Jenny's was a sign of Burnside's realising that we were not well socialised in terms of the world outside. They made it their business to work on this.

Us older girls get enrolled in a Physical Culture class at Parramatta. We're picked up at our various homes and taken to the hall Physical Jerks, or Fizzy. Here we stick to each other like glue rather than mix with the outsiders who outnumber us three to one. We arrive in a group, wait together, line up to start together, march around and exercise together and go home together. Not exactly achieving Burnside's purpose.

I like Fizzy, all of us in uniform, moving to the regular plonk, plonk, plonking of the piano, all doing exactly the same movement, each with its exact name for where arms and legs had to be.

'Oblique,' yells the teacher and all arms move together.

'Acute,' and they all move to that position together.

Marching is fun. There are proper ways to do corners, exact places to march to without bashing into other girls who were doing their part of the pattern and proper posture that makes everyone seem very poised and tidy.

Getting home from Fizzy improves just about every week for a while. First it's hot chocolate to warm us up ready for bed. The kitchen has always been closed after the washing up from tea is done. Now a little group of eight or so stand around sipping our sweet drinks and feeling special because of our double treat. Later Mum Perry decides to add cake to our Fizzy night delights. But that's not the best addition.

The Outer Limits. That's the best. We have just got television at Ivanhoe and we're only allowed to watch Shirley Temple movies at lunchtime on Sundays. Us big kids always have to leave before the end to get to Sunday school on time.

Now we're allowed to stay up late and watch the scariest things I can imagine. We sit pop-eyed, sipping hot chocolate while bits of dust change inside vacuum cleaners to become evil forces from other planets that suck the life out of innocent women and children. Or innocent women and children are really ghastly aliens living in stolen human bodies, waiting to do dastardly deeds to all living things on Earth.

It all seems so real and so possible. The juniors get too upset so Mum Perry sends them to bed but they can stay up later to make up for missing out on telly. Us seniors feel very important but we almost envy the juniors being rescued. We don't get to sleep quickly on Fizzy nights, despite the hot chocolate.

'I don't believe in men from Mars. Do you?'

'No. I don't believe in 'em.'

'How could they get here anyway, even if they were true?'

'Yeah. There's no such thing as space ships.'

'And how could they get here without a space ship. They couldn't.'

'Hey! What if we've been making us clean up the dust 'cause they know it's real!'

'Oh shut up. Go to sleep will ya!'

There was a Fizzy Night when I couldn't get to sleep for ages because of the outer limits of my arms. That night I wished we didn't have a mirror too.

We were learning a new sequence ready for a competition. The teacher never got angry with me, so I'd assumed I was pretty good at Fizzy.

'Then acute,' she yelled.

All arms stretched to acute.

'Now you'll have to pay attention to your lines. The tip of your fingers right up to your shoulder should be one straight line.'

I stretched my hands out. Yes, mine are straight.

'Stretch them out, girls. I want to see straight lines.'

Yep. I've done it. Stretched and straight.

186

She walked around adjusting the odd finger or arm. She didn't come near me. Mine were perfect.

'Straight lines! Not bent hands,' again.

Oh, come on! My arms'll drop off soon. Can't you all just look at mine then you'll see what straight is. Why doesn't she tell 'em?

She seemed to give up in disgust and go on to the next position.

I went home feeling very proud that our teacher hadn't had to come to correct me. I was so good without her help. After The Outer Limits I stood in the purple room at the mirror and stretched my arms to acute again, feeling their poker straight lines and their strength.

Let's see. There were my arms stretched into faultless lines. But look at my hands, stretched so far they almost formed right angles to my arms, looking as if they were ready to balance trays of porridge, one on each!

I wished a space ship would appear and disgorge a thousand aliens to devour my body and smash this wretched truth telling mirror.

We kept going to Fizzy for quite a while and some girls got medals. I got 'Hardest Trier' in the senior section.

The staff had another scheme to help us learn to be sociable but this time they restricted it to Burnsiders. All children over twelve were 'invited' to a social at Eskdale where senior girls usually went for Sunday school.

'What's a social?'

'Dunno. S'pose it's where yer sit round talkin'.'

'What about?'

'Dunno.'

'I don't wanna go.'

'Me either.'

''Cept there's soft drinks an' that. They reckon there's top forty songs too.'

I still don't want to go.

'The boys are goin' too.'

'Oh sugar. What do they have to be invited for!'

Now I definitely don't want to go. Mum Perry says it'll be good. She says it's what people our age do and it's planned so we'll enjoy it.

We get dressed in our best play clothes. The truly sophisticated ones of us even put rollers in our hair the night before. Off we go to the social pretending we're coping very well, thank you very much.

The social workers and some of the house parents from other homes are there to welcome us. Ivanhoe girls stand in a group beside the food that we have to leave for later. Blackwood boys stand in a group up the far end, then along come the Dunkeld girls who stand in their group. And so on until the room buzzes with each group's own erratic conversation. We steal glances at other groups to see what they're wearing, whether they're talking too and whether they're mixing with kids from other homes. Girls peep at boys then giggle back comments to their friends. Boys don't know what to do with their comments, except that they know not to deliver them here the way they normally do. This is all so painful but it gets worse.

Staff are watching, judging, looking confused but trying to smile.

'Come on, girls. We want you to mix with the others. That's why we brought you all here.'

We all grudgingly move closer to another group of girls. Then we keep doing what we were doing before. I'm not the only one who can't find my social switch to turn on. 'Girls and boys,' this time it's a general announcement, 'we hope you're having a good time this afternoon. We hope that this will be the first of many socials for you. Now perhaps it's time for some music. If any of you would like to dance, please do so. Boys, remember your manners.'

The record player blares out but beyond all the groans, sniggers and whispered hopes, not a single foot ventures towards a person of the opposite sex.

'Oh, come on, girls. If I can get the boys to ask you to dance, will you dance with them?' begs a desperate house mother.

'No.' I'm definite about that.

'Oh! Why ever not?'

'Can't dance.'

An honest definite answer. We learn ballroom dancing in PE but I always volunteer to do the boy's part with girls who didn't get a boy partner. I never have to dance with boys.

Some girls say they'll dance but when the awkward, self-conscious boys who were brave enough to try to imitate rock n' roll stars start their performances, the other girls change their minds. It's back to lining the walls again in boys groups and girls groups. At least now the girls are mixing with each other and so are the boys with each other. At last it's time to eat and drink. That's something we all do well although us girls think we should pretend we don't like eating much when boys are around. Boys don't have to pretend any such thing. Soon all the food is gone and there's nothing left to do. We're allowed to go back to the safety of our homes.

Efforts to turn us into social creatures weren't entirely abandoned by the Burnside staff but whatever they arranged, we usually congealed into a lump of awkward joviality rather than drifting gracefully, confidently in all directions as they'd hoped.

Meanwhile hints were dropped by social workers, every now and then, that soon I'd have to start preparing for my future with my family. I thought I'd be able to cope with anything the future held. It seemed a long way off as the world I lived in now became brighter.

RESPONSIBLE BIG GIRL

I was the eldest girl at Ivanhoe now and I'd been there the longest too. I liked the responsibilities this brought. Mum Perry relied on me when staff let her down or when she had no official assistant. Sometimes my confidence was challenged and it was sent tumbling backwards but never too far. Most of the time I could laugh or at least smile about my failures and feel proud of my successes. In two years time I'd be leaving and my emerging confidence let me think I could cope with anything life presented here or outside.

A tiny ragged girl with tangled hair and wild hunted look eyes comes to Ivanhoe. I'm ready to be her Analise when Mum Perry's finished with her.

'We'll have to get her into some clean clothes,' Mum Perry announces. 'The hide of some people sending children to us in rags like that!'

The little girl stands rigid. Huge strength. Tiny, bony body.

'Come on. Off with those rags.'

Mum Perry backs off suddenly as the clenched fists lash out, the little jaw stiffens, ready to bite.

190

Sh . . . ugar. What if Mum Perry loses her temper? Watch it, little girl. You'll cop a belting!

I think I'm too busy to wait here. I'd better go and . . . I can't go. I have to help. The new kid has only taken her blouse off. She's absolutely rigid in her filthy singlet and skirt. Mum Perry's demands that she get the rest off but Mum Perry gets whacked away by the little fists.

'Lan sakes! Kate! Where are you? Take her into the spare room and see what you can do?' Clean clothes are shoved into my middle.

What am I supposed to do?

'Come on,' I say softly, so the new kid won't know I'm out of my depth. She follows me.

Now what am I supposed to do? I sit on the end of the bed away from the teeth.

'You have to put these on.'

I know she won't.

'All right,' the tiny voice replies.

What? Just like that!

'Want me to help you?' Promise you won't bite?

The tangled hair nods as the grubby bag of bones raises its arms. I get the singlet off. The eyes that were so fierce are now wet and red. The hard chin begins to tremble.

'You'll be all right. What's your name?'

'Dianne Cameron.' Dianne Cameron puts her clean singlet on and I help smooth it down over her ribs.

'Now, here's your dress.'

'Nah. That's not mine.'

'It is now.'

I like the little smile that creeps around the corners of her mouth.

'We'll put your name on it later.'

'For keeps?'

'Yeah. 'Til you get too big for it.'

She smiles again. I can't imagine her getting too big for anything.

I take Dianne Cameron to the washroom where we rub hard to get the dirt off her face. I'm afraid she'll break. She doesn't. She's tough. We leave the hair for later. There she stands in her new clean clothes, an almost clean face and a bit of a smile that stops her tears, at least for a while.

I smile. I'm good with little kids. I'm a big kid, an Analise for new kids. I let Dianne stay with me for a while then she has to go off to play with the little kids.

One thing I won't have to show kids ever again is how to use towels and elastic and whopper safety pins when they get their monthlies.

I'm on boiling duty and the kerosene tin full of towels starts leaking on the stove.

'You'll have to go and ask Mr Duncan for another one.'

Mr Duncan doesn't have to be told what the tin was for. My red hot blush is wasted. He gives me the only tin he has left.

'Oh well. It won't have to last much longer,' Mum Perry says.

She tells me about the new invention, disposable pads, that we'll be getting. Sounds like the things new girls have been grumbling about for a few years.

'No more bloody nappy pins and great chunks of elastic 'round yer middle!'

'Yeah. And no more washing. Just burn 'em.'

'No more accidents!'

I hope Linda's heard about them. I remember her walking proudly out in front of the whole school with a bright red stain on her very white shorts to be presented with her high jump trophy.

'You'll have to collect all the towels and burn them,' Mum Perry says. 'We won't be needing them when these new things come.'

'Hey guess what. We're getting those pads things. We have to burn the towels!'

Soon we are gathered around the heater like a coven of witches, cackling as we commit past injustices to the flames.

'What the dickens is going on here?' Miss Perryman's furious.

'We're burning our towels,' replies the chief witch. Why's she so angry. Too noisy I s'pose.

'Lord give me strength! Not now. Not yet!' she almost shrieks. 'Who told you to do that!'

'You told me t . . .'

'I told you it was going to happen soon, not now!'

Miss Perryman's withering stare shrinks the flames and my pride. The spell is broken.

'Are there any towels left?' She's almost hysterical.

'I've only got two.'

'I haven't got any.'

Hands, clutching towels, move slowly behind backs.

'None here.'

Another groan from Miss Perryman.

'You'd better go to Mr Duncan and see if you can get the Modess now.'

She leaves to write a hasty note to the storeman while I stand there feeling foolish.

'Good on ya, Shayley. Good trick.'

I soon cheer up.

'Yeah. Who wants to wait any more for 'em!'

I let them think I'd plotted a clever scheme. We have a quick ceremony to burn what was hidden behind backs.

I go off with Mum Perry's note and a smile. I come back with a big light bundle and a very red face. Mr Duncan had asked me how many I needed!

A Tuesday afternoon, fourteen years old.

'Matron Rogers wants to talk to you, Kate. Go up now and do your work when you get back.'

I walk to the hospital calmly. Last time I came here I had German measles. I was forced to loll about in the sun and do nothing but listen to the glorious chorus of a thousand magpies in the bush. The bush is heaven and I was near it. That's how it felt. It's not clinic time now so Matron Rogers must want me, a responsible older girl, to help her. She takes me into the clinic. She chatters on about nothing much. I steal glances at the silver trays. Instruments all in place, gauze dish full and the ones for . . .

'. . . you get very smelly . . .'

Eh!

'. . . under the arms.'

Stink? 'Course I don't. Mustn't have heard right. Better listen.

'You're surprised, aren't you. Hasn't anyone told you?'

'Nuh.' Why should they?

'. . . use this after your bath. It'll stop the smell.'

I feel like a freak. She shows me how to twist the thing out to expose the waxy bit. Looks like a flamin' candle. I have to rub a candle under my arms so I won't stink! Why doesn't anyone else have to do it?

'. . . nicer to be near you and they won't want . . .'

Yeah. All right. You don't have to rub it in. I have to rub de-something-or-other on. Can I go to work now?

I'm keen to have a private whiff under my arms as soon as she's out of sight and prove the old battleaxe is wrong. I walk home contorting my head, trying to steal sniffs of my underarms. There, see. No pong. She's wrong. But what if she's not! I clutch the candle, just in case.

Jenny and I are on our usual seat.

Go on. Ask her. Don't be a chicken.

Another bite into the peanut butter and beetroot sandwich to disguise my dilemma. I have to know. Ask her. Quick.

'Jenny, do I thsting?' My sandwich plots against this being short, sweet and over.

'What!'

'Do I stink? Smell?'

'What did you say that for?' Jenny fidgets with her purse. 'You've never said anything like that before!'

194

This is different. I have to know.

'It's just that I've got to put deodorant on. They reckon I smell.'

'Oh, is that all! I've got some of that. Had it for ages.'

'You don't smell!'

'No. But I would,' she grins.

'Well, how did you know to get?'

'Mum got it for me.'

A little pause.

'You can't smell yourself, you know.'

Oh no! Matron Rogers must've been right. Sugaar! I've been walking round stinking and I didn't even know! I wonder what else there is that I don't know about.

Another summons to the clinic and this time Kerry has been called too. Perhaps Matron Rogers wants me to teach clinic work to my sister.

We sit together in the clinic. Matron Rogers yabbers on.

Looks like all the bandages are rolled, trays full. Can we get on with the wards then?

'. . . you are just too fat . . .'

What? Too what!

'. . . girls your age . . . breasts and hips and tummy . . .'

Red fury creeps up from an explosion in my chest.

I'm just never all right, am I. You've conned me again and now you've dragged Kerry into it too. Shut up, you dirty old hag. Just leave me alone. And Kerry. Leave us alone.

She drones on and on. We're too fat, ugly, boys won't like us.

Who cares! Who cares what boys think. I don't. Jenny and I don't care. Kerry doesn't either.

Torn between thinking Matron Rogers might be right again and grasping at my wavering certainty that although I'm big, I'm not fat.

How come no-one else gets told they're too fat! We're just like everyone else except we're stronger. You just pick on us because you hate us. I'm gunna tell Dad . . . No. Not about this.

Anger seethes. I look at Kerry whose face is as red as mine feels.

She's not fat. Look at her. Lovely hair, rosy cheeks, big muscles. She's all right.

'. . . you'll have to go on a special diet. We'll see to that but get on the scales first and we'll weigh you.'

I stand there, caring, trying not to care. I want to be normal, to be worthy. Perhaps I do care about boys. Boys like Warren Garland anyway. I thought I was all right but now there are numbers that prove I'm not.

Matron Rogers thinks it's important to plot our progress towards acceptability each week so she makes a graph before we leave the clinic.

I'm confused about myself. What's the truth? What she said or what we knew before she said it?

At home I look in the mirror. I look the same. I dismiss Matron Rogers' criticism.

Big strong girls like me are very helpful. Matron Rogers ought to ask Mum Perry if I'm too fat. She'd tell her.

Among our farm supplies sit two huge green melons. I know they're good because the more experienced girls are excited.

'Look. Watermelon!'

'Bet they're for staff but.'

'Kate, take the watermelons to the pantry. And don't drop them.' Mum Perry's always snarly when stores come in.

I lift one big, cold melon, cradle it and reel under its weight.

'Like my baby?' I ask as I lug the thing past salivating lips.

I've seen kids play mothers like that. With a toss of my maternal head I put them out of their excitement.

'We're not getting it now. It's for later. Meanwhile I shall look after you, my little darling.' I plant kisses on his cool green cheek as I rest him on the table. 'Mwah. Mwah.'

'Get a move on, Kate. There's work to be done,' Mum Perry snaps.

I lift my green baby off the table, take a few steps, feel it slipping. A little hoick up. Can't hold . . . Splat!

'Eh look. Shayley's dropped 'er baby!'

The melon lies splattered all over the floor. A puddle of juice spreads like Mum Perry's anger. The temptation for a public expression of grief is urgent but I know better.

'Oops. Sorry Mum Perry.'

'It's not much use being sorry now. Why couldn't you just carry the thing inside without all that confounded shenanigans!'

The last of the juice finds the drain. Girl vultures gather. They see the solution. 'Get a knife. We'll have to eat it now.'

Oh no. Poor us!

'On ya, Shayley,' a few whisper as I pass.

I flex my muscles and grin. I am big and strong. Clumsy, but big and strong. And popular.

Next week, back to the clinic, back on the scales. Matron Rogers is disappointed with her flat graph. She starts on again about how we're too fat, boys won't like us, blah, blah, blah.

'. . . I must write a letter to your father and ask his help on visiting . . .'

No! You can't. Don't write. Not about my body. Don't!

My body is everyone else's again. I'm afraid of the darkness of being my father's daughter, though the reason is now buried, intangible.

'We'll have to try you on some tablets, Kate.'

She reaches for the Tenuate Dospan packet that already has my name on it.

No-one else has to take tablets. How come I have to?

'You'll have to remember to take one every day.'

'Yeah. All right.'

If I get skinny, she'll only find something else wrong with me.

At home I tell my friends what's happened. We compare our muscles again. I'm still all right, without Matron Rogers judging. Or boys.

Jenny and I don't discuss our common 'fault' much. Until recently it's been a fact for us but not a fault. We know it's a fault according to some snobby kids. And boys. Apparently. But sometimes boys smile at us and talk to us. Or try to.

'Oh. You've got a salad!' says Jenny.

'Yeah. Gotta go on a diet. Matron Rogers reckons I'm too fat.'

'Who's she?'

'Oh. At the hospital.'

'Heavens. Have you been to hospital?'

Burnside at school gets complicated.

'No. Well, yes. Just Burnside's. It's where we go if we're sick or something. Where I got the deodorant.'

'So why did you go this time?'

''Cause I'm too fat.'

'Yeah, me too.'

No you're not! You're just bigger than some kids.

'Mum says I shouldn't worry about it.'

Jenny eats her cake. I like her mum. She's right. Jenny's all right. Why should she worry? Why should she feel less acceptable than those other twits with little bikinis?

But I feel a rift. My great big unworthiness is between us. It's just me. I'm too fat. Matron Rogers is always lurking in the background, graphing the evidence. I envy Jenny with her Mum who tells her she's all right.

Matron Rogers sent a letter to my father. He gets it out of his pocket while we're having lunch in his kitchen.

'I got a letter from Burnside about a diet for you two girls.'

Don't talk about it. Shut up. Mind your own business.

'I don't know what all the fuss is about. Do you?' Dad says.

No. And don't talk about it. It's not your . . . Wait on. Do you mean we're all right? Not ugly? I need to know. Need to think he is a good judge of things like this.

'It's 'cause they say we're too fat.' Kerry hasn't got a single subtle bone in her body.

'No you're not! What do they expect me to do about it anyway?' My father seems annoyed. He rarely criticises the keepers of his daughters. He puts his letter back in his pocket.

That's the end of it! Our father has pronounced us acceptable. I'm so relieved. My body isn't up for discussion or anything. But still I have to carry on with Matron Rogers' diet.

Then on one visit to the clinic Matron Rogers announces, 'Mm. I think we can stop the diet now.'

'All right.' Who cares!

'Don't you feel better now that weight is off?'

'No.' Was I sick?

'You don't feel any better or healthier?'

'No.' I'm the same.

I can't believe she thinks I'm all right now. She's sure to find something else wrong with me soon. I try not to care.

Meanwhile it's back to the chocolate cream, homemade honeycomb and marshmallow for snacks and cake instead of carrot sticks with sandwiches for lunch.

I try hard not to care about how I look and what people think of me, people outside Ivanhoe. I feel accepted where I am and I try to ignore the outside world that I'll have to survive in in two years time.

I wish I didn't have those aweful nightmares. Sometimes they start as dreams. I'm walking peacefully down a path and Roger, Nanna's beloved dog, runs up to meet me. I'm thrilled to see him. I've missed him since he died. Suddenly he lunges at my throat, baring his fangs. Chill terror gives me strength to grab his jaws, like the Tarzans Grip figure does to the lion. I rip Roger's head apart, realising as I do that I love him but being unable to stop myself mutilating his lovely head. As I tear him apart I see deep into his eyes, pools of sorrow. His tears roll slowly out of his faithful eyes and my own sorrow confuses my terror. As I cry into his mangled mane he is still a threat yet I know he still loves me. Waking is the only solution. Terror fades eventually and, finally, sleep returns.

Except for one night when I couldn't get back to sleep, even after the terror had gone. I started thinking about stars and the universe that went on for ever and about me, a tiny speck, drifting aimlessly out and out, completely and utterly alone, forever in cold, endless time and space. The chilling nothingness was far worse than any loneliness I knew.

A rich powerful voice, that was not a voice but an awareness, said to me, inside, 'I Am with you.'

I Am came with me through the universe and I was enfolded in an incredible, warm stillness where I knew I belonged among the stars, on the earth and with I Am. I knew with an unfamiliar but sure part of me, that I Am was God. Not God who they talked about at church or Sunday school. I Am was bigger, stiller, safer, stronger.

The world outside mightn't be too big. I'll be right. I can do anything anyone tells me. I know about the world outside. After all I've got make-up, well sort of, and deodorant, a hairstyle, a bra and a nice face. I can survive visits to people's houses and I've got thin enough too. What more could there be to know!

A FAMILY HOLIDAY

Changes kept happening. The most dramatic was that anyone with any sort of family was allowed to go home for two weeks of the summer school holidays. Again I was so proud of my father who made us a family, who made us somebodies. Kerry and I imagined that we'd have all sorts of adventures in this burst of freedom. We would come back for our final years so worldly wise and sophisticated. We'd practise for what we'd been waiting ten years for: leaving Burnside and being a real family.

Miss Molesworth, the new social worker, wants to talk about our plans.

'You've heard that people are going home for holidays at Christmas, haven't you, girls?'

'Yeah.'

'You're really looking forward to going to your Dad's, aren't you!'

'Yeah.'

'You know your father hasn't been well, don't you?'

'He's better now.' Come on. Get on with the plans!

'Yes. That's true. He is a little better but he's still very frail.'

201

Dad's all right. He said so. What's this about?

'Now I don't want you to get upset but I want you to think about the strain it will put on your Dad having you at home for the holiday.'

Stunned. My world starts falling apart.

'Do you see what I mean, Kate? Kerry?' Miss Molesworth asks.

'Nuh.'

'We'll behave ourselves. We won't be a strain.'

'Yes, of course you'll behave. But Kate, your father is old. He's seventy-six and he isn't well. Looking after two teenage girls could be too much for him. I'd like you both to think about staying here with us for the holidays.'

Stay here? We can't. The nobody who I sometimes am, shivers.

'Dad said we're going.'

'Yes, he wants you to go home. But what I want you to think about is that he is very frail and it might be too much for him. There'll be other children left here and there'll be special activities for those who stay.'

Left here! I just can't conceive of being fatherless. That's what it would be like. Like he was dead. Acid tears burn my eyes.

'Are you going to make us stay?' Kerry challenges.

'No. Kerry, I'm not going to make you stay. I just want you to think about your father. Will you do that for me?'

'Yes.' No. There's nothing to think about.

We walk home confused and frightened. We hardly speak beyond confirming what we need to hear.

'Dad said we're goin', didn't he!'

'Yeah. And they can't stop us. He's our father, not them.'

I make myself know that my father is well, that he can cope with having us at home. I talk to Mum Perry so that she'll make my knowing stronger.

'Your Dad hasn't been well. What did he say about it?'

'That we're going. So we must be.'

'We'll talk to him about it when he comes up then, see what he thinks. You girls give him his will to live. I doubt that he'd want you to stay here for the holidays.'

Will to live? He'll die if we don't go then! We are going home.

The holidays are here. We pack excitedly and wait for our taxi. Other kids are packing too. It feels like going to Huskisson.

Dad's house is so quiet, too quiet, for so long. Nothing to do but watch TV. No rules except the ones about not prying into cupboards and not going out by ourselves. This house is our father's and Ken's but it's not ours yet.

A few nights after we arrive I wake up to a voice shouting in panic not far away. I'm terrified. I listen. It's coming from my father's room. What's going on? Is someone trying to kill him? Couldn't be. There's only Dad's voice shouting words that can't find meaning in the darkness. I lie rigid listening through the shouting until he's quiet again. Eventually I fall asleep.

'Did you hear someone shouting last night?' I ask Kerry when we wake up.

'You mean Dad?'

'S'pose so. Was it him?'

'Yeah,' Kerry brushes it off.

'What was it . . . What . . . Well what was he doing?'

'Ken reckons he has nightmares about Nazis and the war and that. Haven't you heard him before?'

'No.'

'He goes on all night sometimes. Ken reckons he won't tell him what it's about, so it's no use asking.'

I'd always thought the story Dad told me about being a spy was just a story. But now I want to know more and Dad always dodges talk about the war. Kerry says that Ken told her not to ask him. The nightmares were never explained.

Other mysteries are about to unfold.

Ken's gone to work and Kerry's busy outside with Dad.

I test the cupboard where Dad put that little grey book. I'm sure I'm mature enough to understand whatever is in it. The door opens and there it is. The little grey book, 'Treasured Memories'. I feel guilty disobeying my father but curiosity gets me over that.

I open the book. Yes, there's that poem, 'My Pal'. Here's another:

We speak of the past as the good old days,
Those days we spent together;
When the world was young and our hearts were gay,
Come sun or chilly weather.
Now we travel along to the Great Unseen,
With many regrets for the Might-have-been.
But come, grow old along with me,
And you'll find God's best is yet to be.

That's a mystery. I dismiss it as I remember the other mystery that Dad snatched away from me. Is it still there? Turn back a few pages. Yes, here it is. The folded paper, browning, slipped between the cover and the first page. I tug it gently and it comes to me. I unfold the secret words, written in my father's familiar hand.

A few weeks after Norma died,
Kate said to me one day:
'Daddy, will Mummy ever come back to us?'
Before I could answer, Kenny (aged 6) said:
'She won't come back.'
Only one ever came back
That was Jesus.

I stare at it.

This is what Dad got so upset about! This is the big secret! It's just Sunday school stuff. They always tell us that Jesus rose from the dead. Everyone knows that. What a secret! I put the book away, satisfied that I've seen enough. I still don't understand why Dad got so angry but some things about him are a mystery. It's better to leave them alone. He doesn't like talking about our mother or our life with her. He gets sad when we try to.

Another thing I find while poking about in the cupboard is a long wooden box covered with leather and bordered with a fine gold line. It's held shut with tiny etched gold clasps. It looks very important but it's harder to examine without my father seeing so I don't try to hide what I'm up to.

I open the box expecting to find jewels or perhaps just one fabulous necklace. I don't. Instead I find a set of six round metal discs and a slightly rusty tin marked 'Tea Bushell's. 1/6'. I stack the discs in a neat pile. They fit perfectly into each other. I leave the tin until I've got the two metal dishes out and hung them by their gold chains on a bar with a leather tab. Scales. I know what they are. I hold them up and wait for the dishes to settle.

'Ah. You've found the scales,' my father's voice beside me is animated, not cranky.

'Yeah. What are these round things for?'

He explains that they're troy weights and that there should be a set of pennyweights somewhere too.

I turn the little Bushells tin over to see how it opens. There's something scratched into the back. 'S. Wade'. Twice it's written, the second time to get the 'S' the right way around. Who is this S. Wade who doesn't know how to do 'S' properly? Am I going to find old tea in here? Is that all?

The lid is hard to twist off but I get it at last. Inside there's the complete set of pennyweights accompanied by a set of thin rectangular grain weights. The full set. The only things left in the tin now are some little bits of rock or something. I take them all to my father and ask, 'Who's S. Wade, Dad?'

'Who?'

'S. Wade. It's on this tin with the scales.'

He turns the tin over and replies, 'Hmm. I don't know any S. Wade. S. Wade? No. Doesn't ring any bells.'

'Where did all this come from? Whose is it? What's it all for?'

Although I wouldn't discover that S. Wade was my mother's uncle for another thirty years, I discover now that it's good to load Dad up with lots of questions.

He tells me that in the Depression, he didn't have anywhere to live so he and lots of other men went to live in the bush.

'Were you a swaggie?'

'A swaggie? Yes, I suppose I was. Or a tramp. There were lots of us camped out then, looking for work. We came to town for rations then went bush again.'

I'm caught up in the magic of my father the swagman. I'm amazed that he's had a life that was so different to the parts I've been in. Sometimes we go bushwalking with Mum Perry. Sometimes we take lunch. But my Dad lived there! Out in the bush!

'What did you do in the bush?'

'Oh, we'd trap rabbits for stew, sold the skins or we'd pan for gold, tell yarns . . .'

'Gold? Did you get any?'

'Not much,' he chuckles. 'Some blokes, coves we called them, I think, had scales just like those to weigh their gold before they cashed it in.'

'Are these your scales then?'

'Mm. They must have been mine. Wouldn't have had much work to do though, not with the pittance of gold I found!'

'Who's S. Wade then?'

'Don't remember him. Must be some bloke I met out there. Could have bought some tea from him I suppose. Could've thrown in the tin for luck.'

'Why would you buy tea from a bloke in the bush?'

'There were no shops out there. You only went to town for supplies once a month and if you ran out of anything you bought it from other men, or swapped it, or waited 'til you went to town again.'

As Dad talks I see a different man to the one I know. He's lived in a world that's totally foreign to me. I feel removed from him, yet pleased that he's so interesting. Maybe he could be a war hero too. I don't know why he won't talk about it. At least he belongs with the heroic explorer sort of people who lived in the bush.

Now Dad's in the world of the scales. He shows me how to use them. We weigh the tiny nuggets that are kept in the

Bushells tea tin. I'm surprised and disappointed that they are gold. They're not shiny and smooth. They don't sparkle and, worst of all, they're very small. Dad chats about the different people he met on the road but I don't care about them. I just want him to keep telling me about himself. I'm hungry for more hero stories. I don't get them. Bingo gets in the way.

Bing is Dad's oldest friend. He's a cranky, old cat who never comes home on visiting days unless he's hungry. Dad feeds him and off he goes to mind his own business in his own world. We love our Bingo because Dad does. We don't mind the distance between us. He's in our family.

I asked Dad how the cat got its funny name. He had to talk about our mother then. He said that she had named the cat after Bing Crosby because they sang the same. I liked that my mother was funny, that she'd made such a permanent joke.

Now Dad's poor old Bingo is sick. He lies about the house in puddles and drags his back legs just the small distance that his front legs can manage. He looks as if he's almost dead. It's frightening to see him dragging himself along as if he's trying to catch up with his life, but not quite making it.

'We'll have to get the vet up to look at him.'

The vet won't come so Ken gets the lucky job of taking Bingo to the vet on his motor bike. Bingo is gently bundled in a towel and then into Dad's work bag. His feeble yowls and futile swipes of his front paws let us know he isn't impressed with this indignity.

When they get back, Ken says the vet thinks it would be better to have Bingo put down.

'I won't have that,' Dad says angrily. 'He doesn't deserve that kind of treatment.'

I don't understand the emotion in it. Bing is only a cat and he's old, smelly and sick. It seems sad to leave him dragging himself about in puddles all day. We could easily get another cat.

Ken and Dad start arguing. I go away. It's a quiet argument but it feels dangerous. Ken seems young and strong and he's being cheeky and Dad's getting upset and he seems . . . he seems so . . . little.

All the things that Dad was and is are so confusing and worrying.

A few days later Bingo dies. Dad's tears fall as he strokes the dead cat clumsily and says a shaky goodbye.

'We'll give him a good Christian burial,' he announces. 'He deserves that at least. Don't you old friend. A good Christian send off.'

'Is he . . . Can he . . . I mean how can you have a Christian burial for a cat? And we haven't got . . . you know . . . like Mr Hardie or Mr Ross at church anyway.'

'We don't need a minister here,' my father says with a bitterness that's so out of character. 'We can do it ourselves. We'll say a prayer or have a hymn. You girls know some prayers don't you?'

'Yeah, but just Our Father and that. Not for cats.'

'Our Father will do. He's been in the family for a long time and I want him to have a proper send off.'

My brother starts by digging a hole while Dad sits almost lifeless in the kitchen, waiting. I tell him I have to go and do something so start without me. I tell him I'll be back soon but I know I won't. I'm frightened of Dad like this, small and crying. What's the matter with him? He's gone all weird. I don't want to watch him bury Bing and say stupid prayers or whatever he's going to do.

He's cranky with me when I get back. I took so long that they couldn't wait for me. I hope he gets back to his old self again soon.

Dad is still allowed to go to work sometimes to do maintenance work at R.B. Davies, makers of locks and other such devices. He's been there for years and he calls it 'the works'. It's as much a part of the father we know as his work coat, work bag and hat.

'I want you to come to the works today,' he says. 'I want the men to meet you. I've been telling them about my three Ks for years and now they can meet you.'

Panic. I'm going to be inspected by a factory full of men. I'm frightened. Deep inside I'm afraid they might be dark fathers whose work coats hang on the hooks behind the bedroom doors.

'But we have to go to town to do the Christmas shopping today.' I'm so relieved to have a good reason not to go to the factory. We've got our pocket money to spend on presents. 'We can't go any other day. It'll be after Christmas, too late.'

'Oh yes. Well, try to get back in time. The men would love to meet you. What bus are you getting?' He's not going to give up. He works out how long it should all take. He reckons that if we don't waste time we'll be able to get to the factory before the hooter goes.

'All right. We'll try.'

'Do you want to go to the factory?' Kerry asks when we get on the bus.

'No! I don't wanna.'

'Let's not go. I don't wanna either.'

'Yeah. Let's just say we ran out of time.'

'He really wants us to, doesn't he?'

'Yeah.'

I feel so guilty about letting Dad down. He's obviously so proud of us and we're going to disappoint him. But I'll lie and disappoint him if I have to, to keep away from darkness. Kerry's not wanting to go either makes it easier.

We spend the day window shopping and buying presents. It takes ages because we have little idea of what there is to buy. We stick mostly to Coles and Woolworths. I've been in the hardware shop with Dad and I've seen so many fascinating things there that you can look at without being disturbed. I go back there to wander around and fidget with the gadgets whose purpose I have no idea about. That takes up, wastes, lots of time.

'You didn't come to the works,' Dad says.

'Sorry, Dad. We ran out of time.'

'The men were very disappointed.'

We know who was the most disappointed.

'Sorry, Dad,' we say, full of guilt and relief in equal parts.

Christmas is like the other days of our holiday but we exchange presents after breakfast. More pink nail polish, stockings, socks, hankies and tie. We don't know what to do about Christmas after that so we have an ordinary day, watching television, playing shuttlecock with screwed up paper and exploring cupboards.

I've found a photo by itself in a cupboard. A handsome man with a thatch of thick black hair sits behind a bench looking quite serious. He's wearing a vest and the sleeves of his striped shirt are rolled up just above his sinewy forearms. Behind him is a wall and behind that, the big sky.

'Who's this, Dad?'

'Show me.'

He gets his magnifying glass and holds it to the little photo for a long time. 'Oh, yes,' he says eventually. 'It's Charley Shayler.'

'Charley Shayler? That's you. Is it you? Doesn't look like you.'

I tried to cut his thatch of thick white hair a few days ago.

'At the works.'

He slides the photo back to me and I look again. There on the wall behind him are the huge letters 'R.B. Da'. There are some pipes on the bench in front of him.

'Why did they take your picture?'

'I found a way to make a join. They reckoned you couldn't do it. They'd tried everything. Then I found a way.'

'Wow. Did you invent it?' Now my Dad is an inventor too.

'Yes, I suppose I did. I invented it.'

'What is it you invented exactly?' I want details that I can skite about.

'I don't remember the name of the material. Anyway Princess, I don't think you'd understand even if I could. They gave me a bonus that day. It wasn't much, mind you, but it was good to get some recognition.'

The holiday passes. It's a curious mixture of boredom, of getting to know Dad and of companionship with Kerry that isn't beset with fear of her getting into trouble.

Now I saw our father as separate from us. He'd had so much life without us. That life became who he was for me. It stopped me seeing his frailty. It stopped me recognising my need for him to be strong and capable. I recreated him to be who I wanted and needed him to be. I was coming home for good soon.

MY LAST YEAR

My last year at Burnside is filled with people telling me who I am or who I should try to be.

The school Careers Adviser sits at her desk opposite me.

'Will you be going on at school, Katherine?'

'No.' I'm leaving so I can get out of Burnside and live with my Dad 'til a nice boy finds me. It's what I've been wanting for years.

'Are you sure? Your results show you could go on.'

'No. I'm leaving.' What's the use of studying when you're just going to be a housewife?

'Have you thought about what you want to do when you leave then.'

'Yes. I'm going to be a clerk.' Whatever that is. Or a secretary or a nurse. Just until I get married.

'You could do a business course. Have you thought of that?'

'Yes, but my father can't afford it.' And I won't need it.

'Well. Um. Perhaps you should wait for your Vocational Guidance Test before you decide.'

I loved doing the Vocational Guidance Test, especially the patterns and puzzles. By the time the test results came I was mentally headed for home and so they were set aside. My superior sense of design would not be needed where I was going.

Miss Molesworth calls me to her office regularly to pour out her worries about my leaving. I resent any suggestion that I might not be able to cope with what lies ahead for me.

Everyone else has coped. Well, there was Bob Jones who people reckon committed suicide, but that's just a rumour. Idle gossip, as Mum Perry would say.

'You know that your father is very weak and old don't you, Kate. I've been to see him and we've made arrangements for him to go away for a holiday. He needs a rest.'

'Yeah. He told us.'

He hadn't had a holiday for twenty years and he said it might be good to be spoilt for a while.

'Kate, you have to try to understand that your father might not be able to look after you. We've talked about how he might need to go and live in a nursing home.'

'How long will he have to stay there?'

'People usually go there when they're too old to be at home. He wouldn't come back to the house at Marrickville. He'd have to sell it.'

Sell it? But we're going to live there! We've always been going to live there. What will happen to me? My head spins. I shiver.

'I know this is hard for you to face up to, Kate, but your father may not have long to live. He's a very old man.'

Shut up. You don't know!

I hate the tears that fall, that might mean I know she's right.

'You can stay at Burnside if you want to and finish your Higher School Certificate. Then we could find you a place to live and you could get a job. Your Aunty Dot has offered to take you.'

I'm going home to Dad. Aunty Dot isn't my real aunty. I didn't even know she existed until a few months ago when someone said, 'How come the Westons go with your relations on visiting days?'

'What relations? We haven't got any relations.'

213

'Yeah ya have. That lot the Westons go out with. They said they're your relations and Joanne told everyone. Didn't you know?'

The Westons live in Cumbrae and we see them at school and church but we hardly know them.

I ask my Dad, keeper of all family knowledge, about the relations.

'Oh, they're just some distant relations of your mother's I suppose,' he says dismissively.

Dad talks with them next visiting day and we're invited over to sit with them.

'Oh! You're just like your mother! It's so good to see you at last. We've often wondered how you were.'

Kerry and I sidle away and become very concerned for the well being of the Weston girls. We're not comfortable with all that affection.

'Charley, you'll have to bring the girls to see Mum,' Aunty Dot enthuses while I stare at the first person I've heard call my father by his christian name. 'She'd love to see them!'

So next outing day Dad takes us to Aunty Dot's house at Lane Cove. Aunty Marj lives next door with Uncle George. We meet Uncle George and their children. Susanne, they tell us proudly, is in the Miss Australia Quest. I feel so drab. The worst is yet to come. Meeting Brendon who is definitely the most handsome boy in the universe. Warren Garland fades from significance as I give my heart to Brendon, who doesn't even notice.

Another person appears. Her name is Jane. She's my godmother.

'What's that?'

'It means I was a friend of your mother's,' says Jane who suddenly looks uncomfortable.

I dismiss her as nice but irrelevant. My mother died ages ago and she is irrelevant to me now too.

Although I resent that these relations have chosen other girls to take out, I'm relieved too. I don't have to try to fit in with them, to be like them. It would be too hard. Cousins feel superior and sophisticated and the aunts are better at a distance. No. I'm not going to Aunty Dot when I leave Burnside. I belong with Dad.

'We'll send your Dad some new clothes from you girls,' Miss Molesworth says. 'That should cheer him up and, you never know, the holiday might just give him a new lease of life. But we have to be realistic, Kate. He is seventy-seven and he's not well.'

I sob all the way home. To Ivanhoe, not home. Marrickville is home, my real home. Where my father lives. Lives.

Our new assistant house mother at Ivanhoe is Miss Driver. She sees my red eyes and asks what's wrong. Although she'll become important later, she can't help me right now. Miss Driver sits knitting. I'm cold deep inside but she can't warm me. She usually listens to us and discusses our gripes but right now she doesn't know what to say. She's been all over Australia but not to Marrickville. She recognises other girls' home towns. Tibooburra, Nyngan, Boggabri and Canowindra. She's been everywhere but she can't get me safely to Marrickville.

Mum Perry isn't her new self when she has an assistant who doesn't like her. Miss Driver doesn't and so we see more of the old Miss Perryman nowadays. Mum Perry isn't about to warm me.

Although Miss Driver is detached, I've come to like her. She listens, advises and discusses. I don't realise how much I like her until she tells us some months later that she's leaving. I'm devastated. There's nothing I can do to make her stay, so I want to hurt her, to make her go away quickly.

'You're a deserter. You just pretend you like us,' I yell.

'Kate, that's not true,' she says calmly.

''Tis so. Or else you wouldn't be going.'

'You know that's not true.'

'It is true.' You're going 'cause you hate us. Well, good riddance to bad rubbish. I'm trying to crack her cool calm. I fail. I want to break her heart, make her hurt. Like I am. She tells me, calmly, that she can't do all she wants to do for young people when she's working here.

'Yeah. You're just deserting us to go and be nice to some other kids. Better ones. Somewhere else.'

She tries to reason it through but I'm hurting and she still isn't. I pronounce her a deserter again and I tell everyone her new name is Deserter Driver and that's what we'll call her.

The hurting ones start up a chant, 'Deserter Driver's leaving. Deserter Driver's leaving.' She lets this go on for a while then, 'All right! This has gone far enough. It's got to stop. Now. There's work to be done.'

I don't talk to her much before she leaves. I won't pretend that all's well, that it doesn't hurt.

My father has his holiday at Camden. A week after he goes, a letter comes from him. I rip it open as if my life depends on it. The writing is shaky and doesn't sit neatly on the lines. That's just because of his blind eye, not because he's dying. He sounds cheerful and well and, what's more, he says he's well. He says that he's looking forward to having us all together again at his home.

I go to my next appointment with Miss Molesworth, armed with the letter.

'That's nice. It's just what he needed.' She smiles warmly.

'Thank you for arranging it.'

I mean it and I'm glad I know about good manners.

'It's the kind of care he needs, Kate. We'll have to see how he goes looking after himself when he gets back. Meanwhile we should be looking at your options.'

I don't need any options. The letter! He's going to be all right.

Miss Molesworth knows her truth, so she talks about staying at Burnside or going to live with Aunty Dot. I know my truth so I let her words get to my ears but not to my brain. They aren't needed there. I like that she speaks to me as if I'm mature and good but I wish she'd see that I am going home to live with my father.

Meanwhile there's the trial School Certificate to get done. I'm very nervous being the only Burnsider doing it. Jenny and I decide we'll do our best but we don't care about it. It's only the trial and neither of us wants to do the Higher School Certificate anyway. Jenny is going to be a secretary and I'm going home to my father and I'll be a clerk or typist or something. We both pass the trial and feel proud.

Jenny is bridesmaid at her sister's wedding and she brings a photo in to show me. The photo is proof that there's no need for us to try to do more time at school.

'But Kate, what if you don't meet a nice boy?' Miss Molesworth asks.

Everyone meets a nice boy and gets married. Everyone says so.

'I will,' I shrug. I feel rather foolish claiming the miracle that I really don't know the mechanics of.

'You probably will, Kate, but until you do you'll have to be able to support yourself. Your Dad won't be able to help, not on the pension.'

'Yeah but I'm going to be a clerk in a bank.'

'You could have a much more interesting career if you did more study.'

'Yeah but then I couldn't get out of Burnside.'

'You're very sure you want to leave us aren't you?'

'Yeah.'

'You've been looking forward to it for a long time. You and your Dad. We'll look into a job with one of the big insurance companies. Meanwhile I'd like you to try something to help you get to know some people your own age.'

I suspect another social or something is on the agenda.

'I know people my age.'

'People outside Burnside.'

'I know an outsider. Jenny at school.'

'Kate, you don't get much practice at meeting young people and you won't get over your shyness with them by hiding away.'

She wants me to go to a church at Parramatta with a teacher from school because they have a fellowship there for people my age. She wants me to think about it and we'll talk it through next week.

All I can think about her idea is that I don't want to go. I'm too shy. I won't fit and they won't want me around.

I tell Christine about it and she reckons it sounds like fun. It's all right for her. She doesn't have to go. I talk with Mum Perry and she thinks it would be good for me. So is castor oil.

'Why don't you ask if Christine can go with you?' she suggests.

Miss Molesworth isn't impressed with the idea.

'Kate, Christine won't be with you when you're trying to make your way in the world. You need to go by yourself. Well, you won't be by yourself completely. Miss Laws is picking you up.'

'Do I have to go?' I ask, not even trying to hide my resentment at being forced to torture myself.

'It will be good for you, Kate.'

'Do I have to go?'

'Yes. You have to go. You'll be fine. Don't get worried about it. Just go along and see what happens.'

I stew about Christine not coming with me through a week of scrubbing my face with special soap and plastering it with medicated cream.

Miss Laws and her boyfriend pick me up and after hello we don't know what to say. They talk together all the way there, deposit me in the hall and go to talk with some people their age. I hang around wondering what to do until Miss Laws remembers I'm her burden.

'That's the fellowship group over there,' she says pointing to a group of cheerful friends.

All right. I've got to go over there and say something. I feel drab and insignificant despite my deodorant and other trimmings.

I stand near the circle of friends hoping someone might say hello and make a space for me. They don't. Are all the trimmings making me invisible? Can't they see my hairstyle and my medicated cream, my lovely eyes, waiting, hoping, losing hope? Maybe the disguises aren't doing their job. Every pair of eyes mine meet turn back to familiar ones as if they haven't seen mine.

I wait and wait. What else can I do? I can't stand waiting somewhere else. I can't go home.

Suddenly a girl steps back and nearly trips over me.

'Oh sorry. Didn't know you were there.'

'It's all right,' I mumble as she floats happily away.

Now's my chance. I step into her place feeling like a clumsy hippo in the company of swans. At last a swan sees that the hippo is real.

'Hello. New, are you?'

'Yes. I've come for fellowship.' I try to smile but it might have been a mistake. I manoeuvre my lip off my dry gums. Wow at least I said something! Now it's all supposed to start happening. Conversation. Fellowship.

'Oh,' says the happy swan and turns back to her friends.

I stand in the same place not knowing what else to do. Happy swans giggle with each other and watch for others to arrive. Gradually they turn away from me so there are two groups and I'm the hippo in the middle. Alone waiting for fellowship. Angry. Wanting to pull their stupid feathers out and trip them over in their stupid high heels. Wanting to shout that I've done all the right things with deodorant and all that so why am I invisible again. Surely you can see a hippo bloody potamus. I hate them all. I'm never coming back here. Never.

Miss Laws and what's his name call everyone to sit down so fellowship can start. I sit at the back. When they introduce me, I glow even redder. When they say how nice it is to have me, my eyes burn with angry tears trying not to roll out. When they say they hope everyone will make me welcome, I want to spit at them all. When they talk about spreading the gospel of the love of Jesus wherever you are, I mumble inside, 'Oh shut up. Take me home.'

At home I cry and Mum Perry finds me. I tell her how awful it was, how hopeless I was.

'I'm not going back,' I splutter. 'They can't make me.'

Mum Perry doesn't think it sounded much good and she doesn't think I was the problem. She doesn't think I should get too upset about it. She'll talk to Miss Molesworth.

'Kate, things are often difficult the first time you try them,' says Miss Molesworth.

'I'm not going back.'

'Just try it one more time. I'm sure the next time wi . . .'

'I'm not going back.'

I'm surprised by my speaking so forcefully. I'm pleased too as Miss Molesworth agrees to let it go for now.

'I've arranged an interview for you with Mrs Collins at the Colonial Mutual next Friday,' she says a week later.

'Do I have to go by myself? Do I have to get time off school?'

These are only some of the questions whirling around in my head now that it's actually happening. What do I do there? What do I say? What if she thinks I'm too fat or too ugly too? What is colonial mutual?

'I'll go with you. I'll pick you up after school.'

What a relief! But I suppose we'll have to talk about how frail she reckons Dad is all the way there and all the way back.

Miss Molesworth concludes today's chat with, 'I'll see you next Friday, Kate. And don't worry. You'll be fine. You've been brought up well and you present yourself well. You'll get over your shyness.'

'Thank you, Miss Molesworth,' to prove I have good manners, to put a seal on her words and trap them in my mind. She likes me! She thinks I'm all right.

It's Friday at last. I feel very important having a car to get in instead of the Burnside bus. Miss Molesworth chats happily about how nice it will be when I have a job and how I'll be able to save up and buy nice clothes and perhaps even a sewing machine so that I can make whatever I want. At last we arrive in Martin Place where the sandstone edifice of the Colonial Mutual office stands like a foreboding castle. I'm not terrified. I'm too numb for that.

'How do you feel?' the ever chirpy Miss Molesworth asks.

'Good, thank you.' At least I know the right answer to that.

'I know you're good, Kate,' Miss Molesworth grins, 'but I asked you how you are. It's better to say "fine thank you".'

'All right.' A handy tip but why confuse me with such trivial stuff now!

We cross the foyer and get in the lift where man in uniform smiles as he holds the doors open.

'Seventh floor. Personnel. Thank you,' smiles Miss Molesworth. At least she knows where she's going.

The lift driver closes a heavy metal gate, closes two chunky doors and pushes a lever to take us up to Mrs Collins. My stomach lurches up to me just before we get out. We're released into a room full of people who look up from their desks disinterestedly, then down again. They look so neat and tidy with nice hairdos and make-up and clothes from shops. I feel so very dowdy and plain in my brown school uniform. I follow Miss Molesworth through a doorway.

'How do you do, Mary. It's good to see you,' says a smooth, warm voice.

I'm introduced to a movie star who Miss Molesworth reckons is Mrs Collins. She's so beautiful! I'm thoroughly intimidated by her perfection. I'm ashamed of my clumsiness, my grubby, creased school uniform that only just makes the distance around me and of my glasses and my pimply face. Mrs Collins, tall, elegant, immaculate, asks, 'How are you, Kate?'

'Good thank you.' I dare not look at Miss Molesworth.

'Come in and sit down, won't you.'

Miss Molesworth makes me go in first.

Where do I sit? There's two chairs.

'Kate Shayler, isn't it.'

Mrs Collins takes some papers out and puts them in front of her. She writes my name in perfect handwriting. She smiles through perfect, movie star teeth. 'You told me on the phone, Mary, that Kate has been with Burnside for quite a while and that she does well at school.'

'Yes that's right. She is a very responsible girl at the home too.' My social worker smiles at me as if she's proud.

'Good. That's good. Now Kate, you want to work for the Colonial Mutual do you?'

'No. I mean, yes . . . I mean Miss Molesworth said I have to. I mean, I think um . . .' I don't have a clue! My face is already burning up and we've only just begun.

'Kate's very shy but we're sure she'll grow out of it. We know she's well spoken and a very trustworthy girl. Very reliable and a hard worker too.' Miss Molesworth, best ever social worker to the rescue.

Mrs Collins nods and smiles. She says she's sure that working here will help me get over being shy. She says I'll meet lots of people my own age and they'll invite me out and show me around.

'Well, what do you think, Kate? Would you like to come and work with us?'

'Yes please.'

My employer tells me about the conditions of my employment. I agree to everything. I don't let on that I haven't a clue what the Colonial Mutual is or does, except that people work at desks and watch lifts arrive and depart.

After the formalities are over Mrs Collins talks about how she likes Burnside because it reminds her of her Scottish relatives. My eyes try hard to stay in their sockets as she says that she envies girls who learn highland dancing.

At last she flows gracefully to a standing position that tells me the torture's nearly over. She reassures me that I'll fit in well at the CML. I can start work as soon as the exams are over.

'That went well I think,' Miss Molesworth says as we head back to the car.

'Oh! But I was really, you know. Shy!'

'Yes but you'll get over that. You've got a job. Won't your Dad be pleased!'

'Do I have to start straight after the exams?'

'What do you mean?'

'Jenny's having a holiday first and she asked if I could go with her.'

'Kate, that costs money and you don't have any.'

'I could ask Dad.'

'He's only getting a pension now. He couldn't afford it.'

I see the chance for my first great adventure fade away but I'm relieved really. I wouldn't know what to do in Queensland and Jenny would be so embarrassed by all my dreadful Burnside clothes. They're nothing like the ones she's going to buy.

At home I tell everyone I've got a job. I hope I look very office workerish and more mature than the others. Most of all I hope I don't look as mystified and terrified as I feel. Thank goodness we have bedrooms to hide in. I can do my worrying and secret crying with only one other person. I cry under my blanket after lights out.

A wonderful surprise comes my way a few weeks before the School Certificate starts. Deserter Driver's room hasn't been filled with another assistant. Mum Perry calls me to the sewing room.

'I've got an idea to help you study for your exams,' she says, with a rare twinkle in her eye. 'Would you like to have Miss Driver's room?'

'Have it? What . . . How do you mean?'

'I mean you can move in to that room so you'll have a quiet place to study. It must be hard with the others around talking and playing and interrupting, so I thought you might be better off there.'

I'm not shy with Mum Perry and this is the first time for a long time that I've been lost for words with her.

'Would you like to?'

'Yes please. Am I really allowed?' I'm bursting. The words only use up a millionth of my excitement.

'Yes. No-one else is using it and we want you to do well.'

I move all my stuff out of the purple room into the staff room. I check all the drawers and the wardrobe to see if Deserter Driver has left anything, preferably money or jewels. Next I set out my brush, comb and mirror on the dressing table. I put all my school books in subject piles on the floor and sit on the bed, my bed, trying to let the bedspread soak up my excess energy. Totally alone, I feel whole somehow. I feel believed in. While I sit gazing at my luck, I realise that the other kids will call me a crawler and tease me relentlessly. I won't like that but I feel somehow separate from them now. Anyway, I wouldn't give this up for anything.

I've misread those girls. There's a bit of teasing but they're almost as excited as I am about my good fortune. They think I'm a genius and that I'll know every answer to every question in the School Certificate because I'm allowed to be in the staff room. I want to study really hard and do well for us all.

But I'm still going home to Dad after it.

I, the student, am excused from work when I get home in the afternoons. Matron Rogers has excused me for being too fat so I don't have to go to the clinic either. Miss Molesworth still has occasional talks with me but mostly she leaves me to study too, with a promise that we'll talk again before I leave.

It's heaven getting home. We all have afternoon tea then I go up to my very own room to study, whatever that is. I lie on my bed and feel the stillness. I daydream about trips to England and being dressed in beautiful clothes and being surrounded by boys who all want to talk with me and marry me. This is how it will be when I get out. Then I remember that I'm here to study.

I read my textbooks over and over again and I read my class notes. I work through all the maths problems in the textbook and all the exercises in my science books. I work on trial balances for commerce and translate passages to and from French. I hope this is studying. As the exams get closer teachers pile on homework and I wonder how I ever had time to do anything but study.

I do my best at the School Certificate and I'm sure I'll pass because I studied so hard. Jenny and I don't really say goodbye. We make plans to ring each other and meet when she gets back from her holiday. I begin to feel like a stranger to her. I feel like I've become someone else who has to keep up the old life for a short time before leaving to become who I really am. The framework in which our friendship exists is melting away. I want to hold on to it. I can't see the dimensions for the world outside clearly and I can't see where Jenny fits.

My twelve years here are about to end and the future stretches out ahead. I'm going to be . . . who? I'm beginning to feel like a stranger, even to myself.

PERFECT FAMILY

My day arrives. I'm really, really getting out! I'm nervous, excited. I'm a person to be envied. I feel heroic. I push aside all Miss Molesworth's concerns about how difficult my life is going to be. What would she know! Everyone thinks, no, knows, everyone knows that getting out marks the beginning of a life of utter bliss.

Girls who leave often make promises to come back to see their friends or ask their parents to adopt them. No-one ever keeps these promises. Life outside must be so good it makes you forget about the girls back at Ivanhoe. I'm not going to. I'll come back and bring presents and take kids out who don't get visitors.

Oh wait! I don't want to . . . It's not until right now that I realise that leaving means not living here any more, not being around all the familiar people who have been my life so far. Leaving means leaving them behind!

Frightening new emptiness. No. Push it away. I'll be coming back. I'll stay connected. Mum Perry keeps snapping at me. Do this. Do that. Clean out your locker, thoroughly. Put everything into the brown cardboard hat box. Yes, it's yours to keep. Put your linen in the basket. Snap. Snap. Snap. At least I won't have her snapping at me any more.

I pack my brush, comb and mirror set carefully and my sewing basket too. I keep my solitaire set, some comics and pencils. I give away other childish things to those less fortunate. I put my hat box of treasures beside the suitcase Mum Perry has packed my clothes into.

I consign everything to do with school, except my Merit Certificates, to the hungry flames of the heater. I've heard the shrieks of joy as some other girls have punished their teachers this way. I don't want to punish mine. I just want a dramatic ritual to farewell my struggle to be brainy. I want a symbol that shows I'm now free to be found by a nice boy, swept away in a flood of romance and married to produce six perfect children and live happily ever after.

Mum Perry keeps snapping. I wonder what she reckons I've done wrong now. No-one will boss me around or pick on me for nothing from now on.

There's nothing to do but hang around 'til Miss Molesworth comes to take me home. To my real home. I carry my bags to the back road to wait. Other kids play around and I join in a bit but I feel separate. I am not a homes kid any more. I wish I didn't feel this sadness that keeps creeping up, threatening to spoil my moment. Oh anyway, I'll be so busy when I get home.

Mr and Mrs Ross arrive.

Gawd. What have I done now? What are they gunna tell me off for?

'Well Kate, your day is here at last,' Mr Ross smiles.

'Mm.' Get on with it will you. Tell me off and go away. I'm leaving.

'We've just come to say goodbye, dear, and to wish you all the best,' says Mrs Ross.

'Oh.'

'Come back and see us sometime, won't you. I'm sure your Dad will be very proud of you.'

'I'll come back.'

The Rosses shake my hand and go.

Mum Perry wipes her eyes as the car arrives. Suddenly I feel so very confused and anxious. Miss Molesworth chats about how excited I must be and how different life is going to be, as my bags are put in the boot. Slow down! Slow down. I don't want this. Yes I do. I'm leaving but why does it feel so . . . so . . .

'Well, it's time to say goodbye to Mum Perry.'

No, wait on. I don't want this. Not goodbye! I don't want her not to be in my life!

'Goodbye, Mum Perry. Thank you for . . . everything.'

I don't know the words for what I'm feeling. I'm too choked up anyway. I hope Mum Perry will save me by interrupting my inadequacy and making her own little speech, like she does sometimes when other girls leave. She doesn't. She just turns away and walks quickly inside.

Come back. Say something. Don't be angry. What have I done? Don't get cranky. Not now!

Kerry comes to say, 'Bye, sis. See ya soon.'

She has to finish this year of school before she comes home for a holiday and camp. She wants to stay at Marrickville. She still hates Burnside. So they've said that if all goes well she might be allowed to stay. We know they want her to come back to Burnside but she's very stubborn.

The other kids come to say goodbye, to wish me good luck and tell me what a lucky thing I am. Their cheery farewells fill the street as we drive off.

'How does it feel?' asks Miss Molesworth.

'Good but why didn't Mum Perry say goodbye or anything?'

'She's upset.'

'But why? I did all my work.'

'It's not about doing your work, Kate. Think about it. You've been with Mum Perry for a long time. You've been like a daughter to her, like family. She's sad that you're going, not angry. She's losing one of her family.'

'The Burnside family.' They've said that to us so often it's become trite. It doesn't mean what it means when we say it in the Shayler family. Does it? Did it?

Mum Perry's family! Have I been in it for so long without realising? That means she loves me. Yeah. That's why she didn't talk. She was all choked up because she didn't want me to go.

We started off so badly yet I've grown to love Mum Perry without recognising it as love. Until now. When I'm losing her.

Us girls have only thought of love, in the Burnside context, in terms of the tacky comics and in dirty jokes told to shock and disgust. And more recently in the sentimental syrup of Shirley Temple movies on television. Other love, family love, is what I'm going to, not what I'm leaving behind. Isn't it?

I'll miss Mum Perry. Fight tears. Exciting day. Beginning of wonderful adventure. Squash sadness, emptiness down. Get on with getting home.

The journey seems to take forever and no time at all.

Dad is waiting at the gate. I love him for being there. I love him for meaning to make everything right at last and for keeping his promises to be here when I finish school and get out of Burnside. I love him for the family he's about to make us into.

'I've got a wonderful surprise for you, Princess,' he grins. 'Come inside.'

Push the emptiness away. Push away the dark shadow. Go in to happiness.

Inside I see a blank where the lounge room used to be! A wall hides what it's become.

Dad proudly pushes the door open and stands back, beaming.

I can't believe my eyes. This is for me. So beautiful! Two beds with matching green bedspreads, a dressing table with doilies on it, wardrobes and a rug on the floor. Curtains on the window and soft green walls. Of course, it's for Kerry too but she's not here so, for now, it's mine. I can't think of anything to say. This room confirms that life is about to be perfect.

'Where did it all come from?' The Aunties?

'From the Smith Family.'

'Who are they?' Must be neighbours or other relatives.

Miss Molesworth explains who they are and how they help poor people get on their feet. I want to tell the Smith Family how much I love my new room. I want to tell them that I'll look after us now because I'm going to work, but thank you for the start.

'Let's all have a cup of tea and then I'll leave you to your family.'

My father leads the procession down the hall to the kitchen. Why is he going so slowly?

Miss Molesworth stays for a quick cuppa. We chat about what I'll wear to work on Monday and what bus and train I'll have to get and so on and then she's got to go. I walk to the door with her, trying to ward off the emptiness again.

After she goes, with a promise to ring and see how I'm going, Dad, Ken and I sit trying to be a family. We soon run out of things to say.

What do I do now? Wash the cups! That must be what you do next.

'Don't bother with that now, Princess. We'll put them through after dinner,' my father says. He's in charge.

I can't keep not knowing what to do in front of them so I go to my room. My perfect room.

I unpack my things slowly, being very careful not to take more than my share of the space. Kerry will want exactly half when she comes home. I put my brush, comb and mirror on my side of the dressing table and feel like I belong here, at this dressing table at least.

After unpacking there's nothing to do. No-one.

I wander through the house wondering what I'm allowed to touch, now that I live here. I see the things that I've longed to get my hands on for the last twelve years, ones I didn't get to in the holiday here. I assume I still can't touch them without permission, so I don't. I see a lot of things that need cleaning too. I haven't noticed them before. There are smells that I haven't noticed either. Repulsive smells that come from my father's room and the bathroom. I don't know if I'm allowed to clean anything without being told. I might offend someone because it's their job. No-one tells me what I have to do here and I don't want to ask. Although I've forgotten why, I don't want to be alone with my father and ask him anything. I go back to my room.

I'm sick of doing nothing here in my room. I wander back down the hall to the kitchen where my father and my brother are.

'Well, I'll get going then. Bye,' says Ken.

He didn't ask if he could! He just said he's going!

'All right, son. When will you be back?'

'Don't know. Don't make any tea for me, Kate. I'll get mine.'

Make tea? Do I make tea? Oh. Yeah. Miss Molesworth said I'd have to.

My brother rides off on his prized motor bike and I feel relief that he won't see my first attempt at tea. Then I feel . . . feel . . . emptiness.

Keep busy.

'Roll you some smokes, Dad?'

'Oh, I've got enough done thanks.'

Doesn't he remember that I know not to pack too much tobacco in? I used to do that when I was young but now I know.

I know he likes cups of tea but we've just had one.

'Will I get you a shandy then?'

'Huh. No. It's a bit early for that!'

'What time do you have it then?' Trying to define myself with rituals.

'Oh, later perhaps. We'll see.'

I wander back to my room and do nothing for a long while 'til I get an idea.

I find Dad hunched over the form guide with a magnifying glass jammed into the inch between his good eye and the paper. The radio blares out an incomprehensible drone that escalates to screaming madness every now and then. I've seen him like this on visiting days and I know he prefers to be left alone by his children who can't help because they don't understand. We can help look for his lottery ticket numbers although they're never there. For now though it's the form guide so I can't help.

'Dad, can I go for a walk?'

'Can you wait 'til this is over?'

'Why?'

'So I can go with you. Mind you I'm pretty slow on my pegs these days.'

'I was going to go by myself.'

'You can't go wandering about the streets by yourself!'

'Why not?'

'Anything might happen to you. There are all sorts of deviants out there, Princess.'

'But I'm just going down to the shop and around the hill.'

'No. You can't go by yourself. I'll go with you later.'

I wish I could do it Ken's way but I'm still a Burnside girl after all.

'Can I go to Nina's place then?'

I don't want to go there. It just feels better than doing nothing with nobody. Nina's family is Italian. Kerry and I have been invited in a few times on visiting days. I'm always nervous there but I'm fascinated too, watching and listening to these people who don't seem to mind my staring. They live two doors away. There's Mr and Mrs Maranos who hug the breath out of us and talk endlessly in Italian, some of which Nina translates for us. There are two brothers, Theo and Phil, who are both so handsome and romantic. I'm already shy but in their presence, I'm a totally speechless, brightly blushing wreck.

'No. You can't just go to their place without being invited. You'll have to wait for Nina to ask you.'

I go back to my room wondering who'd want to attack me if I went for a walk. There are only people like the Maranoses and the Bakers out there.

The Bakers, Mr and Mrs and their daughter Irene, live across the road. They invite us over sometimes too, more after we made friends with their dog Pixie during our holiday with Dad. The Bakers are much less interesting than the Maranoses and since Irene got a boyfriend she's hardly ever at home anyway. I suppose I'm not allowed to go over there without an invitation either.

So I do nothing again for another long time. Looking at the floor, the walls, the curtains and out the window is nothing. It just fills in time. So much time.

At last it's dinner time. Something to do. Dad says I can help him cook mashed potatoes, frozen peas and sausages. He shows me where we keep our saucepans and things. I'm disgusted at how dirty everything is. He keeps saying that he can't keep up with things now. His arthritis and his bad eyes make it very hard. He doesn't mention my brother, but he says it will be nice to have me at home to help. We help each other get dinner. Mercifully, he says he'd like to watch the telly so we sit in the dining room not having to talk while we eat. I wait for him to say Grace. He doesn't, so when he starts eating I do too.

When he's finished he shuffles out to the kitchen with our plates, his slippered feet barely leaving the ground with each step. His old hands clatter the plates onto the sink.

'I'll wash up, Dad.'

'Yes all right. Good.'

He seems relieved and shuffles back to his chair close to the TV.

I open the cupboard to reach for detergent. Waves of cockroaches scatter to the dark places in the sea of empty coke bottles. Some are drowning in dregs in the bottles. I slam the door shut before they can take refuge up my legs and before the stench can knock me out. I go to ask Dad where we keep detergent but he's snoring, mouth agape and teeth resting half way out. I wash up quickly with laundry soap, bending carefully away from the sink and the cupboard.

I sit by my sleeping father, watching television. Whatever's on I'm enthralled. This isn't Burnside. I can watch anything I like. Everything! What luxury. Except for the bad smells, the cockroaches and the absence of twenty-nine other girls to giggle with. Should I wake Dad to tell him I'm going to bed or should I leave him? There are no rules for that. I've never had to wake an adult. I don't know how to do it. So I leave Dad there and get ready for bed, very noisily, hoping to wake him. I don't.

'Goodnight, Dad,' I say as loudly as I can without shouting.

'Goodnight, Dad,' again. Loudly but still not shouting. No response. It wouldn't be right to shout at him, would it? He's an adult and you don't shout at adults. One more try, louder.

'Goodnight, Dad.'

'Umm. Oh, you're off to bed then?'

'Yeah.'

'Give me a kiss then.'

Fear. Confusion. Small child. I don't understand my fear. Something surfaces quickly then vanishes. The fact that I can't recognise it is just as scary and confusing as the thing itself, whatever it is. I kiss him quickly. Run up the hall. To my bedroom. Shut the door tight.

Pushing it all away I go to bed and drift off to sleep wondering how I'll fill a whole day tomorrow. Sunday. I just have to get through Sunday then everything will be all right.

On Monday I'll go to work.

Waking on Sunday is empty. No, 'Good morning girls. All rise,' followed by frantic, purposeful activity. No anything. Just silence. Blurry images of the previous day push me fully into this one. I'm flat. No rules to define me. Dirt, smells and cockroaches won't do it. That's not who I am. And later the screaming radio, the faithful, scary father who doesn't, can't do anything much, the brother who hardly knows me, who doesn't want me around. Where am I? Awake in a vacuum. Who am I?

'Give it time,' Miss Molesworth said.

No-one to make this right, to make me belong. No-one but me though I can't see that yet.

Should I get up? What's the right time to get up?

I lie still, using up time. Imagining what the girls at Ivanhoe will be doing. Remember belonging with them. Move on to other busyness.

Might as well get up. Get dressed. That'll be the first thing, then make my bed. Slowly. Use up time.

I make the bed absolutely perfectly, hospital corners and all. Matron Rogers would be proud. I do a long, slow Matron Rogers inspection.

Yep. That's good. Might as well have breakfast. S'pose I'm allowed.

I creep down the hall trying to avoid the creaky floorboards. It would be inconsiderate to wake anyone else with my carelessness. I creep past the gentle snoring in my father's room, past raucous snoring in my brother's room and into the kitchen.

Cornflakes. Alone, except for cockroaches creeping through cupboards. Eat slowly. Rinse plate. Ready for more nothing.

Walk past the twin laundry tubs. Wish there were some washing to do. No ironing either. Sunday. Another day of wandering about using up the endless time, imagining what the girls are doing, trying not to miss them. What movie would they miss the end of because they had to go to Sunday school? Perhaps I could watch it. No. I don't have permission. Nor do I want to sit with my father.

I resort to obsessively checking and rechecking all things related to starting work tomorrow. This keeps me from staring at the walls, the floor and the curtains in my room all over again, at least for a while. I worry about missing the bus, getting on the wrong train, getting out at the wrong station. Whatever there is to worry about, I've got it covered. No-one but me is responsible for me now. No-one will be checking on me. I have to be mature and independent now. In charge of myself. They told me that a lot.

How do I do it?

'You'll need to get up at six. Don't forget to set the alarm clock before you go to bed. Oh dear. Well, don't worry, we'll have to get you one. Have a good breakfast . . . the blue dress, the pearl brooch . . . white shoes . . . handbag . . . money for fares . . .

your lunch.' Miss Molesworth has been through it all and I've listened carefully. It was obviously relevant.

I know it all but I go over and over it. So many new things happening and I'm alone. It's all up to me.

'Dad, can I go down to the bus stop?'

'Why do you want to go there?'

'To make sure I know where it is. For going to work.'

'You shouldn't go walking around the streets by yourself.'

'But I have to make sure. What if I miss the bus tomorrow?'

My father relents. I'd been single minded in my request but, now that I'm on my way, I recognise other possibilities. Perhaps I'll bump into the Maranoses or the Bakers and they'll invite me in or talk to me.

I sit on a seat at the top of our hill watching planes landing and taking off at the airport. Not that I'm interested. I have no idea where they're all going, except England. I just watch without seeing. It's something to do to make being out take longer. Sundays are very quiet days when no-one does anything. They all go to England or somewhere. That's why I'm the only person left in Marrickville. The others will be back for church tonight. I'll be going with Miss Molesworth next Sunday. Not by myself. With Miss Molesworth.

Might as well go home and worry some more. I don't worry much about actually being at work. I don't know what there is to worry about. Yet.

So my first days back with my much longed for perfect family passed. Waiting to be told to do something, anything. Being deafened by the silence. Being disoriented by the absence of twenty-nine girls to do something with. Being lost without rules and rituals to define who I am. Waiting for something to happen in my life. Waiting for tomorrow.

Monday morning. Acid screech at six o'clock. Where am I? Fumble the alarm off. Add actions to the ritual I've rehearsed in my mind for getting ready for work. All goes well. Getting to work is easy, apart from all those strangers in the train, bodies pressing too close, breaths on my face, hands on mine as we lurch to stops and grab for the handrails. A fog of nervousness follows me up Wynyard station tunnel. It thickens to gloom as I arrive at Mrs Collins' Personnel Office on the dot of 8.30 am. She smiles her perfect, humbling smile as she welcomes me to the family of the Colonial Mutual Life. She rings someone to come and get me.

'Katherine is it?' the someone asks, but there's no time to bravely tell her I prefer Kate.

'I'll show you the bundy clock and then we'll go to your department. Which one is it? Oh yes, Collector Claims.' She's got all the details on her clipboard, like a sports teacher.

I trot along behind the voice as it floats down a passageway.

'Bundy on every morning as soon as you get here. If you're late your pay will be docked. The red numbers show you're within five minutes of the cut off time and you'll be called in to the office if you make a habit of getting to work in that five minutes. If you make a habit of being late, you'll get the sack.'

A potato sack jumps into my head as she hands me my card. An efficient clunk shows that my time is red when I bundy on today. I trot along behind her into the lift.

'Fourteen, thanks John.'

'A new lass, are you?' the lift driver smiles gently as he closes the cage and the heavy doors.

'Yes.'

'Good luck. I hope you enjoy your time here,' he says as he lets us out.

I'm more nervous than I thought I knew how to be. I'm politely dispatched to my boss, Mr Mansouriani, whose name I forget as soon as we pass the second syllable.

'Sit down, please,' he says, pointing to a chair. He sits too, straightens his tie and pulls his shirt sleeves up over the silver bands around his arms. He runs his freckled fingers through his

237

tight ginger curls then clasps his hands on his desk.

He talks at me. He's very serious. I try to look as if I understand. Why am I so anxious in this little room with this ginger man? Must be my shyness.

Eventually I hear, 'Come on out then. I'll get one of the girls to show you around.'

One of the girls. That sounds better.

People at their desks look up and smile as I'm introduced. I forget their names straightaway too.

'So, that's the Collector Claims Department,' says Mr Soupisomething. 'That's Accounts and there's the Typing Pool . . .' He might as well be telling me the composition of Sputnik fuel. 'I'll leave you with Pat now. She'll be able to tell you whatever you need to know. If you have any questions, just ask. Otherwise just do as she tells you. All right, Pat?'

Pat gives the boss a cold glare and a grunt. She tries a smile for me but it doesn't quite turn out. I'm ready to like her, to be looked after by her. She's supposed to be one of the girls. She looks like Elly, the widgie from Burnside's hospital, but she's much less cheerful.

'Don't judge a book by its cover,' says Mum Perry.

'This is your desk. Put your handbag in this drawer and your pens and stuff in the top one.' I like having a desk of my own. I wish it could be one of the ones at the back. My desk has a blotter on it and two wire trays, one empty and one full of bunches of papers with the 'Quote' forms clipped to the front.

'You've got to fill these out when someone makes a claim. Grab a biro and I'll show you the records. Oh! Wait a minute.'

Pat struts to the counter, on heels higher than I knew were possible, to talk to a man there. I try to recall what she and Mr Man . . . Soup . . . have told me in case it helps. It doesn't.

Pat comes back with more papers as the door clunks shut behind the man.

'Yeah, we'll do this one. He wants to surrender his policy so come around here and I'll show you the records.'

Anita Bryant, Cliff Richard, Bing Crosby, Dean Martin.

I follow her around a corner to a wall covered with long thin books, not round black records. As we walk I'm sifting through my mental dictionary for the word 'surrender'. 'All to Jesus I surrender' from Sunday school, is the best I can do. I watch Pat. She runs her painted talons along the books, digs them into a cover and pulls down one volume. She pokes it under my nose.

'With these numbers it's the proponent on this side,' she explains, or she thinks she does. 'Copy that name on the quote. There! Where it says "proponent"!'

'Kate would do better if her handwriting improved,' whispers Mrs Brack from sixth class.

'Now the one on this side is the life assured so put that beside "life assured".'

On and on she goes in Sputnikese while I strain to be neat, to understand and remember. I can do this copying when Pat's there interpreting, directing.

'These numbers are the other way round so you have to remember the year they changed. Fifty-seven to sixty-three. No! You can't write it on your hand! What if you have to talk to a customer!'

Me! Talk to a customer? What about?

'I'll go back to my work now and you grab the quotes in your basket and fill them out. Just do it like I told you.'

But . . . but . . . I don't know what I'm . . .

I grab a bundle of papers and go back around the corner to the books. I look up the first number. Got it. I begin copying names and numbers. I'm sure all the typists are watching, knowing that I don't know what I'm doing.

Eventually Pat comes to check up on me.

'Where are the ones you've done? Is that all? Gee. You'll have to speed up! It's all right for now but you can't keep being this slow. I'll check these.'

She checks. I seem to have done all right, but then, 'I told you

239

they changed the names around. These are wrong.' She chucks them down in front of me. 'It's from June 1957 to May 1963. Listen and do as I tell you, will you.'

I write the dates on my hand after she's gone. I bury my red face into my work. I check everything twice.

Other people come to use the books. Sometimes they say, 'Hello'. The friendly ones add, 'How are you going?'

'Good' I always say. If only I could say, 'What on earth am I doing?'

At last my work is interrupted by a bell and then Pat.

'That's the morning tea bell. We'll go to first.'

I don't know what 'going to first' is but I follow her there.

'No, don't leave those there. Put them on your desk. We only get twenty minutes, so hurry up.'

We take the lift to the sixteenth floor. This time we don't have to say where we're going. The lift is packed with people all going to the canteen. I hate the closeness of all these strangers. Pat talks and giggles with some men. She gives knowing looks to her women friends.

The canteen is huge, its dreariness is compensated for by the fullness of chatter and the clatter of cups and saucers. Pat forgets me but I follow her on a queue that snakes slowly past the ladies who pour tea from Burnside sized teapots. I follow Pat to a table where she sits on the last chair.

'Oh.' I hear her disappointment that I'm still standing there. 'Pull a chair over.'

She turns away quickly, not wanting a new girl to hang around her. My chair only just squeezes in at the corner of the table.

'Hello,' some people say while others ignore the new kid and keep talking. I drink my tea silently, listening to them and stealing glances. How comfortable they all are. Talking and smiling and smoking and laughing. No-one looks as if they don't belong. They can all think of what to say. They all have make-up and nice clothes and hairdos.

'You'll be able to save up your money and buy some nice

clothes,' Miss Molesworth whispers, reminding me of how terribly drab I am.

Another bell rings. They all stand up.

'Back to work. Put your cup here,' says the stranger I sat beside. I wish I'd been able to think of something to say to her at morning tea.

Back to the office and the rest of the people go to second morning tea. I fill out more forms and Pat gets cranky when I ask her anything. I can't break the news that I've got absolutely no idea what all this means. She keeps putting more work in my tray. I keep filling in forms.

After lunch, which comes and goes like morning tea but so much longer, I continue until three o'clock when my mentor tells me to stop.

'These go to Melbourne now. I'll take them.' She picks up all my work and vanishes. In five minutes she's back again, empty-handed.

Surely Melbourne is further away than that! No, better not say that.

My next lesson is 'filing'. I manage to do this well. The alphabet isn't a problem. I sort 'pending', whatever that means, from 'completed' files and put them in the right drawers. Easy.

'Home in five minutes,' says Pat later, applying bright red lipstick to the circle of her mouth. She judges her reflection as perfect, clips her compact shut and casually tosses it and the lipstick into her handbag. She sits waiting, handbag over her arm, legs crossed, top leg bouncing impatiently.

I keep working.

'You don't stop until it's time to,' says Burnside me.

The bell goes at ten to five and everyone but me swarms out of our office, through the door to freedom.

'Well. How was your first day?' Mr Something asks as I pack up and get my purse.

'Good, thank you.' Go away.

'Think you'll get the hang of it?'

'Yes.' Go away. I'm shy. And nervous.

Dash away into the lift where people press too close again.

At home my father and the cockroaches and chaos and foul smells of the house are waiting.

'Well. Tell me how your first day was.'

Dad seems energetic. He's so sure my first day has been wonderful, that I've been a success.

'Good.' But don't ask me what it's all about. I can't tell him I'm a failure.

'What are your duties?' he asks, smiling at his businesslike formality.

'Oh, I fill out forms.'

'What are they for?'

'They're quotes.'

'Oh. Quotes, eh Princess. And what are the quotes for?' The very question I least want him to ask.

'Dunno.' My shoulders shrug up to my glowing face. I'm not much of a princess.

'And did you meet some nice people?'

No.

'Yeah. Pat. She shows me what to do.'

'That's good. Maybe she'd like to come home one day and have tea with us.'

What? Pat here? Why?

Dad's work friends don't come for tea do they? If Pat is the best I'm going to do for friends, I won't ever invite friends here.

Cockroaches run out of my way and the smell of boiling cabbage pushes a less inviting smell back up the hall as I cook tea. I try to imagine Pat and other nameless faces here. I can see the faces but not why they'd want to come or what they'd do if I got them here.

'Tea's ready, Dad.'

He's fallen asleep in front of the TV, his top denture in its resting position on his bottom lip, filtering his gentle snores. His bad eye is open and only the white of the glass eyeball shows. It weeps as if it knows me inside.

I wake Dad and we eat in front of the television. Ken has rung to say he's working overtime and won't be home 'til later. I put the washing up in the small clean space I've made at the sink. After I've done the dishes I scrub the bench. The pale grey grime turns dark and wet. Yellow wood begins to show through the foreign scratches in the slime. The cockroaches have retreated to their bottles.

'Leave that 'til the weekend,' says Dad who's standing at the door. 'You must be tired after your day at work.'

'It's all right.'

I am tired but I'm doing this without permission because I can't stand the filth. I'm claiming a place for myself here at the sink. I hope I get it all clean before Kerry comes. What will she think if she sees all this muck?

'Come and watch some telly. Keep your old Dad company.'

Burnside girls do as they're told. I sit and watch telly but what I see is a clean smooth yellow bench with a pile of sparkling dishes waiting to be stored in a sweet smelling cupboard.

Ken comes home. He drowns his dinner in tomato sauce and eats it in three minutes. He puts his plate on the pile of newspapers on the floor.

'Well, I'm going out now.'

I envy that he knows places to go.

My father is asleep again. I creep out with my brother's plate.

I decide to run a bath while I clean my teeth. Suddenly Dad's at my elbow. I freeze then force myself to squeeze out some toothpaste.

'Going to have a bath now eh?'

'Yeah.' Go away. This is the bathroom. I want privacy.

'Have you got everything?'

'Yeah.' I point to my bath bag.

We stand in the uneasy silence. What happens next? I feel cold inside. I shiver. I clean my teeth. Dad's still standing there. I wait. I can't take my clothes off while he's there. I swish the bath water around. Eventually he moves.

'Say goodnight before you go to bed then.'

243

'All right.'

He shuffles out. I lock the door and undress. I lie in warmth trying to be blank. A stray cat yowls near the back door, the other door to the bathroom. Is it all right to shoo the thing away? Other cats join in the chorus. A chill runs up my spine and I feel like a stranger.

It's early but I say goodnight to my father and go to my room to be alone. Sleep comes between proponent and life assured and then settles in, erasing all quotes. The clerk's first day ends.

GIVING IT TIME

I start to feel part of the rush to get to work although I'll never be comfortable in the close, pressing crowds on the train and the hands that I'm not sure of. I bundy on each morning before the red line can mark my card 'late' for the paymaster.

Each day is the same. Fill out the quotes, morning tea, fill out the quotes, lunch, fill out the quotes, bundle them up for Pat to take to her Melbourne, filing, fill out more quotes, go home. In time there's some variety because my mistakes begin to show as my quote forms come back from head office.

'Look at this! You've got to get the details right. They'll think we're idiots.'

'All right.'

'I'll show you again.' Pat's cranky. Again. 'Blah, blah, blah . . . Have you got it this time?'

'Yes.' I'm not going to let my tears out until she goes back around the corner.

'It's no use crying about it. Just do it right!' Pat snarls.

When the ten to five bell goes I'm relieved about the day ending but I don't really want to go home. I wander down to Wynyard station, not like the hundreds of people rushing for their trains. I dawdle, staring without seeing what's in the shop windows.

When I'm nearly home Nina catches up to me.

'Why don't you come to our place for dinner?'

'Now?'

The shyness that will embarrass me there is better than being alone, more or less, at home.

'Oh. I can't. I have to cook tea for Dad.'

'Come after then.'

'All right. Thank you.'

I'm lighter. Somewhere to go. Someone who won't be disappointed that I'm a failure, because I won't tell her. She won't know. Nina's a hairdresser. She doesn't know how to be a clerk.

When Dad asks how work went, I hesitate before I lie.

'All right.'

I don't want him to know I make mistakes and Pat shouts at me and I cry and I can't remember things and I don't know what it's all for. We'd both be ashamed. Dad guesses the truth.

'Give it time,' he says. 'Give it time.'

We have tea and I wash up.

'I'm going to Nina's place now.' I feel like I'm being insolent but I'm determined to go.

'Don't be long then.' He's too tired to argue.

Nina is busy. Her boyfriend has rung and she's going out. My jealous stomach turns.

'Stay and talk to me 'til he gets here.'

I watch her brush her glossy black hair.

'You'd look good in really short hair,' she says. 'Bring out your eyes, your face. Get Theo to do it one day.'

I watch her put make-up on her flawless skin. No medicated cream. She talks about what she should wear. I agree with whatever she suggests. I stand in awe. She's got lovely, lacy underwear. It's black and shiny, not plain white cotton, and it fits perfectly. I wonder where she got it from and whether I'm allowed to get some too. She slips a cotton dress over her head. It falls perfectly down over the gypsy princess. She checks her reflection, as if she needs to, and we wait for the boyfriend.

I walk home slowly after he comes. He's not handsome like boyfriends are supposed to be but his eyes sparkle when he talks to Nina. I wonder if I'll ever be good enough for a boyfriend.

'You're too fat,' Matron Rogers whispers. 'Boys won't like it.'

'Boys don't make passes at girls who wear glasses,' jeer the Carlingford girls.

'You're back early.' Dad says, interrupting my gloom.

'Yeah. Nina's boyfriend came.'

'Oh. Are there any nice boys at work?'

'Dunno.'

I don't want to talk about that. It's another failure. But there's something that makes me shy away from my father too. It's not just this misery that I can't shake off.

'There's a letter here for you. It came today.'

'For me?' Who'd write to me?

Mr and Mrs Ross. Why? They hardly know me. I realise I'd hoped it might be from Mum Perry.

Dear Kate,

Since you left us on Saturday we have thought of you quite a lot as we realise this is such a big step for you, and although you will have many moments of loneliness and no doubt nervousness too as you meet new people, you will soon adapt to this. This really happens to all of us, particularly as we go off to our first positions and have to start standing on our own feet. But do not get anxious, Kate, as after a time it will all pass.

I stop reading as two worlds collide. I can't see through the tears. I don't understand why they come so easily.

How do they know I'm nervous? Will it really pass? How long will it take?

My father is watching, waiting.

'It's from Mrs Ross,' I gulp.

'Oh?'

'Saying they hope it's good.'

'Oh. That's nice of them.'

I rush away to my room knowing it's rude not to let him look too, but it's my letter. Just mine.

I read the first part again. 'Loneliness?' Is that what it is? I don't want it named. Naming will make it more real. Make it true, that I have no friends, that no-one at work likes me because I'm dumb and I'll never have a boyfriend because I'm fat and I've got glasses. I read on.

We can guess how quiet it must seem after being with so many, but I am sure that the thought you are able to be with your father, who has been so wonderful to you all for so many years, will help.

Dad? Yeah but it's different now. He isn't the same. He feels like a stranger, like there's a world between us. I don't know how to talk to him. Why can't I be normal with him? Why do I keep crying? It feels like something's waiting to crush me. It's getting closer, too close.

Try to make new friends as this too will help you, Kate, and, although it is not easy at first, when we try to be friendly it is amazing how friendly others will be to us.

Make friends. That's what I've got to do. But I'm no good at that. I've had all those failures at Burnside to prove it. Remember fellowship? Anyway, I'm not unfriendly to Pat and she hates me.

As you know we did not say much to you on Saturday because we realised just how you felt and we did not want to further upset you, but we hope it will help you to know that we are all thinking of you a lot.

Should you visit Burnside be sure to come and say 'hello' as we will be delighted to see you.

Can they make things right? Can they tell me exactly what to do to make this sadness go away and make me understand work and my father? Make Ken like me, talk to me, help me sometimes?

Suddenly that last paragraph jumps out at me and I'm filled with a certainty that overwhelms and relieves all my anxieties.

I'm going back to Burnside where I belong.

I won't ever leave again. They want me back. They said so. I could go back and work there. I won't have to worry about how to make friends. I know how to do it there, without even trying.

I breathe deeply. I let my mind and heart sit in the stillness of belonging.

The stillness can't last. It can't sit beside the truth.

Will they really let me come back? Robyn has moved into my room. A new kid has come to take my place. What about my father? I'm supposed to look after him so he won't have to go to a nursing home or worse. If I go back to Burnside he'll lose his will to live. I'll be nobody with nowhere to go. And Kerry will too.

A steel cage crashes around me. There's no way out. I can almost breathe the dark cloud of dust that rises inside it. This lonely cage is where I live. There's no going back, except to visit. Through the tears I read at the bottom of the letter.

Give our best wishes to your Dad and Ken. With much love from Mr and Mrs Ross.

No! Don't spoil it. Don't let them be in my letter. It's mine.

I sob hopelessly before I read the letter again. I stop before I get to the end but I know the spoiling lines are there.

I try to find some stillness but anger and confusion get in my way. More tears, interrupted by a burst of crackling as my father turns the television on again. I take a deep breath and escape from my thoughts by sitting with Dad mindlessly watching. I keep my head down so he won't see my puffy eyes.

Soon he's asleep. His snoring drives me back into my

thoughts. Tears again. I retreat to my room in case he wakes up and sees them. I start to read my letter. When will these tears stop? When will everything be all right?

'After a time it will pass.'

There'll be an end to it. I just have to wait. But how long? Please, please tell me. How Long?

I meet my brother as I go to the bathroom. I give him his tea.

'Humph! Not this again. Can't we have something different.'

I don't answer. I tell myself, sadly, that I'll have to try to find something different. I'll have to stop being too scared to go into a butcher's shop. When will I ever get things right?

Pat doesn't even pretend to be friendly any more. I'm garbage. Not worth the effort. I stay away from my desk beside her as much as I can. I spend hours with the records around the corner, fighting back tears, hoping I look as if I'm actually using the book in front of me.

Other people come sometimes but I dare not talk beyond 'hello'. What if I try to smile and cry instead? Mrs Ross said this would pass. I try to believe her while I barely hold myself together.

Morning tea and lunchtimes are even worse now. I can't sit at Pat's table, pretending I belong. I sit at any table where there's an empty chair. Sometimes I'm asked if I'd mind moving so that so-and-so, who usually sits there, can have his or her seat. I drink my tea slowly. Sometimes I watch the door, pretending I'm waiting for a friend to come through it. Pretending I'm not lonely.

This will pass.

One day I happen to sit at the table where Denise, the girl who sits behind me in the office, always sits.

'Hello. Kate, isn't it?'

'Yes.'

'Sitting with us today are you?'

'Is it all right?'

''Course it is! Better than sitting with that lot,' Denise says rolling her eyes towards Pat's table. 'Sit here any time. We'll talk to you.'

She introduces me to her friends.

'Be friendly,' Miss Molesworth and Mrs Ross whisper.

'Hello. It's nice to meet you,' I say.

'You should have come here first, instead of all those other tables,' someone says.

I smile. Top lip sticks to gums. Tea to rescue it. Hope they don't notice burning red eyes.

At lunchtime I head for Denise's table. She isn't there.

'She's probably gone shopping again. Doesn't matter. Sit here anyway.'

I sit and after 'thank you' I can't think of anything to say. They don't seem to mind.

Sometimes they ask me things and I answer in monosyllables. They don't seem to mind that either. I do.

After lunch Denise comes to my desk and shows me what she's bought for her nephew's birthday and her friend's wedding. I admire them. I'm good at that. Denise takes a little black book out of her handbag. She asks if she can write my phone number in it in case there's a party on that she could invite me to. I don't think Dad will let me go to parties but I'm too embarrassed to say so. I'm secretly relieved as images of the Burnside social creep through my mind.

'LL 4505. It's my father's.'

'Your father's?' She looks puzzled. 'Oh! Are your parents divorced?' Now she looks shocked. Divorce is rare and scandalous.

'No.'

Divorce seems like a weird explanation. The real one is so obvious.

'Where's your mother then?'

'She's dead.'

'Oh! Sorry.'

251

Now poor Denise is shocked and, for the first time in ages, I feel like a freak because of my mother.

'It's all right.' It's irrelevant! I don't need a mother. I just need friends.

Denise relieves the uncomfortable silence with, 'This is my phone number. Ring up if you . . .'

'Busy are you, girls?' Miss Samuels, Denise's boss, sings her threatening song.

'Ring if you're having a party or something,' Denise whispers quickly then she hands me a piece of paper and goes off to work.

I put the number away in my purse thinking I'll never use it.

All the same there's a tiny spring in my step to Wynyard today. I call in to the fish shop. I have to make a nice dinner. My father likes fish and my brother might too. I look over all the dead fish lying, waiting on the ice. I'll have to cut their heads off so I'm not buying them.

'Fish Cocktails' a sign says. Golden balls of batter with bits of fish inside lie around the sign.

'How do I cook them?' I have to get it right or Ken will be angry.

'They're cooked. Just heat them up in the oven.'

'All right. I'll have some.'

'How much?'

'Oh, er . . .'

'How many people?'

She's such a nice lady. She tells me what to do as if she wants it to be a good meal too. I know from Home Economics that it isn't good to do this every day and that soon I'll have to get brave enough to go into a butcher's shop and buy some meat. I can't keep going to Mrs Guy's shop. Or this one. I have to stop being shy.

At home I open the package of fish cocktails. Dad's out the back so I'll just pop them in the oven . . .

Ye gods! What's this? Little slimy grey and yellow blobs! I didn't ask for this! They don't even look like food! 'Fish cocktails.'

That's what I'd asked for. What'll I do? I'll have to go to Mrs Guy's. I haven't got any money.

I bundle up the slimy blobs and hide them in the fridge. I go to my room and cry because I'm hopeless. I read my letter again and cry because there's no-one here.

It's my job to get tea. I have to do it. I can't let the others know how hopeless I am. The slime balls and I glare at each other. They don't give me any hints about how I should cook them. They just lie there looking disgusting. I could ring Aunty Dot. No. I can't tell her I've made a mistake. And I might have to tell her about Ken getting angry. And she'll ask how work is and . . . But I have to get tea ready.

'Hello, Aunty Dot. This is Kate.'

'Who is it?'

'It's Kate.'

Silence. Maybe she didn't hear.

'It's Kate Shayler.'

Silence.

'From Burnside.'

'Oh. Kate. How are you, dear? You haven't ever rung me before. I didn't recognise your voice.'

'I'm good, thank you.' What are these slimy balls?

'You're working now, aren't you. And at home with Dad at last too. You must come and see me and tell me how everything's going. Oh. How nice to hear from you. How are you?'

'I'm good, thank you,' except for these slimy balls?

'And how is your job? With the Colonial Mutual isn't it?'

'Yes. It's good.' How do you cook these rotten things?

'That's good and when are you coming to see me, dear?'

'I don't know.' I just want to know how to . . .

'Well. You know I'd love you to come. You could stay for a weekend and keep me company.'

'Yes. All right.' But what about these . . .

'Well, you just ring when you want to come, dear. You know I'd love to have you.'

'Thank you, Aunty Dot. Could you t . . .'

'Goodbye, dear. It was so nice of you to ring me.'

'Goodbye.'

The horrid things, staring at me from the kitchen, demand that I wonder about them instead of wondering about visiting my aunty. I'll have to ring Aunty Marj.

The conversation is very much like the one with Aunty Dot but I can't let this aunt escape without telling me what to do. I describe what I need to cook.

'Hmm. I don't know what they could be. Do you think you could batter them?'

'I don't know,' how to make batter.

'Well. I think that's all you can do. Either that or have something else,' she suggests lightly.

It's not bloody well funny!

'All right. Thank you, Aunty Marj.'

'Ring again if you need help, Kate. And do come and see us won't you.'

'All right. Thank you.'

'Bye bye, Kate.'

'Bye.'

Everyone seems to want me to visit them when all I want is to turn slime balls into tea. To disguise them as food.

The phone rings.

'Hello, Kate. It's Ken. I won't be home for tea. I've got overtime.'

My father says, before he's seen my purchase, that he still has his Meals on Wheels lunch left and he'll just have that for tea. I hurl the wretched balls into the garbage and hope garbage night is soon. I have devon again. And I don't care. Tomorrow I'll work out where there's a butcher and I'll go in.

Later in the bath, my worries don't dissolve. How much time will it take for everything to be all right, how long before I get the quotes right, how long 'til the house is clean, how long 'til the smells go, how long 'til I get friends, how long 'til a boy takes me out? Will I get it all right before Kerry comes for the holidays?

My father's in his chair. The sight of his teeth out and his glass eye turned around are becoming familiar. But what else is it? Why is he frightening this time? He's still. He's so very still! I can't see, can't hear him breathing. Closer, hardly daring to breathe myself, choked by need, confusion, compassion and panic. He's d . . .

'Goodnight Dad.' I force it out.

No response. No breath.

'Goodnight Dad.' Louder. For nothing.

Please, please answer me.

'Dad,' hysterically higher, louder.

The relief when he stirs in his chair! Tears in my eyes with the slow, shallow breath of his life.

'Uh. Oh. You're off to bed then?'

'Yes. Goodnight.'

I rush away to the safety of my room. My mind keeps harking back to Dad in the chair. What if he had been . . . been . . . dead in his chair. I can't control the shaking as I sob fear and relief and confusion. I don't want to need him.

The letter. Perhaps it will help. I read it again.

'. . . after a time it will pass.'

That's about loneliness and nervousness. I admit now that I'm lonely. Very lonely. I can name it and own it. No-one to be with and talk to. No friends who know me. Everyone telling me from the outside. No-one knowing me inside. No-one knowing how desperately I need to know, inside, that I'll be all right. And my father . . . I'm lonely. How can I go and see Mum Perry when I'm such a failure! And what about when Kerry comes and I'm . . . like this.

'. . . after a time it will pass.'

I read that over and over again as if the reading will make it more true and make time pass.

I know the letter almost off by heart. Reading it again gives me an idea. It's polite to answer letters. We've always had to at

Burnside. Dad wrote, then we replied, every month without fail.

I start politely. Perhaps, if they see how lonely I am, even though I'm trying my best not to be, they'll let me come back. But I must let them know that I haven't forgotten my debt to Dad.

> Dear Mr and Mrs Ross,
> I received your welcome letter yesterday. Thank you very much for writing to me. I found it a great comfort. When I am feeling lonely I read it and I feel a bit better.
>
> You have no idea how much I miss my friends at Burnside. I often think about it. I would much rather be living at Burnside. I cannot say I like it here.
>
> Of course I like being with Dad and Ken but I get very worried about Dad. Do you know if I could get someone to look after him during the day?

The relief of 'talking' to someone takes charge of the letter. I know I'm unburdening, manipulating and hoping.

> I don't think it's only homesickness that makes me miserable. It is the worry over Dad and, no matter how much I clean the house, it is still very dirty and untidy and so I get very tired and miserable.
>
> To tell the truth I would much rather be living somewhere clean and tidy but I know that Dad has been very good to us for all these years and so I must think of him now instead of myself. I owe it to him to care for him when he is like he is.

The worry about him staying alive is so real I can't bear to write the words. The responsibility is too heavy.

> I wish we had a mother like Mum Perry. She was understanding and loving. I can't wait to see her and all my friends when I come up on Saturday and to be in a clean, tidy house.
>
> Some people have told me I can ring them if I had a problem

but I can't because I don't want Dad to know how lonely I am. Sometimes I would just like Mum Perry's shoulder to cry on but I know it's impossible when we are so far away.

Do you think that perhaps one day I would end up working at Burnside? I often think about it and I'm pretty sure I'd love it.

Then you've got to write back and say, 'Yes. Change your visit to a moving back day. You belong with us, Kate. Bring your Dad too and we'll help look after him.'

Last night I rang up Aunty Dot and Aunty Marj and they said I could ring up if I wanted to know anything and sometimes I am going to go out to see Aunty Dot.

Everyone at work is nice and helpful. I have made friends. Pat, the girl who teaches me and Denise whose table I sit at for lunch and morning tea. Today Denise and I exchanged phone numbers so we can ring each other up if we want to.

I can't tell them Pat hates my guts. I can't say Denise wants me to go to parties and that I'm afraid that if I do I'll be such a spectacular failure that she won't want to be my friend anyway.

I finish work at 4.50 and I get home at 6.30 if I don't hurry. I get tea and clean up. Sometimes I go to Nina's.

It's getting late now so I must close. Once again, thank you for your letter and for everything you have done for me. I hope we can be friends forever. I will write back later if you do not mind. With lots of love, from Kate.

I know I've gone way beyond the well-mannered reply. I cram the pages into an envelope.

My only real hope is that I'll be accepted back into the Burnside fold. I'll do my best while I wait for the reply. I have some hope now. I'll check the letterbox as soon as I get home every day.

GOING BACK

'Thank goodness it's the weekend!'
   'Oh yes! What are you doing?'
The Friday ritual at the office. People with plans to see friends, to go out with boyfriends, to go to places I've never heard of. People with no plans but they don't mind. They say they're doing nothing but their nothing is very different to mine. At least on Sunday night I'll be going to church with Miss Molesworth. No-one thinks that's very interesting.

On Saturday I do washing, ironing and cleaning. I see my brother for long enough for him to complain that I haven't found his washing and done it with mine and Dad's. He sees the Coke bottles lined up for washing and tells me he'll get money for them when he returns them to Mrs Guy's shop.

'Just leave them,' he orders. 'I'll take 'em when I get time.'

I will not leave them. I live here.

When he's gone I wash some. At least it might make the cockroaches think about going somewhere else to live and taking their stink with them.

At the end of the day I stand cooking dinner, immersed in

fantasy about how friendly all the people at church will be tomorrow. My letter won't have got to Burnside yet so Miss Molesworth won't tell me yet that I can come back. Perhaps I'll make friends at the church. I won't count the Parramatta fellowship experience in this. God says people in churches have to be friendly and so at least they won't hate me. And Miss Molesworth will be there to tell me what to do and say. And there's that lady who told Miss Molesworth she'll look after me, in a motherly way, at church.

Suddenly my father is close, too close, behind me at the stove. His thick voice, that voice that brought fear years ago, mumbling again in my ear, gnarled hands squeezing my breasts. Panic rises, explodes. Then rage. Shove the old man away. Run. Run to my room. Slam the door. Scream inside myself inside my room.

Why? Scream in the shadows of years ago. Why? I hate you. I don't care who you are. I hate you.

Guilt threatens my anger, gets in its way, blurs it into shame. I'm so ashamed.

How long do I stare at the wall, waiting? Waiting for what? I can't think beyond the thick voice. I can't move away from that moment when rage boiled with hatred in me. Can't move my mind backwards to remember details of the first time I heard that voice. Can't move forward to this room and beyond to escape. I'm frozen in icy now with boiling rage inside me. I try to bury it deep down where dark things have been buried for years. It won't go. Shame stays near the surface. I'm ashamed of what my father did. Shame freezes too and stops me seeing the truth about where it belongs.

I manage to return to the kitchen and I finish cooking in silence. What is there to say? I give the old man his tea and take mine to my room.

I wash up in silence. There's not a single word that will feel right, normal. I am frozen.

I wedge a chair hard up against the bathroom door and fill the room with steam as I run a bath. The handle rattles.

'What are you doing?' says the voice I hate.

'Nothing.' Stay away. Leave me alone. I hate you. Shame drifts around in the steam.

'You've been very quiet.'

'I'm having a bath.' Go away. Leave me alone.

I wait until I can't hear any sound but the television. I undress for a quick bath. The wind rattles the back door to the bathroom. Creep out and make sure, again, the bolt is across. Finish quickly. Wrap my dressing gown around me. Tightly.

Past the sleeping old man to the safety of my room, lock my bedroom door and go to bed to the yowling of the wretched cats on the verandah. I hate them. I hate and I'm ashamed.

Sleep comes slowly. My self-loathing blinds me to I Am and the wolf invades my dreams. I am alone. So alone.

On Sunday I see my brother for long enough to hear his complaint that I haven't ironed his shirts. He's cranky and I don't care. I don't care about anything. I wait for Miss Molesworth. Long for her to come. I hardly know her but she's somebody. I'll make myself find words to tell her what's wrong here. I long for a letter from the Rosses too. I need Burnside people. Predictable, safe people. I will this day to hurry along.

Late in the morning there's a knock on the front door. A young couple stands there, smiling.

'Yes?'

'Hello. Are you Kate?'

'Yes.'

'I'm Jane and this is Errol. We're from St Mark's. We just came to say hello. We wondered if you might like to come up to church or fellowship with us sometime.'

'I don't know,' what to say.

'We could pick you up, if you like.'

If I like? They smile a lot. They seem so nice and friendly. Clean. Yes take me. Now. And don't bring me back. Make me like you. Clean. Smiling.

260

'Well, you think about it and if you like we'll come back another time to see what you've decided. Is that all right?'

'Yes.' Don't go. Take me with you. Don't leave me in this stinking cage.

My father wants to know who I've been talking to.

'Some people from the church.'

'Hmph. What did they want? Money, I suppose.'

'No.' I hate his scathing tone. 'They asked me if I wanted to go to fellowship. And church.' And they made the sun shine through the bars for a moment.

'What would you want to go to church for? They're only after your money.'

'I'm going tonight with Miss Molesworth to the Methodist one,' I reply defiantly. And I'm going to tell her what you did.

The afternoon drags on. I go for a walk without permission. Nina's mamma waves to me and speaks in Italian. I think she means Nina's out, so I keep going. I walk around streets I don't know, not caring if I get lost. I try not to think about loneliness and shame and being brainless and ugly. I walk on and see people getting off the bus. I don't know any of them. Someone walks in front of the bus just as it pulls out. The bus driver shouts at him and he shouts back and keeps going. I dawdle home and wait. My father's sleeping in his chair and I hope he's dead. Then I'm ashamed again, guilty and lonely.

I read my letter and remember my reply. I hope Mr and Mrs Ross have written the answer I want. Tonight I'll find words for Miss Molesworth about the unspeakable. At last she arrives. She's cheerful and sunny. She says a warm hello to my father and we drive off.

'Your Dad seems tired.'

'Yeah. He's always like that.'

Tell her. Tell her what he did.

'And how have you been?'

Words. If only I could find them. Words strong enough to get me past the shame I'm frozen in. I need to find words louder than

261

the thick voice that gags me with shame. I need to remember the child, terrified, and tell about the darkness that is buried without words for it. Shame and fear always stop me but I know the thing is there. How can I say it? What are the words?

I need to get past what they all know, those Burnside people, that my father is a good, loyal man who lives for his children. I know and love that part of him but there's the other.

And what if I find the words and Miss Molesworth doesn't believe me? She'll hate me then and I'll never be allowed back.

'Good,' I say.

Miss Molesworth chuckles.

'Don't you mean "fine"?'

'Yeah. Fine.'

She's so warm. Safe. I want to go back.

'Do you like your work?'

'Yeah. It's good.' I won't be doing it for much longer.

'That's good. Here we are. Now remember, Kate, just relax and be yourself.'

Be myself! She must have forgotten about that fellowship.

Miss Molesworth walks into the church hall so confidently. She introduces us both to the minister. They chat quietly and then he nods towards the woman who's going to look after me. Miss Molesworth introduces us both.

'Mrs Charles is the lady I told you about, Kate. She lives near you. She has two sons about your age.'

'Oh.'

I know the silence is waiting for me to fill it.

'Kate's really been looking forward to meeting you, haven't you, Kate?'

'Yes.'

Another waiting silence.

'You must come and visit us. Come to church with us too. Wouldn't that be nice?'

Another waiting cage.

'Yes. Thank you.' No. I'd hate it. I hate boys. I don't want you or them.

'Where do you live?'

'378 Cressey Street.'

'Who's there with you?'

'Dad and Ken, my brother.'

'Bring them along too then.'

'All right.' Never!

'Good. Well let's go in now and sit together for the service. Afterwards I'll introduce you to some of our young people.'

The service passes with some familiar songs that Mrs Charles makes sure I can find in the hymn book. I'm not interested. I don't belong here. I'm a Burnsider. They'll have to take me back. What's the use of embarrassing myself with Mrs Charles and the young people? I'm going back. I don't even like Mrs Charles. She's bossy and her hat's bommy and she's a sticky beak and she's ugly and she's got sons who she says I have to make friends with.

The introductions to the young people are dreadful. I know I'm disastrously different. They dress differently. They speak confidently. They don't need grown ups to take them to church and they aren't covered in acne. They don't keep looking around to see if escape is possible yet.

Eventually Miss Molesworth says it's time to go.

'How was it? Still shy aren't you. Don't worry, Kate. You'll get over it.'

We talk for a while about how hard it is to keep the house clean and how tired I get. I manage to tell her that I don't like living here but words for the other won't come.

'Kerry will be home soon, for a while. Perhaps she'll cheer you up, eh?'

I say what I'm expected to say and Miss Molesworth goes home with a promise to ring me soon.

Mr and Mrs Ross's reply is waiting when I get home from work on Monday. The solution! Tell me. Tell me. Quickly.

Dear Kate,

We were so pleased to get your letter and very happy to know you like your new position and have already made some friends. This will help you tremendously.

It is a big thing for you to have to face up to big responsibilities at home, but you will find that as time passes you will gain much more confidence in yourself and though you will often feel weary and perhaps miserable you'll adjust and all this will become easier for you.

No. Oh no. This is wrong. You're saying that it's because something's wrong with me. Say I can come back, not that I have to be different!

I throw the letter away. My breath is heavy, loaded with anger and frustration. It rattles the bars of my cage. I can't leave the letter, my only hope, on the floor. I reach through the bars and pick it up.

When you have lived for twelve years under certain conditions without having to shoulder heavy responsibilities and then be thrust into more or less taking the 'Mother' position in the home I can quite understand that you are really feeling quite out of your depth but try not to be too concerned, do as much as you can, try and keep your high standard and at times close your eyes to things that are not as pleasant as you may like.

Oh shut up. Shut up. I didn't make the conditions I lived in for twelve years! Anyway, I did all my work. Really well. I did shoulder my responsibilities and I was so good at . . . How can closing my eyes make this place clean and block out the stench? And I'm not the mother? I'm not. I'm the daughter.

Write to us as much as you like and talk to people who you can trust and find understanding of your problems . . .

Who? There's no-one. No-one!

I am sorry we will not be here when you come up on Saturday
. . .

Angry, jealous, hopeless sobs rack my body. I bury my head in my pillow so my father won't hear. I finish the letter, just so it will be finished, not because there's hope.

. . . you will find Mum Perry a great help and comfort and she
will listen sympathetically to you. She has helped and advised you
now for many years and if you try to remember and put into effect
all that she has taught you, you will find that all your problems
will gradually diminish in size.

Not about this. She never told me about this.

Keep faith in yourself, Kate, and remember that many people are
thinking of you as you settle into your new and grown up life.
It will cheer you up immensely seeing all your friends again on
Saturday.
For the time being, lots of love from us both, Mr & Mrs Ross.

I hate them for not saying I belong there, for not saying I can come back. I realise, again, that I can't go back. I don't belong there. I don't belong anywhere. I can never be the same person I was there. I feel damaged now. How can I go back and let Mum Perry see what a miserable failure I am? That I can't even stay and look after my loyal, loving father? And what about Kerry? She hasn't even tried it yet.

The years I've spent at Burnside wanting better have become a habit. The irony of my father teaching me that habit is not obvious to me yet. All I know is that now I want things to be better. I desperately want, need to belong somewhere where I won't feel so vulnerable, so hopeless, so violated. My wanting better drives me to keep struggling, to not give up. Not yet.

THE FRIEND

Last Sunday Miss Molesworth said I could ring her any time I want to. She gave me her home phone number. Every day I come home and want the warmth of her. I wonder what I can ring her about. My father's company makes me so angry when Miss Molesworth is who I need. What I want to tell her is so important but I can't think of another reason to ring, to pad it, to sneak up on it, give it a context and find the words. I get her phone number, hold my breath and dial. Maybe I'll think up something to say when she answers.

'Hello. Is that Miss Molesworth?'

'Yes, it is.'

'This is Kate.'

'Oh. It's good to hear from you, Kate. How are you?'

'Fine, thank you.'

'Have you had a good day at work?'

Miss Molesworth carries the conversation through the uncomfortable pauses where I try to think of something to say.

'How about coming to have lunch with me next Saturday? . . . Kate? Are you still there?'

Of course I am but I can't believe it. This is better than the best thing I can imagine.

Me having lunch with Miss Molesworth! But I don't want to see other Burnside people.

'At your house, do you mean?'

'Well, it's a unit not a house. But yes. Here. Would you like that?'

'Oh yes!'

'Well, that's what friends do, so that's what we'll do.'

She gives me the exact directions for getting there. My hand floats across the lovely piece of ordinary paper as I write. She said we're friends and I'm invited to her house. No, unit. Whatever that is.

I can't wait for people at work to ask me what I'm doing on the weekend. I'll say, 'I am going to my friend's unit for lunch.'

Having this to look forward to gets me through work. It gets me past all the mistakes and past Pat's irritation. Coming home at night is lighter.

But how quickly darkness obscures sunshine. My father has kept his hands off me for a few days but tonight I didn't wake him to say goodnight. As I drift off to sleep I hear a knock on my door.

'Are you in there?' his thick voice asks.

I freeze.

'Are you there, Princess?'

'Yes.' The door's locked. It's all right.

'You didn't say goodnight.'

'Goodnight.'

'That's not right. Say it properly.'

If I lie here quietly he'll go away.

'Say goodnight to your old Dad properly.'

I get up, open the door and say, 'Goodnight'.

He pushes the door open further and grabs my arm.

'Say it properly, with a kiss.'

I kiss his prickly cheek, wrench my arm free, back away.

'Let me lie down with you, Princess.'

'No.'

I push the frail old man out the door where he can't crush me. I bang the door shut. Oh, I hate him so much.

Cats wail on the verandah outside my window. I stay frozen, listening to them, wanting to kill them. To catch them and rip their yowling jaws apart and hurl them to hell. Afraid of my own dark side I fall, exhausted, to sleep where the wolf lurks.

The next time I see my father asleep in his chair I hope he's dead. Again I'm overcome with shame.

Saturday. I get up early. Today I'll tell Miss Molesworth what I hate most about being here. I'll get her to help.

I take my piece of paper and follow the instructions exactly. It'll be worth going to new places, in the packed trains today. I check the indicator board so many times before I get on the train. It isn't crowded at all. I sit near an old lady who smiles and goes on knitting. I check each station name as we pull in.

'Is Chatswood next?' I ask the woman beside me. I'll even risk talking to a stranger to make sure I get to Miss Molesworth's unit.

'Yes, dear. That's the next stop.'

'Thank you.' I breathe again.

'Going for a visit are you?'

'Yes.'

'Family?'

'No,' awkwardly, wondering how much to say.

'Friends, is it?'

'Yes.' I smile.

'I'm going to see my grandchildren. I'm trying to get this finished so I can leave it with the little bloke.'

I smile and she chats on happily about her little bloke.

'Well, here's your stop. Enjoy yourself, dear.'

'Thank you.'

I check the number on the bus and ask the driver if he's going down Burns Bay Road.

He says he is and asks where I want to get off.

'Just sit there, love. I'll tell you when to get off.'

Soon I'm knocking on Miss Molesworth's door. I've checked the number with my paper.

'Well, here you are! It's good to see you, Kate. Come in.'

It isn't the kind of room where particular things stand out so as to stay in the memory. It isn't a perfect Burnside room. It's a warm, friendly room that admits to getting in a mess of papers sometimes but invites you to come in and feel comfortable anyway. Everything is fine here.

I don't want to spoil this with my problems. Every time my father is mentioned, panic rises and I feel I must find the words. Not finding them is a kind of relief though. This time and this place stay clean and good.

At last Miss Molesworth says she'd better get ready for something that she's going to tonight at church. Jealousy comes with the realisation that she has a life without me. She says it'd be nice if I could come with her but I'd be too late getting home if I did.

'Anyway, you have your own church now, don't you. Are you going tomorrow?'

'Yes. I think so.' If you want me to.

Two friends drive to the station together. One cries on the train while the other goes to other friends.

At home I cry again. About the loneliness. About the helplessness. About the words I hadn't found.

There's hope now though. Miss Molesworth said she knew it was hard for me at home. She didn't say, 'I told you so.' She just said she knew and yet she didn't know the worst of it. She told me to try to hold out until Kerry got here but if things didn't improve she'd talk to my father about my living somewhere else. What will Kerry think? I worry but I can't see that she'll make much difference, especially as she's going back to Burnside. I envy her.

'Call me Mary, if you like,' Miss Molesworth had said. We'd chuckled that her name was the same as my middle name and we'd joked that I could call her 'Mary Middlename'. I don't want to call her Mary anything. It would mean that we're equals and I don't want to be equal with her. No. It's more like I don't want her to be equal to me. She has to stay older, wiser and stronger. She has to make things right.

Sunday seems lighter. There's hope for an end to this . . . this sadness. Miss Molesworth rings to make sure I got home safely. She encourages me to go to church. It'll be easier this time and it's important for me to make friends of my own age. Mrs Charles will be friendly and will help me and I'll be able to ring her too. My friend Miss Molesworth says she'll ring me to see how things are going during the week.

I have all the friends I need now. I don't need church. I'll only go if that nice couple from the Church of England come. It'll only be to please Miss Molesworth. And because I won't know how to say 'no'.

The nice couple don't come. I'm relieved. I don't want to cloud friendship by going back to Mrs Charles' church and grinding through that again. It won't be easier. I know. I shut myself in my room and struggle through an old paperback I found in the shed out the back. It's a romantic story called *Beyond Pardon*. 'N. Lyford' is written inside the cover. The book takes me into another world where people struggle because they've fallen in love with other people's wives and husbands. It must be a rude book but I don't care. No-one will know I'm reading it and it's better than being alone with my life.

Miss Molesworth is so disappointed when I confess I didn't go to church. I'm ashamed that I've let her down. She's cross too and that's worse than her disappointment. I don't want to be in trouble with her and lose her. I'll go to church next Sunday, however hard it is.

Errol, of the nice couple, comes to the house during the week.

'G'day, Kate. Just popped around to see if you'd like to come to church next Sunday.' Smiling words through sparkling eyes.

'Yes, please.' It won't be with just you though, will it? Where's the lady, Jane, the one who was with you before. It has to be with her too. Not just a man.

'Good. Good. We'll pick you up at, say, a quarter to seven?'

'All right. Thank you.'

'Bye then. Mum's got dinner waiting. See you then.'

'We'll pick you up,' he'd said. 'We'll' not 'I'll'. I'll be all right then. Miss Molesworth will be so glad.

The next time they ask me at work what I'm doing on the weekend, I say, 'I'm going to church with my friends.'

The reaction is puzzling but conversations about me are usually short. They often end with, 'Oh', followed by awkward silence.

When Jane and Errol come on Sunday night I'm relieved to be getting away from my father. From his hands. From the glass eye that stares at me through his sleep. From the teeth that grin at my guilty thoughts.

At church there are lots of friendly people who smile but don't want me to come to their homes and be friends with their sons. I sit near a stranger, who smiles and whispers that her name is Cheryl. Jane and Errol had to get ready for choir. Cheryl kneels on a little bench. She must be praying. I can't imagine why it takes so long. Eventually she gets up and sits quietly.

Gradually a hum fills the little church and swells in a flood of triumphant organ music. Everyone stands as a procession of two rows of robed singers walk down the aisle. They look so neat and ordered with their snow-white smocks, flat black hats and deep black skirts. Some are men and one must be the minister. I'm intrigued. The best thing isn't what I'm seeing though. It's what I'm hearing. The singing! It hums around in a beautiful harmony that fills my head and drives out everything else. Soprano voices soar ever higher in the drone of deeper ones that hold them steady and strong.

Cheryl is singing too. I want to be in this. I can't find the words. Cheryl sees me fumbling in the wrong book and points to the hymn book. I'm not game to sing as loudly as I want to, so I join in whispering, hardly believing that I'm allowed to be part of something so utterly beautiful.

When the singing stops we change to *the Book of Common Prayer*. Keeping up with when to stand and sit and kneel is confusing but if I keep a second or two behind Heather and don't shut my eyes for prayers, I'll be right. There are parts when the minister speaks and then the people answer. The minister speaks again and the people respond again. I love it. It's like having a conversation but you know what to say because it's all written down, there, in front of you. You can't go wrong and there's none of those awkward pauses. And at the end, my favourite benediction from Burnside,

> *May the Lord bless you and keep you.*
> *May the Lord lift up the light of His countenance*
> *upon you*
> *and give you His peace. Amen.*

If I could stay here and be still I think I could find I Am. I swallow my tears as Cheryl kneels again, then we all file out, shaking hands with the minister as we go. He says it's nice to see me and he hopes I'll come again. Cheryl says it's been nice too and that maybe I'd like to come to the fellowship that Jane and Errol run. Fellowship! No thanks. I've tried fellowship before. I'll come to church again though. If I time it right I won't have to talk to anyone but I can be in the singing and so on. And Miss Molesworth will be pleased with me.

Jane and Errol take me home. They won't be able to pick me up next week because they have family Christmas things to do. I wonder what other families do at Christmas. Kerry will be home by then. We'll try to do a family thing too, like last year.

My father is waiting at home, to poke fun at my going to

church. I hate him again while I feel a longing for him to tell me it's all right. He doesn't. He keeps up the banter. What a coward. Not game to do it when Miss Molesworth's here. Well, what does he know anyway.

I say goodnight just to stop him talking. And to stop him coming to my room. I hate this place. I refuse to think about how I need my father or that there's something of him that I still love.

Miss Molesworth is so pleased about church. She says she can tell by my voice that I enjoyed it. She can't tell that it's talking to her that makes me sound happy, not what I'm telling her about. She reckons this is the beginning of my finding new friends my own age and that I'll gradually become more confident as I realise that people like me.

'Kerry will be coming home on Friday. Bet you're looking forward to that.'

'Hm.'

'You can take her with you next Sunday.'

Why do I feel angry that I have to share this with my sister?

'I'll be in town on Thursday. What time do you have lunch?'

'Um. Twelve-thirty.' Why? Has work told Burnside on me? Is Mr Mans-something going to give me the sack?

'Good! How would you like to meet me for lunch?'

Oh, what a relief! Lunch!

'We can talk about arrangements for Kerry coming home.'

'Good.'

I don't know what there is to say about Kerry coming home but I want to see my friend.

I imagine telling Denise that I'm meeting a friend for lunch. One of my own.

'You'll have to try to help Kerry feel good about being at home, Kate. We can talk about how we're going to do it at lunch. See if you can help each other be a bit more happy. All right?'

The week's looking brighter.

The telegram that's waiting for me on Wednesday spoils my anticipation of a sunny Thursday.

'Gone away Stop Cancel lunch Stop Ring next week Stop Mary Molesworth Stop'.

I cry so easily these days. Disappointment. Resentment. Something has got in the way of our lunch.

Kerry is here when I get home on Friday. I know because of the mess in my room first. My haven is spoiled. She's even chucked her stuff on my bed. Is she going to invade every crack of my existence? Mess it up? I try to be glad to see her as she beams in the hope of the freedom she thinks she's found.

'Hi there, sis. Back from work?'

'Yeah. Back from work. Back from Burnside, are ya?'

'Yeah. Never goin' back to that dump.'

Oh, if only you knew how you're going to feel in this dump! We make tea together.

'What time's Ken get home?'

'Dunno. Depends if he's got overtime.'

'Oh well. Where's the tommy sauce?'

We smother our dinner with Fountain and sit down with our father in front of the TV. He's so pleased that his three Ks are together again at last. Ken's absence is overlooked.

'We should have a celebration!' our father says with more enthusiasm and more light in his old eyes than I've seen for weeks. 'We could go to town. To a restaurant and have a posh dinner,' he says, laughing.

While I wonder what going out to a restaurant with him would be like, he eats some dinner and falls asleep. Kerry and I finish ours, trying not to notice. We try to pretend everything is all right, normal.

I beat her to the sink. I'm washing up, not wiping. Some things will never change. Nothing is going to spoil Kerry's freedom though. She whacks at a few cockroaches with the tea towel and cheerfully wipes up.

'Well. That's that. What do we do now?' She talks as if the day's just beginning.

'Nothin' much. We could watch TV. Or we could unpack your stuff.' Naming our choices is lonely.

'Let's go out.'

'Where?'

'Dunno. Where is there?'

'Dunno. Nina's. No. She's probably gone out with her boyfriend.' I think of something just to show I haven't really spent the last three weeks doing nothing but watching TV. And that I know about boyfriends.

'I can't wait for camp. Monday and I'll be off canoein' and bush-walkin' and all that stuff. It's gunna be really good.'

Oh, shut up will you!

We watch TV but I go to bed soon. Kerry still has energy and hope. The mark of true freedom, apart from gallons of tomato sauce, is to stay up watching TV 'til whatever time you like. Dad won't say anything. He's asleep.

On Christmas Day we tell Dad we're going to church. Kerry thinks it's better than just hangin' around doin' nothin'. Dad says it's stupid. What do we want to do that for? He hopes we're leaving our purses at home.

Again I love the singing, especially the carols that we know. Kerry and I grin when we get things wrong and we grin when they announce a hymn we know. I like the Christmas conversations in *the Book of Common Prayer*. Cheryl's here to show us the right book to use.

'Is this your sister? It must be. You're so alike.'

'Yeah. This is Kerry.'

'Hello, Kerry. It's nice to meet you. Gosh, are you twins?'

'No. Just sisters.'

'Well. Happy Christmas. I've got to rush home and help Mum with dinner. The family's coming over. See you next time.'

'Crumbs. She's a bit of a square isn't she!' Kerry's assessment of Heather offends me. I claim her strongly as a friend.

Back at home we exchange Christmas cards. Ken's here for that. We have lunch together and sit wondering what to do next.

'Well. Um. Happy Christmas everyone. Um. Sorry, but I have to go out now. Bye. Happy Christmas.'

And our brother's gone.

'Where's he goin'?'

'Dunno. He never says.'

'Must have a girlfriend.'

'Yeah.' I'm amazed that my sister is so worldly wise.

Dad's asleep again so Kerry and I go for a walk after we make our beds and tidy our room. I wish she'd make her bed properly, like mine, so they'd be matching perfectly. Instead she just throws the blankets up and tosses the bedspread on top.

In the street we hear all sorts of shrieking laughter from other people's houses. The smells of Christmas envelop us. We see little kids with balloons and ice-creams and bad tempers and mothers and fathers fussing over them or shouting at them. We don't talk much. The day passes slowly. I'm filled with a confusion of resentment about Kerry's presence emphasising the emptiness of my life, Kerry's presence bringing the hope of company and safety and Kerry's presence threatening to intrude and spoil the tiny rays of light that have filtered in to it.

By Sunday night we're sad. We cry in our room without saying anything and without knowing the extent to which our separate sorrows entwine. Words for it won't come for another twenty-five years. Now we just cry.

Kerry's tears stop when she realises she'll have to check what she's packed and repacked for camp so many times already. Mine stop when I have to iron my clothes for work.

More sobs under my blanket that night. Where's the life we hoped for for so many years? What's wrong with me? Why can't I do it right? I long for Miss Molesworth to tell us how to make all this sadness go away.

Kerry's gone off to her next adventure by the time I get home on Monday. She's at camp. I miss her. I put aside the resentments and the fears of her spoiling things that are mine and I miss her. Tears come easily.

My father's hands are always trying to invade my body now and my rage and hatred grow. I have to get out. The only way out is to tell Miss Molesworth. On Wednesday.

I look at my father asleep in his chair. The glass eye stares at my conscience, the teeth grin at what it sees. I wonder how I could make him die, that old wolf man. Am I strong enough to hold a pillow over his head and stop his breath? Would I be game to stab him? My head whirls in a morass of guilt and shame and hatred. The knowing glass eye keeps staring. The teeth keep grinning. I can't feel anything but feelings I shouldn't have. I don't want to hurt him. I just want to stop him touching me, stop him making me feel dirty, shameful, stop him from stopping me being whole, stop him from crushing me. Just stop him. Not hurt him. Just stop the part of him that I hate so much. Oh but there's always the part that I love and need, getting in the way, bringing more guilt and shame.

Wednesday night. I can scarcely breathe. I'm going to tell Miss Molesworth that my father keeps putting his hands on me and saying rude things to me. I don't think I can say it on the phone but we're going to have lunch together. I'll say it then.

'Who are you ringing?' My father is beside me.

'Miss Molesworth.' Mind your own business.

'You can't keep bothering her. What do you want to ring her for now?'

I can if I want to. She's my friend. I need her. So shut up.

'She told me to. On the telegram.'

'Oh yes. Well, I'd like to say hello to her too.'

'All right.'

'Hello. Miss Molesworth?' It doesn't sound like her but I dialled so carefully.

'No. Who is this?'

'It's Kate. I want to talk to Miss Molesworth, please.'

'Who is it?'

'It's Kate. From Burnside. Well I used to be.' Just get Miss Molesworth. She knows who I am.

'Oh. Kate. Well, I'm Miss Molesworth's sister. Are you alone?' What's going on? Just put Miss Molesworth on.

'No. My Dad's here.' What's it got to do with him?

'Would you put him on please?'

I just want to talk to Miss Molesworth. If she isn't . . . Something's wrong. Very wrong.

'Can't I talk to Miss Molesworth?' Quickly. Panic. No breath.

'You'd better put your father on.'

I stop breathing, thinking.

'This is Mr Shayler. Who am I talking to? Oh. Oh no. I see. Yes. When is the funeral?'

No, don't say it. Not that word. Don't say it, I scream at him inside. It can't be. I saw her. We're going to have lunch. No don't say it. It Is Not True.

I watch the old shaky hand hang up the receiver. My father turns slowly and looks at me.

'You know what's happened don't you?'

'No!'

I run away to my room. I won't let him say those words to me. Won't let him make them true.

He follows me up the hall. I slam the door.

'Princess. Open the door. Let me in. You have to know what's happened.'

I sit frozen on my bed, knowing. Cold, unspeakable, knowing.

I walk slowly to the door, open it.

'Miss Molesworth died this morning. They don't know why and they don't know when the funeral will be.'

There are tears in his eyes. I should comfort him. No.

I stand quietly. There are no words for this either.

'Are you all right?' He cares, I think in the haze.

'Yes. Thank you.'

I shut the door. I shut him out.

LIFE AND DEATH

I'm numb. That's how I get to work. All the strangers here bring me to tears. Denise sees my puffy eyes and asks what's wrong.

'My friend died yesterday.'

People stay away. Even Pat. And when tears threaten I can no more stop them than I can stop the emptiness of being lost.

'Would you like to go home?' Mr Mansouriani asks quietly.

'No, thank you.'

'Is there someone there you could talk to?'

'There's no-one.'

And I cry again.

At home that night, 'We've got a letter from Burnside. From Mr Hardie.'

My father hands it to me.

Something about he knows we'll miss her. Something about helping us if we want them to. Mr and Mrs Ross have left now and Mr Hardie is the superintendent. Mr Hardie, who taught us that God and happiness are not far, far away like the hymn says. Mr Hardie reckons happiness with God is here and now.

There's no place for Mr Hardie here. I leave the letter on the table. I go to stare at the wall in my room. I put my wall between me and my father, between me and the letter.

I wish Kerry were here. No I don't. She doesn't like my friend because she's a Burnside worker. But she isn't just that.

Wasn't.

Saturday. Cold in New Year's Day's sweltering heat. Wanting to be enclosed in something warm and soft. To be rocked. Rocked to sleep. Stay in bed. Lie still. Thoughts come. Feelings. Get up. It's no use staying in bed.

Get dressed. Anything will do. I don't care. I don't care about anything. I go for a walk. I might meet someone who I can tell that my friend has died.

I don't meet anyone.

I come home. Wanting, aching to be held somewhere warm and soft. Somewhere rocking. Safe and strong. It's so cold here in this life that's left.

'Are you all right, Princess?'

'Yes.' Not there! Not held there.

We have breakfast.

'We'll miss her, won't we. She was a good woman.'

Why can't I have my own missing her, I think dully. I don't want mine tied to yours. You didn't love her. You didn't need her. You just made me need her. And now she's gone.

'There'll be a good Christian funeral. We'll go and pay our respects. She was very good to us, wasn't she.'

'Hmm.' He does care. He will miss her. I pour his tea.

I'll miss her so much. How will I go on without the hope of her? I don't know how to bear it.

Walking again. Not caring where. Someone might find me. Someone who might say, 'Why are you so sad and cold?'

Then I could tell them, 'My friend is dead and I am lost.'

Knowing there won't be anyone.

Looking down the hill to the bus stop. Remembering the person who got shouted at for walking in front of the bus.

Walking in front of the bus.

In front of the bus.

That's it. I'll walk in front of a bus and it'll all be over. It will stop the sorrow, stop the emptiness, stop it all.

Walking down the hill, slowly, calmly, knowing it'll all be over soon. No need to rush. It'll be over soon. Take step by step. Nearly over.

Waiting at the bus stop.

A bus comes. Slowly. Pulls in. Stops. I step back. Ones that stop are no good. People get off. This isn't my bus. Mine has to keep going.

Staring at the noiseless traffic. Mindless waiting. Another bus. Slows. Pulls in. No-one gets off.

'Getting on love?'

The driver looks right into my eyes and smiles.

'No.'

Tears come with nowhere to go. I can't make him run over me. He smiled into my eyes. What if my driver's like him! What if he smiles at me then . . .

Standing there. Trying not to cry. Trying not to break up. Knowing it isn't going to end. I can't even do this right. No end. Not here. Not now. Holding my breath. Pushing the pain down. Down. Down. There won't be an end.

Walking aimlessly home.

A car pulls in and drives along beside me.

'G'day sexy. Want a ride or somethin'?' says a greasy stinking boy inside.

'No.'

'Ah come on. Jump in the back,' another boy hanging out the window leers.

'Go away. Leave me alone.'

'Just get in an' help us find Hill Street.'

'Leave me alone.'

I walk away from them, up the path where there's no road, just a mossy stone wall.

*

Sitting in my room. How can I make it stop?

What did Bob Jones do? Did himself in when he left Burnside. No-one knew how.

People on television take poison. We haven't got any. Where do you get poison? I need it now. I don't know where to get it. Shoot myself. No gun. Cut myself. Too frightened. What if it goes wrong! What if I don't die?

I don't die? I don't want to die. Bob Jones might have. I know that now, but I don't want to. Not exactly die. I just don't want to be alive. How do you be alive without being alive? How do you not be alive without being dead?

Falling asleep, falling, falling, falling.

Knocking on the door wakes me.

'Kate. It's Dot on the phone. Come and talk to her.'

'Hello Aunty Dot.' Don't cry. Don't let her know you're crying. She's a stranger.

Almost.

'Hello, dear. I've just heard the terrible news. About Mary Molesworth.'

'She's dead.' Tears burn my eyes. Words choke me.

'Are you upset, Kate?'

'I'm so . . . so sad.'

'Oh dear.'

Neither of us can fill the space for a while but the connection is still there.

'Why don't you come up and see me. We can have a talk and the change will do you good.'

'When?' I don't care.

'When could you come?'

'Next week.' Whenever that is. Talking through fog, grasping for something real, something to focus on, something to contain the emptiness.

'Yes. That would be good. Next Sunday. Would you like to bring Kerry? I suppose she's sad too.'

'She doesn't know yet.' This is just mine. 'She's at camp.'

'Oh. She's at camp. Well, when she comes back you ask her if she'd like to come and see me one day too. You know I love you both very much. Your mother was such a dear friend to me.'

'All right.'

'Do you know how to get here?'

Aunty Dot gives instructions. Writing them down gives me something to do. I rewrite them after she's hung up. I might as well go and see her. There's nothing else to do. She got so excited about my mother being her friend. I'm not a part of them but I might as well go.

Sunday. Another cold day. Wanting warmth. No reason to go to church. Nothing bright and beautiful. Only hurting great and small.

Sweeping dust from the verandah. Wanting somewhere to be clean, ordered. With sunshine on it.

'Good morning.' Two people walking up the path. Strangers. Drab looking. Plastic smiles.

Go away. Get off my path.

'How are you?'

I stare at them coldly.

Get off my path.

'Isn't it a glorious day!'

'No.' Stupid, stupid, fakin' idiots.

'We're going to all the houses in the area to tell people about the Lord.'

'What?'

'About the Lord. Have you read the Bible?'

'Yes.' What's it to you?

'Oh! Perhaps you'd like to have a copy of our magazine. Its feature article is about why God allows suffering in the world.'

'I'd like to know that.' More venom than I intended. Bad luck. I snatch their magazine. I turn to go inside, not wanting them to see me searching.

'Oh good. Well. We'll come back and see you next week if . . .'

'No.' I'm inside now and my father is waiting.

'Who were they?'

'I don't know. They gave me this.'

'Humph. "Watchtower". You should've just slammed the door in their faces. Coming here peddling their rubbish.'

I can't be bothered arguing. I chuck the magazine on my bed and go back to sweeping.

If I have to live here, I'm damn well not going to live in a pigsty. Anger drives me to the laundry where I've boiled the copper. I fill the tubs, add Coke bottles, cockroaches and all. Disinfectant stings my bloodshot eyes, makes my nose run. I don't care. I pour more and more steaming water on the bottles. Cockroaches scramble and die. I don't care. I'm frantic. Scrubbing, shaking, dumping bottles into the empty copper to drain. Carting clean bottles to the verandah. Shiny, clean bottles. I stand them in rows like shiny soldiers. A whole army of them. All exactly the same size and shape. Sparkling in the sun. Waiting. Near the wall.

Back to the tub with any whose cockroach remains haven't come out. More and more soldiers join the army at the wall til the whole verandah is covered. Shimmering, perfect soldiers. Waiting.

'What's this?' my brother, the general, demands.

'Bottles. I'm cleaning up.'

'I told you to leave them.'

'I'm cleaning up.'

'You can't leave them here.'

'Where should they go?'

'I said I'd take them to the shop when I get time.'

'They can wait here then.'

He gets his bags and throws bottles into them. He straps them on his bike and rides away, revving too hard. Winning with noise he thinks. I'm right. I'll keep washing the bloody things 'til they're all gone. No matter how much he revs and grumbles. And every garbage night I'll fill the garbage with old newspapers. And cockroaches.

The bathroom is next. I open the cupboard, shoe ready to pulverise any creature that dares get in my way. I take out all the little bottles, read the labels and throw the old ones in the bin.

'N. Lyford' some labels said. 'Take as directed.'

'N. Lyford. Take one per day with meal.'

Whoever N. Lyford is, these bottles don't belong here. I hurl them into the bin. Each crash applauding my anger.

'What are you up to?' This time my father wants to know.

'Cleaning up.'

'Don't throw out any medicines.'

'Which ones are medicines?'

'The ones with doctor's instructions on them.'

'You mean like this. N. Lyford?'

'Yes. Those ones.'

'Who's N. Lyford?'

'Norma. Norma Lyford. Your mother.'

'Oh yeah. This must be from before you got married.'

I'd forgotten that was her name. She's so far away. My father shuffles away, to sit with her, to be close. He never likes talking about her. She's just his.

What do we have to keep her tablets for? Ones from before she was married to him even! She's been dead for twelve years! I put some of her bottles aside for him. I throw the rest out. Surely she wouldn't want to be among this stink!

I clean through to exhaustion. I lie on my bed plotting my life through awful smells.

The bathroom cupboard still stinks of old medicine. The kitchen cupboard still stinks of old bottles. The laundry still stinks of rotten floorboards and disinfectant. There's still so much to do. So many stenches I can't get rid of and more that I don't want to track down. Miss Molesworth said Ken should do the ones in Dad's room.

Miss Molesworth. I haven't thought of my friend much while I've been cleaning but now it all comes flooding back. Too tired to cry but I feel tears roll out of the corners of my eyes, wetting my hair.

'Tired?' My father is standing over me.

I'm not too tired to scramble off the bed. I will not let you crush me.

'No. I'm going to get dinner.' I push past him and march to the kitchen.

After dinner I run a hot bath, lock the door and prop the chair hard against the other. I lie in the warmth. I feel sorrow swirling about in the steam. Oh, why did you have to die? Why did you leave me so alone? You in Heaven. Me in . . . is this hell? It's so cold without you. If only I could have found the words soon enough. You would have known what to do.

I know I can't stay here, no matter how clean I make it. I have to live somewhere else. I have to live.

There has to be a way out. I find Mr Hardie's letter and read it. I put his offer of help to the test.

1/1/67.
Dear Mr Hardie,
Thank you very much for your letter. I was very glad to hear from a friend from Burnside.

At the moment I feel very sad and lonely but I suppose what has happened is for the best. Miss Molesworth has received the greatest gift anyone could have.

Start it right. Good manners. Remember where I once belonged. Remember church and Sunday school. God gave us all His greatest gift, His son to die so that we could go to Heaven. Miss Molesworth is with God who she loves. Ignore the pain that I'm left with. No, just don't let it stop the right words coming. Mr Hardie has to find the answer.

I was going to have lunch with Miss Molesworth this week but she sent a telegram saying she had to go away. We were going to discuss leaving here, maybe in mid-January, but now I don't know what will happen. I am still very anxious to leave but I don't know whether I should or not. Could we please talk it over sometime?

There. I've said it. Some of it anyway. As much as I can. Miss Molesworth knew I had to go. That ought to be enough. I found the words to tell her but I didn't get a chance to say them. I can't say them to Mr Hardie though.

> *Miss Molesworth's sister rang me to tell me when the funeral is. It's in Longueville but I don't know how to get there. Do you know where it is?*

Ken took the message. He can find his way anywhere. He doesn't know how scared I am of new places. I hope Mr Hardie will ring and say he'll pick me up. I don't want to be alone. Not alone with my father. And he can't walk very far and he can hardly see and how will he get to the funeral?

> *I would like to go alone but I suppose Dad will come with me. I have never been to a funeral before so I don't know what goes on at them.*
>
> *Well that is about all I can say for now. Looking forward to seeing you soon.*
>
> *Yours sincerely, Kate*

Please be at the funeral. And tell me what to do as soon as you see me.

Funeral day. I bathe and get dressed.

'Are you going to change? We'll have to be going soon,' my father says as he scrapes the last bit of shaving cream off his cheek.

'I'm ready.' You'd better hurry up yourself.

'You can't wear blue to a funeral!' He's incredulous.

'Why not?' I want to do this properly.

'You have to wear black to a funeral. It's a mark of respect.'

'I haven't got anything black.'

There's nothing in my wardrobe to express the loss better than the blue dress.

Oh. Miss Molesworth. I want to do this right. You said this

dress looks nice, matches my eyes, the brooch 'set it off nicely'. Remember. You don't mind if I wear it, do you?

'Ah well, Princess. I haven't got a black suit either, so we'll both be misfits.'

I don't want us to be misfits, either of us. Miss Molesworth only saw Dad's goodness. Only that should go to her 'send off', as he calls it.

I wait in my room until the time I've worked out that we'll need to leave. I go to tell my father it's time to go.

Walking down the hall I see the silhouette of him. Is it him? Must be. There's no-one else here. A bent frail shadow fossicking about in a drawer of the sideboard. Below the shirt tails, sticks hold him up. Sticks for legs. Closer. Sticks. Bones covered with skin so thin I'm afraid I'm seeing my father's skeleton! When did he become so frail! So small and fragile! He's almost spent. I can't bear it. Inside I scream.

Don't be frail. Be strong. I need you. You have to be the strong one, the father. You have to get us through this. You have to be the father. Strong. Solid. Not . . . not this!

Anger about my need and my love mixes around inside me. I own only the anger for now. Anger about his being so late getting ready. Why can't he get it right?

'We have to go, Dad.'

'Yes. But I can't find a tie.'

'Aren't there any in your room!'

Don't spoil it. Don't make us miss the funeral, the last chance to connect with my old life.

'No. Ken took them. There might be one here.'

His vulnerability is moving me to where I don't want to be.

'I'll have a look.'

He stands aside and waits. There are no ties among the papers.

'No. None here.'

'Will you ring Ken and ask him while I get ready? We don't want to be late.'

Please don't cry, Dad. Stay strong. I need you to be strong.

He hurries away slowly.

Ken will be cranky with me again if I ring him. Dad has to. No. He hasn't got the strength to face a cranky son. Sadness and compassion. He needs me to be strong. I'm ashamed of my anger at him and annoyed by my weakness.

'Ken? It's Kate. Do you know where the ties are? Yes the ties. Dad needs one to wear to the funeral. We can't . . . Oh.' He's cranky. He's gone.

'He doesn't know where they are.'

'I can't go without one.'

'We'll be late. The bus goes in ten minutes.' I realise my plans haven't allowed for how slowly he moves.

'Oh dear. You'll have to go without me and I'll catch you up.'

'How will you get there?'

'Don't trouble yourself, Princess. I'll catch a cab.'

'You can't afford it.' Miss Molesworth told me lots of times how poor you are. Oh, but I hope you can afford it. Today. Just today, if never again.

'Oh, I can this once. You go.'

'All right. I'll see you there. Goodbye.'

Compassion shakes my anger to sadness. How can it be so hard to turn away and leave him to get somewhere by himself? What if he can't make it? What if he can't see well enough? What if he jaywalks and gets roared at by a policeman again, because I made him hurry. But I have to get there. I have to get there and do the whole thing right. My need to connect with Burnside in the emptiness of death shoves me out the door. Oh Dad, why is it like this? Why are you so old!

There are lots of people at the church, some talking, some smiling, some just sad. All strangers. I thought there'd be mostly Burnsiders here. There are so many strangers. Please see me, someone. Someone who knows that I knew her. See me. Talk to me. Tell me what to do.

People start going inside. I follow. Dad isn't here and it's about to start. Oh hurry up. You can't, I know, but tell the cab to hurry. I need you. I sit at the end of a pew.

Please someone, recognise me. I'm here. They don't seem to notice.

My father shuffles in. He hasn't got a tie. I'm embarrassed but someone smiles at him. People squash up so he can sit near me. He bows his head and closes his good eye. When he's finished praying he whispers, 'There's a lot of people here. She'll have a good send off.'

'Hmm.' Don't talk. Just be here.

'Did you see anyone from Burnside?'

'No. Did you?'

'No. I suppose we'll see them later.'

The service starts. The singing is obscenely joyous. I don't understand. People stand up to read from the Bible. People stand up and talk about her. My father dabs his eyes sometimes. He sleeps sometimes. As people talk, her life unfolds and I hold my pain inside. This doesn't seem to be the time for tears. They are celebrating. When do they cry? When can I? I listen. There are so many things she's done that I know nothing about. She has so many friends who I don't know.

But my part of her, with her, feels so big. Equal to all the rest of her thirty-five years. I want to stand up and shout at them that I knew her too, that I loved her, that she knew me, that she was my friend, that I miss her so badly that I can hardly bear it. Most of all I want one of them to let me into their life so that I can still have a bit of her. The service goes on and no-one knows I'm here. The celebration of her life clashes with my sorrow.

When it's over we go outside. Dad looks around for a Burnside person. I'm dazed but the need for someone familiar gets me back into focus.

'Mr Shayler! So you made it. And Kate too. How are you?'

I know the face. And the posh accent. The bosom. Oh, it's you . . .

'Good day Mrs er. I'm sorry,' says my father, tipping his hat.

'Miss Tarlton. From Burnside.'

My father and Miss Tarlton chat for a while. I'm looking for Mr Hardie.

A little lady who looks rather old but bright comes up to us and smiles a greeting.

'This is Miss Molesworth's mother, Mrs Molesworth. Mr Shayler and his daughter, Kate, one of our Burnside lasses,' says Miss Tarlton.

'Oh.' Miss Molesworth had a mother!

'How do you do, Mr Shayler.'

My father tips his hat again and squeezes Mrs Molesworth's hand. The familiarity in her voice is warming.

'And Kate.'

She squeezes my hand and tears come. Not to her eyes though. Hers are sparkling, smiling. Doesn't she know Mary Molesworth is dead?

'Mary loved her work at Burnside. Which home are you in, Kate?'

'I've left. Miss Molesworth was helping me at home.' She knew me. I need her.

'Oh yes. I remember.' The warmth of the mother is like the warmth of the friend.

'Well, I'm so pleased you could come. I hope I see you again.' Mrs Molesworth walks a little way off and chats with someone else. Her daughter has gone forever and I know I won't see either of them again. Mrs Molesworth is just being polite about seeing me later.

'Let's take your Dad over to the seat,' Miss Tarlton interrupts.

After she's sat my father down Miss Tarlton asks me how I am. I cry. She says Miss Molesworth had told her about how things are at home. She asks if they're any better. She asks if they're likely to be better when Kerry gets home. All I manage is a litany of 'No's'.

'I'll pick Kerry up from the station after camp and then I think the best thing will be for us all to sit down together and talk it through. What do you think, Mr Shayler?'

'I suppose that's best. I know you haven't been happy at home, Princess, but things will be better when Kerry comes home. You'll see. We'll give it another try. It'll be better.' I can feel the cage threatening to fall around me again as my father tries to hold me, tries to hold his family together.

'Kate?' Miss Tarlton asks.

'I want to talk about it with us all there. Like you said.'

I'm so confused. My father really thinks we can work it out. He loves us. He wants his family together. At the end of his life he wants to give us the thing he's promised for so long. I don't want it. I'm about to hurt him so badly. I'm going to have to name the problem. I'll have to shame him and myself in front of the family and in front of Miss Tarlton. And I'll have to embarrass my brother, pimp on him. And I'll have to tell my sister what I hate. I'll have to spoil what she sees as her only chance of freedom. The only life for her now will be back at Burnside. She'll have no choice. She'll hate that and she'll hate me.

I'm so sorry, Kerry. Please don't hate me. I can't wait for you to come because you won't be able to stop him . . . stop his hands . . . stop the crushing. I'm so sorry I can't bear it for you.

I have to tell it all. If I don't I'll have to live in that cage. I'll die in it and I'll have to keep living there, dead in the cage. The weight of it is so heavy as we stand outside the church. It's so hard not to cry.

My father and I don't know what to say to each other about the death or the funeral. 'It was a good send off. It did her proud,' he says as we sit side by side on the bus.

'Hm,' I agree.

That's our only connection. Then we think our unsharable thoughts and feel our own sadnesses as we travel home together.

I didn't really say a proper goodbye to Miss Molesworth. My life got in the way.

A few weeks later Mrs Molesworth rings and asks if I can meet her for lunch.

We meet in a cafeteria in a big department store. There isn't much time. I want her to be like her daughter and be my friend. She is herself though and she wants to meet me just this once because she knows how sad I've been. She knew her Mary had been special to me.

'I want you to have a keepsake,' she says, placing a small paisley box in my hand.

'Mary would want you to have this, I think.'

In the box there's a beautiful mother of pearl disc held gently in a fine gold filigree brooch setting.

'Was it hers?'

'Yes. Do you like it?'

'Yes. I love it! Is it for me?' I say, blinking back tears.

Mrs Molesworth pats my hand. Soon we say goodbye and she merges into the crowd of irrelevant lives. I put the little box at the bottom of my handbag. I'll treasure it always.

SOMEWHERE TO LIVE

A letter comes a few days later, addressed to Kerry and me. My sister is still away so the letter is mine.

Dear Kate and Kerry,
At last the time has come for you both to be at home with your Dad! I hope it will be good for you. You've all waited so long for this.

I work at Punchbowl now. I'm the matron, yes, the matron, at a hostel for girls who come from the country to work in the city. We have ten girls here, quite a different thing to Burnside.

If you would like to come and see me sometime, ring and let me know when. Perhaps you would like to come for lunch at the weekend.

The phone number is 759 0611.
Looking forward to hearing from you.
Yours in Christ, N. Driver

Deserter Driver! How did she know? I don't care. She's stretched out the hand that I need. Oh, but what about when I was so rude

294

. . . No. This seems to be a forgiving letter. I grab the phone while I redefine Deserter Driver.

'Bush Mission Society.'

'Hello. Can I speak to Miss Driver, please?'

'This is Miss Driver.'

'Um. Miss Driver. Um. It's Kate. Kate Shayler.'

'Kate! I thought you might ring. How are you?'

'Good. Well sad. Did you know Miss Molesworth died?'

'Yes. I heard about it.'

I can't wait for polite stuff to be over. I have to get on with my life.

'Can I come and see you next Saturday?'

'Yes. Of course you can.'

There's a pause then she adds, 'I've heard that you're not too happy at home, Kate.'

'No, I'm not.'

I'm offended that Burnside people still discuss me, that they've told her my secret, a private thing that I want to tell her later, if it feels right. I want to be the one to tell her I'm a failure at home. But here's a chance to move out. I grab at it, letting go of the resentment.

'Can I come there?'

'I don't have any beds spare just now.'

My heart sinks.

'But one of the girls might be moving to a flat soon, so you could keep it in mind.'

'All right.' My voice trembles. Keeping it in my mind isn't what I want. I want escape. Now. Desperately.

'So I'll see you on Saturday.' Miss Driver is so matter of fact and cheerful. 'We'll talk about things then.'

I'll ring her and say I . . . what? That I don't want to come and talk? I only want to come and hear her say I can move in? No. Can't tell her that. Bad manners. Well, as soon as I think what to say, I'll ring her and cancel the lunch. Meanwhile I'll just go to work and stay there, or somewhere, for as long as I can until . . . something.

Another night at home and my brother grumbles that I keep buying cheap meat.

'Why can't we have something decent for once?' he wants to know, as he drowns his sausages in tomato sauce.

The phone rings. I wait for my brother to answer. It won't be Miss Molesworth. I don't like the phone these days. My brother waits for me to answer it. It won't be for him. His friends don't ring here. I give in as he stares hard into his dinner.

'Hello. Is that you, Kate?'

'Yes.'

'It's Miss Driver.'

'Oh hello.' She's ringing to say I can't come for lunch.

'Look, I just thought I'd let you know that one of the girls is moving out in a week. We'll have a spare bed here. You might like to think about taking it after you've come to see me.'

'Yes, I'd like to.' What is there to think about?

'Well, don't decide now. Come over on Saturday and have a look around. Then if you think you'd like to move in, we'll see what we can do.'

'All right then.'

I already know.

I hang up. The energy that surges through me won't let me sit down. My whole being twitches with tears and laughter, guilt and freedom. I'll have to tell Miss Mo . . .

'Who was it?' my father's old voice filters through.

'Miss Driver. From Burnside.'

Guilty energy forces me out of the room. Out to the street where I have to walk. Fast. Why does my freedom feel so bad? Pounding feet might squash the guilt about the pain I'm about to inflict on my father. Pain, straight to his heart. Keep walking and try to be mindless.

I tell my father I'm going to see Miss Driver who used to work at Burnside. I don't want to tell him why. Not Yet.

'Where is she now?'

'At Punchbowl.'

He wants to know more. It feels so cruel saying, 'In a hostel.'

'Who lives in this hostel?' He sounds tired.

'Girls from the country.'

His back seems to bend more sadly as I follow him out the door to say goodbye. He knows.

'You'll be home for tea, won't you?'

'Yes. I'll be home.'

I push all thoughts of my father away as I get on the train. I remember Miss Driver instead and the way I'd behaved so badly when she left Burnside. I pray that the forgiveness I thought I heard in her voice is real. She's offering friendship now, offering so much, just when I need it.

There she is at the door of the two-storey house that's modest by Burnside standards but huge compared with its neighbours. Huge compared with my father's house.

'Kate! Come in. Did you find it all right?'

'Yes, thank you.'

Miss Driver looks just the same. Short white hair, thick glasses through which she looks directly into my eyes and smiles, the untouched blackhead on her cheek and the slight lean forward that suggests she's eager to be part of whatever is going on, all still there. She shows me around, downstairs first, where she lives and where the lounge room, kitchen, laundry and office are and then upstairs where the girls' bedrooms and bathroom are.

Neat! Clean! Tidy! All the way through! Yes. I want to live here. Looking around is interesting but I don't need to do it.

'This is the room you'll share if you decide to come. You'll be in with Emily . . . Oh here she is. Emily, this is Kate who's thinking of moving in, in place of Wendy . . .'

I'm not thinking about it. I'm doing it. I don't care that the room is so small we hardly fit in it. I don't care that Emily doesn't seem very friendly. This is where I'm going to live.

Downstairs, Miss Driver rings a little bell. Some girls come into the kitchen for lunch. Merrilyn from Woodenbong, Maxine from Cobar, Emily from Newcastle and Lynne from Narrabri.

I'm shy of them but they don't take any notice of that. They chat on, sometimes including me, sometimes not.

After lunch Miss Driver asks, 'Well, Kate, what do you think?'

'I like it. But . . .'

'Is there something you're not happy about?'

'Yes. Dad. I don't think he'll let me come.'

'Have you asked him yet?'

'No. Miss Molesworth was going to but . . . Miss Tarlton's going to when she comes over on Friday.'

'Well, I'll need to know soon.'

'Is Friday all right, after Miss Tarlton talks to Dad?'

'All right but sooner if you can. If you don't want the bed I'll need to contact the next person on the list.'

Do we have to force things to happen quickly? Can't I have time to get used to the idea? Can't Dad have time to adjust too. No. Miss Driver has a business to run.

'No later than Friday then?'

'Yes. All right.'

'Good. I'd better explain the rules to you before you decide, though I'm sure you won't have any trouble with them after Burnside. You have to be home by ten o'clock during the week and eleven on weekends. If you need to be out later, let me know and we'll discuss it. No visitors inside and no phone calls after nine thirty. Board is $11.80 a week. Can you afford that?'

'I think so.' I don't care if board takes my whole $19.30 per week. I am saving up for a sewing machine like Miss Molesworth suggested but I'll gladly pay all that money as well if I have to.

'Board covers all your meals and so on, so let's see. What else will you need? Fares and clothes. Outings too. Hmm. Well, let me know if you have trouble and we'll see what we can do, although they don't usually reduce board because it's already so low.'

I'm sure I'll be fine.

As we walk to the door Miss Driver explains that she does all the cooking and we're responsible for our own laundry, cleaning our rooms and sharing the cleaning of common rooms as well as washing up after meals. We reach the front door and she shows me a little book that sits on a table near the door.

'When you go out at night you write your name here, then when you come home cross it out. The last person in puts the chain across the door.'

We say goodbye. I'll ring as soon as Miss Tarlton talks to Dad.

I'm about to start my life outside Burnside all over again. I concentrate on learning the rules as I sit in the train, to stop thinking about my father. The rules about going out at night are mysterious, not because they're restrictive but because I can't imagine where there is to go. I can't imagine that I'll ever need to write my name in that little book at the door. Perhaps I'm about to make friends with those girls and they'll let me go out with them.

Miss Molesworth would have been so pleased. She always said I should make friends my own age. This hostel will be just like Burnside. There'll be lots of friends and I won't even have to work on it. It'll just happen, like it did at Burnside.

'How was your visit to the hostel?' Dad asks.

'All right.'

Oh, where are you Miss Molesworth? Miss Tarlton?

I want to be still but then I remember how empty, lonely it feels there. By now I had forgotten about meeting the God who meant I belonged. I'm too afraid to be still and lonely.

Don't think. Don't think about telling Dad. Think about tomorrow and going to Aunty Dot's place.

A disoriented me visits Aunty Dot, because I said I would. What will we find to talk about? I hardly know her but she'll distract me from my life without my friend and the father who I'm about to hurt.

The huge smiling aunty waits eagerly at her door. She knows when the bus is due.

'I'm so glad you've come to see me. Oh dear. You're so like Norma.'

She dabs her eyes.

Is she wiping tears or sweat away? Her welcome is so warm. She squashes me against her huge bosom. There's something comforting about it but her hold is too tight, almost squeezing the breath out of me. I want to tear myself out of its closeness.

I like looking like my mother. It makes me someone. With roots. Clean roots. Apart from the family I'm trying to live in now. The roots have no form or texture but my face proves that I did belong somewhere once.

We sit in the lounge room and Aunty Dot talks. She talks about Norma Shayler.

'She loved you all so much.' More dabbing of the remembering eyes. 'She'd do anything for you kids.'

As she talks, Norma Shayler becomes a living, breathing person, not a painful secret, a shapeless idea, a mere word. Norma Shayler was real, with hands that could ice cakes magnificently and embroider and crochet perfectly, with a creative flair that let her design patterns of perfect colour and balance. Norma Shayler was lovable, clever, creative, patient, accomplished and funny.

No ill is spoken of her. She did no wrong. Aunty Dot's memories and my old unconscious idea that my mother could make everything right combine now to produce a saint. There is no emotional connection with my saint mother. I'm just gathering facts that prove she was perfect. I try to feel her being mine but there's nothing there. It's just a fact that I once belonged with a perfect mother. It's not an emotional truth.

My own fascination intrigues me. I hadn't been aware that I wanted to know about my mother. Now though, I want more and more. I want to know everything about Norma Shayler.

Aunty Dot dabs at her perspiration, finishing again with her eyes.

'It was such a shock when we lost her.'

The old woman sits, weeping quietly, grieving for her dear friend all over again. Why does she still cry after all these years? Is that how it will be . . . No. Leave that. Don't cry here.

Aunty Dot regains control, stuffs her hanky into her dress and goes to gather proof of what she's told me. I look at all the strangers in the photos on her shelf.

'You keep this one, dear. Your mother made it for me.'

She hands me a doily. A lyrebird stands proudly beside a bottlebrush.

'But it's yours!'

'You haven't got much of your mother. I'd like you to have it. Go on.'

She fossicks around and produces another doily from the sideboard, an unfinished tapestry from another room, an embroidered runner from the mantelpiece and so on. My favourite is a milk jug cover whose tiny beads tinkle and seem to call me from somewhere long ago. I put my new possessions in the paper bag my aunty has given me. I'll explore them later.

Aunty Dot sits beside me with a photo album. There are so many strangers here. She flicks quickly backwards through her life until she gets to the photos she's after, the ones of people she thinks I'll recognise.

'You know who this is, of course.'

I look carefully at a large black and white face. Short dark hair, a rather masculine, freckled face that doesn't quite smile but looks calm, content and perhaps tired. I want to recognise the face, for Aunty Dot's sake.

'No. I don't know.'

'Oh! Oh dear. It's Norma!'

I must still look blank. How come I don't recognise my own mother's face! It can't be her.

'It's your mother. Don't you remember her?'

'No.' I'm so embarrassed by my dreadful memory. Surely I should remember her face! Aunty Dot takes the photo out of the album and puts it on the lounge beside her. She turns to the next page.

'Do you know who this is?'

She's pointing to another large black and white portrait.

'No. I don't know that one either.'

'It's Kenny. Little Kenny.'

My brother! I look harder at the little boy sitting up in his best clothes, legs out in front, almost smiling, with a squeaky toy beside him. I don't remember Ken like this. That's all right. Little boys grow and change. Aunty Dot takes little Kenny out of the album and puts him near his mother on the lounge.

'You can probably guess who these two are.'

She points to two photos, side by side on separate pages. Two little girls in embroidered smocks sit with the same almost smile that Kenny has.

'It must be Kerry and me.'

'Yes. This one would be you, wouldn't it? Or do you think this one?'

'I don't know. That one looks more like Kerry I think.'

Aunty Dot takes us out too. She picks up Norma and Kenny and holds us all in her trembling hand.

'Would you like to have these, dear?'

I want them so much but is it polite to take them? She's kept them all those years because she wants them. She's cried about Norma right here in front of me. Now she's giving me all these things, giving me her memories. Yes. I want them. I want to snatch them all and go off and study them by myself.

'I'd like you to have them.' Aunty Dot urges.

'All right. If you can spare them.' I try not to sound as greedy as I feel for proof of my belonging among clever, pretty, beautiful, clean things. I add them to the proof in the paper bag.

Aunty Dot delivers her next surprise.

'I wanted to take you. When Norma . . . went.'

I stare at her. She's almost a stranger.

'You didn't know that, did you, but it's true. I would have taken you and Kerry but Charley wanted you kids to stay together. Oh, I thought about taking the three of you but I knew I wouldn't manage. Two maybe, but not three little ones.'

What do I say? It doesn't bother me that she hadn't taken me. She's a stranger. If it hadn't been the saintly mother who kept me, then Burnside was all right. I know Burnside but I don't know this aunty who's so keen to have me understand.

'Yes, Charley always said that Norma would want you kids to stay together.'

Is she bitter towards my father? It's as if he'd talked it through with his Norma after she'd died and she'd told him what to do. Aunty Dot had just had to accept that she couldn't have Kerry and me without Kenny. But I think she's a little bitter with Dad about it. Well, he won't have . . .

I've got to change the subject. This is too weird.

'Were you actually related to my mother?'

The question has been on my mind since the first time we met at Burnside.

'No. Well, yes. By marriage. We were very close friends.'

'What does that mean, "by marriage"?'

'My Bill was your mother's cousin. They are all Lyfords. And Wades.' I remember S. Wade on the Bushells Tea tin at home. I'm confused and not just by Wades.

'Oh, we had such good times together, going out in that old car . . .'

Wait on! Dad always told us we haven't got any relatives in Australia. Now we have. I try to sort it out while Aunty Dot goes off in the car with her Bill and the others for a while. When she gets back, she picks up the photo album and shows me another photo.

'That's my Bill. He's gone now, of course. And this is me. And that's your mother, oh and Aunty Mary, your mother's mother. That's Charley at the end.'

Charley at the end doesn't look anything like my father. Twenty years later I find that she meant another Charley, my mother's brother, my uncle. Now I assume the only Charley we have is my father and he would have been younger when this photo was taken. Here is a row of strangers all smiling happily in each other's company. They are my family and I've never heard of most of them. I study them, trying to find something familiar. There's nothing.

'Well now, we'd better have lunch. You said you liked baked dinner so that's what we're having. A kind of celebration for you coming to see me at last. You sit here while I dish up.'

I sit wondering what there'll be to talk about over lunch. My move to the hostel seems a long way away. My head is full of questions that are so muddled they can't form words. I hope Aunty Dot, my aunty by marriage, will just keep talking so I can soak up more information about my family.

'I've got a special treat for you, Kate.'

She presents a plate of something curved and brown.

'What is it?'

'It's crackling! Haven't you had it before? It's the best part of a pork roast. Try it.'

She watches while I taste the greasy lump of fat.

'How is it? Good?'

'Hmm.' Remembering my manners. How do I say, politely, that I hate it?

'Put some salt on it. It's even better.'

She watches as I follow her instructions.

'Good?'

'Hmm.'

Pleased with her success, Aunty Dot finishes dishing up lunch. I look around for somewhere to plant the crackling, like the Three Stooges would have. I haven't got any pockets and there are no pot plants. There's nowhere, except my mouth. I chew slowly 'til lunch arrives.

Another surprise comes after questions about how work is going, how much I get paid and what I do on weekends.

'Why don't you come and live here with me, dear?'

Has she guessed that I'm so unhappy at home? How could she know? I don't know what to say. I have plans to move into the hostel. Now, suddenly, I have choices. Too many choices. What would Dad say if I came here? Or went to the hostel? I don't want this to come up here. It has though. I wish Miss Molesworth could tell me what to do.

'You could have your own room and I could look after you. You could still go to work, of course, and you could help me out around the place. I'm not as young as I used to be.'

As she plans my life I feel another cage hovering above my head. I don't understand this feeling. Not here. I want to be looked after by someone, have someone to tell me what to do, where to go, what to say. To tell me who I am. I need someone to tell me, now, what to do. I don't know what's right, what's best. I just don't know. I'm lost among choices.

I hold back my tears.

'I don't know,' I say weakly. 'I might be moving into Miss Driver's hostel.'

'Oh. Yes. Well, you think about which you'd like. I'd love to have you here with me. I couldn't do it for you when your darling mother died but perhaps I could make up for it now.'

'Um. All right. I'll think about it.'

I'm relieved that she knows how to change the subject. Well, I am for a while.

'Have you got a boyfriend yet?' The question becomes inevitable in conversations with adults.

'No.' I'm a failure.

'You will have soon. You have such lovely eyes and teeth. Such a pretty face and you've been brought up so well too. I'm sure you'll make someone a lovely wife.'

My face burns. I wonder what my teeth have to do with it. I want to believe what she says but I don't, not really. I'll never get over being shy.

'You'll get over being shy, dear. Oh, it will be so lovely when you do meet a nice boy and marry and have your own home. Now, you finish up your crackling while I get our pudding.'

I chomp on another curve of fat while I try to sort out the inside of my head. What if the hostel's awful? What if I have to come here to live? Would it be better to just stay at home with . . . No. No!

We talk about work and Ken and Kerry over pudding.

Suddenly Aunty Dot looks at her watch, heaves herself up and says, 'Goodness gracious! Look at the time. You'll miss your bus.'

She bundles me out the door ahead of her. We can't fit through together.

'You think about what I've said, dear. There's no hurry. Just let me know what you decide.'

She presses her words in amongst her farewell hug before releasing me to rush off to the bus.

So many things to think about. New things. My mother, my mother the person, relatives I have, crackling, boyfriends I don't have, how to catch one with my teeth and so on.

I hear Aunty Dot plotting my life again. Why do I baulk at this? Why do I feel I'm suffocating? Many years later I come to understand that I baulked at the possibility of her getting to know me. The real me. Inside. Where dark things are buried. Things that I am so ashamed of, that I sensed she'd loathe me for if she ever found out.

All I know today is that what she offered feels like a gate clanging shut on a different cage. I imagine disappointing her with my failures and, finally, my aunty not wanting me. I feel her expectations bearing down, forcing me to a life and a self that I don't recognise.

I study the photos. Who are these people? Not their names. I know their names but who were they back then when they all smiled together. Who were those little kids with their almost smiles? Who were they when the saint was their mother?

Where are they now?

FAMILY TALK

Walking quickly home from the bus stop after work on Friday. Miss Tarlton will be there. We'll talk about the future. Thinking very hard about the words I have to say so they'll let me go, let me out of the cage, to live in the hostel.

'My father keeps touching me and saying rude things to me.' That's what I'll say. But, does it have to be in front of them all? Do I have to shame my father and myself in front of them all? Do I have to embarrass my brother for being so lazy? And crush my sister's dreams?

Yes. I do. There's no choice. My misery is bigger than all of that. I don't know how to live with it.

Kerry meets me at the door. She looks so young.

'G'day. How was camp?' I try to sound as if I've been wondering.

'Fantastic!' She glows. She's so alive. 'We did swimming and archery and rowing and all that. An' I got this an' I . . . Oh.'

My tears are already spoiling her homecoming.

'Bad news about Miss Molesworth, eh.' She's not particularly sad but she tries to be sympathetic.

'Yeah. Sorry.'

We stand in our room, side by side, the gap between us is filling with what's coming, drawing us to the kitchen where our futures will be decided. Kerry will hate hers. Soon she'll know she has no choice but to go back to the place she hates most.

But it's only for two years, Kerry. It's better than this! If only you knew.

Miss Tarlton has told Kerry what she can of what's happened here in the last week or two but Kerry and I don't know how to talk about it here. We go to meet our father and Miss Tarlton. Small talk jerks uncomfortably on among cups of tea and smokes. We all know we're waiting for the real talk to come out from hiding behind the teapot.

Miss Tarlton begins, awkwardly. She finds some words that mean our father is very frail and needs to be cared for properly, maybe in a nursing home.

'Oh, I'll be better soon. I'll go to the doctor and get something to perk me up.'

He still has some fight in him. I'm torn between admiring his determination and being afraid that he'll block my escape.

'You need proper care, Mr Shayler. Kate can't give you that when she's at work. And Kerry will have to finish at least another two years of school.'

'We can manage. I'll be better soon, then I can help more around the place. I've held on to it for the girls and Ken for a long time now.'

Don't fight for me to stay. Don't. I want to shout at my father who's using all his strength to hold on to his dream. His dream, not mine. Not any more.

Miss Tarlton finds some more words that mean I'm very unhappy and there doesn't seem to be a solution to it here. She thinks it would be just as difficult with Kerry here too. After all, I couldn't be her mother and do all the other things I have to do as well. That's not how a sixteen-year-old girl should be living. She should have time and energy for going out and meeting people her own age, making a life and a future for herself.

'I know how unhappy Kate's been. I've tried to help but . . .'

I can't look at my father's face but I hear his tears falling in his words. I watch his hands tremble. He leaves his shaggy smoke in the ashtray. The empty hands rub each other. They make that same leathery swish they'd made when I was a trusting child sitting on his knee. Now they pull a hanky from his pocket and dry his eyes. The utter sadness of him moves me so deeply that I can hardly see the thing I have to get away from.

'I'll try to do more. I only want my girls to be happy. I'll be better soon. I don't want to lose you. We've waited so long . . .'

The hand takes the hanky upwards again as words fail him.

I want to shout, 'I'll stay with you. I'll look after you and care for you and make sure you're happy before you die. I'll make myself be happy . . .'

Miss Tarlton tries to dull his pain.

'But if Kate moves out you won't be losing her, Mr Shayler. She'll come back to visit, won't you, Kate. And we can take Kerry back and she'll see you on visiting days as usual.'

Miss Tarlton hasn't lost sight of why we're here. I've been lost in the fog of my father's grief but her words bring me out. Now I'm frantically grasping for a way to stop hurting my father when I stand my ground and leave him.

'Yeah. 'Course. I'll come back. Every weekend,' I promise, knowing it will do so little to ease his pain.

'Perhaps we could get someone in to help.' My father's still fighting. 'When Kerry's with us she'll be able to help and it won't be as hard for you, Princess.'

'You could probably only get someone for a few hours a week. The cost for more would be a problem. What would you like to say about that, Kate?'

The cage hovers.

'It would help to have someone to wash and clean and Kerry could help too. But there's . . . It's just . . .'

I must say the shame words. Now. My future depends on it. I try again.

'I wish I could be happy here.' I can't help the tremble in my voice. 'I'm sorry I can't be, Dad. I know it's what you've always wanted. I wish it could be all right but you . . . It's just that . . . It's just . . . I'm so tired . . . so tired of . . .'

I can't do it. They're all waiting. I try again.

'It's just that . . . you . . . when you . . . you keep . . .' The words stick. I can't get them out. My heart is breaking. My father's is too. I can't hurt him more. I can't shame him on top of all that pain.

He will be shamed if I tell what he does. Ashamed of his behaviour as well as heartbroken by its results. Seeing him so vulnerable overwhelms me. It prevents me from looking at the truth, the truth that my father has caused this pain himself. He deserves the shame, not me. I'm blinded by his vulnerability.

Perhaps I could have coped with living here if all I'd had to deal with was his age and his need for care.

'Do you think a part-time housekeeper would help?' asks Miss Tarlton who can't hear what I can't say.

'No.' Because there's the other.

'Then we need to look at alternatives. It's too much to ask of a young girl to run a house and hold down a job, Mr Shayler. Can you see that?' Miss Tarlton asks gently, kindly.

'Yes. Yes. I only want my girls to be happy.'

The shaky old hand picks up the smoke. It's nearly spent. It drops into its ashes.

'How do you feel about Kate going into Miss Driver's hostel?'

'If that's what you think is best for her, I'll have to agree. Is it what you want, Princess?'

'Yes.'

He stops fighting. Relief. And so much hurting.

'I'll arrange for Kerry to come back to Burnside at the end of the holidays. Are you agreeable?'

'If that's what's best. You've looked after her well for so long,

310

another year or two will be all right. It'll go quickly. You can still come on visiting days, Cherry.'

I'm afraid to look at my sister. She'll be so sad, angry, confused. She's losing her freedom. She'll have to struggle on with life at Burnside. She wanted to get out even more than I did. Now she has to go back. She has no choice. She doesn't fuss or shout or blame or argue. She simply says, 'I don't want to go back but I s'pose I'll have to.' Her voice is firm, resolute. It's just for two years so that she can finish high school. She'll move out of Ivanhoe, into Cumbrae where Aunty Mavis will be her house mother.

After my brave little sister agrees to return to her cage, she breaks down. Sobs with her whole body. I understand. Our father decides to fight one last time.

'Could you have a talk to Ken when he gets home. I know he hasn't been much help but we could talk to him, explain things. He'll be home soon.'

The hanky dabs his eyes again.

'We're family. We should be together. It's what we've wanted . . .'

'Yes. All right then. We'll wait for Ken if you think he'll be home soon but I really need to get home myself. Kate, could you make us some more tea?'

Thankful that there's a reason for me not to sit in the charged silence around the table, I make the tea, slowly.

Ken arrives. He looks very awkward. He surveys his family. He surveys the floor as Miss Tarlton explains what's been discussed so far. Miss Tarlton is quite blunt about the need for him to take more responsibility for some housekeeping and for the personal care and hygiene of our father. She says this isn't something young girls should be expected to do. With our father as frail as he is, he can't do it all himself, though he does his best, Ken should help. She explains that I haven't been able to cope by myself and unless we find an alternative, Kerry and I would be moving out.

My brother's face hardens, reddens. He announces angrily, 'If the girls have already made up their minds to go there's nothing I can do about it. What's the use of discussing it!'

'Your father needs to be looked after, Ken. We've discussed selling the house and finding a good nursing home for him but he doesn't want to do that if he can stay here. But he needs care.'

'I'm staying.' Ken's eyes blaze at her as he spits his reply. 'The girls can go if they want to. I'll stay and look after him. He's not selling the house.'

He storms out and the motor bike roars away. Again.

I'm shaken by his passionate vow to care for our father so that he can stay in his own house. I've never seen Ken do anything for my father. Tonight I can't see my brother's need for a home. I only see my father's need and I'm ashamed that I can't make such a solemn promise to him.

We sit in silence for a while, knowing there's only one solution. More tears flow as Miss Tarlton concludes, 'I think we know what has to happen, don't we?' This is my last chance to do what I think is right for my father who is weeping quietly, exhausted. I should stand up like Ken and declare that I'll stay and care for him, give him some happiness, give him back his family before he dies.

'We'll move Kate to the hostel and Kerry will come back to Burnside. You'll visit your dad on weekends, won't you, Kate?'

Miss Tarlton knows that he needs to hear it many, many times.

'I'll see about getting you some home help, Mr Shayler, and we'll see how things are going in a month or two.'

The decision is made. Incredible relief swirls around with the guilt and worry about my father as I cry under my blankets tonight. The only way to stop the tears is to focus my thoughts on Miss Driver's hostel. Not Aunty Dot's offer of family. Family is . . . isn't much . . . If I think about family I'll think about my father then I'll give in and stay. And die inside.

All my things are packed back into the cases they'd come out of just a month ago. My father watches, knowing it's hopeless to fight any more. Kerry has packed too so all there is to do now is wait. Nothing to say. Feelings too strong to frame in words. Guilt too private to speak of. Glimpses of my father show how small and frail he is. The weight of him makes me turn away.

The car arrives. We all help pack our belongings in. Now we have to say something.

'You'll be back soon, won't you?' my father asks.

'Yeah. 'Course I will! On Sunday.' I try to sound cheerful, as if this isn't a big moment.

'And Kerry Cherry. You'll be out next visiting day, won't you.'

'Yeah. I'll be here.'

I think she wonders why he needs to be told so many times.

'Off you go then and I'll see you soon.'

The bony hand holds my shoulder too hard as he kisses my cheek.

'I'm sorry, Dad,' I whisper.

'I know. I know,' he whispers back. He turns to kiss his baby.

'Bye bye, Cherry. 'Til visiting day.'

He stands waving as the car drives away. Kerry and I sit sniffling on the back seat.

We're all starting again, each with our dreams broken. The two of us leaving in the car have separate hopes. The old father, almost hopeless, waves us out of sight.

My biggest hope is that Ken will stand by his promise to care for Dad. Keep him alive. I can't bear the thought of not having a father, the good father who loves me and cares about me. When I think of Dad, I think in terms of my need for him. There's enough pain to deal with just needing to be loved, without letting the dark thing creep to the surface. I won't let it. I need to survive. I won't if I'm hurting too much.

So I push away the fear of his dying too. I'll visit on weekends. I'll think about him then.

Meanwhile I concern myself with hoping I'll belong in the hostel. I hope it will be like Burnside or better. I'll make friends who'll ease my loneliness and show me how to be a girl my age in the world outside Burnside. I'll even ring Jenny and make a plan to see her. Maybe. Miss Driver will guide me through my life until I meet a nice boy who'll marry me and we'll be happy. We'll have children, a house and a car, just like Aunty Dot said.

My room mate, Emily, greets me not quite warmly and leaves me to unpack. There's hardly any space between our beds. I hate the closeness.

I unpack slowly, mapping my space. My brush, comb and mirror set proudly on the dressing table. Ignore the teeth that my now straggly hair has snapped out of the comb. I don't know where to go for a haircut or what to say. Pretend I'm growing my hair. Next my plastic solitaire set, my name still on it in obscene pink nail polish, set to wait in the top drawer, in case it's ever needed. Beside it the green hanky box Nanna made. Cane sewing box in the bottom of the wardrobe. There. My beautiful things, the giver all but forgotten, are now in place. I look them over, defining my self. I am a person who owns lovely things and so I must be all right.

Now I can unpack the rest. I hope Emily doesn't come back and intrude. She doesn't. She's very good friends with the two girls across the hall. She keeps visiting them and I keep wishing she'd stay there. The worst thing is when she comes back and finds me with nothing to do but play solitaire.

I settle into the hostel rules easily. I don't resent them like the other girls do. Rules mean things have been done right. There's even a rule about how to shake the dish mop out so it won't get smelly. Mockery of Miss Driver and her rules usually begins with a dish mop impression. 'You must shake it out,' girls order as they grab other girls, their clothes or their boyfriends and shake them, 'Shake it out, let the air in so you won't get smelly.'

All around me is a bustle of noise, laughter and chatter. On Saturday girls come home with their shopping and plans to go out that night. They spend the afternoon sewing, ironing, painting their nails and curling their hair. They borrow each other's hair dryers, make-up and stockings and they share an excitement that I'm not part of. By dinner time there's only a few girls left and they vanish quickly after washing up.

I'm alone. Miss Driver is home but she's shut herself in her rooms with her own life. This isn't what I hoped for. Oh well. I'll get a boyfriend soon too. I don't know how to but it seems to be inevitable.

On Sunday, I visit Dad. I get away from Emily's watching eyes. I need to know that my father's all right. Now I have to think of things that hurt but I have to know how he is. I let myself into the house in case he's still in bed. I walk down the hall, feeling like a visitor, calling softly to him so he won't get a fright.

He's up and sitting in the kitchen with a newspaper, trying to read the lottery results through his magnifying glass.

'Oh! Hello, Princess.' He smiles his teeth back in. He's cheerful. Some of my tension drifts away. 'Hoped I'd be awake when you got here.' He chuckles and tries to stand up.

The effort is too great.

'Don't get up, Dad.'

'Come and sit down and tell me all about this hostel place. Are you happy there?'

He's more alert than he's been for a while and he's making my visit so easy. I don't understand it but I feel like my father from long ago is back. I like him. We chat about the hostel, the rules, all the girls going out and Miss Driver. He stays with me and asks questions sometimes.

'You seem to be well, Dad. Are you?'

'I'm getting on all right. Kenny's been good and Meals on Wheels come with their muck every day.' He grins mischievously. He enjoys having something to complain about. 'It's better than I could get for myself, so I can't complain.'

'What do they bring?'

'Oh, meat and vegies, cooked to slop. You know. The usual. A nice pudding most days. Have a look. There's some in the fridge.'

'Don't you eat it?'

315

'Sometimes. Depends if I'm up to it. I don't need much these days. Ken brings us good tucker when he hasn't got overtime.'

We sit in a companionable silence for a while. I can't believe how comfortable this is and how much fun my father is having. The comparison with my life at the hostel is almost painful except for the unmentionable threat that means I can't live here.

'What number are you looking for?'

I pull the newspaper closer, remembering how willingly I'd checked the lottery tickets when I was a Burnsider and how I'd never even offered to in the misery of living here.

'I can't see it very well. You look for me, Princess.'

I check his ticket number and, as usual, it isn't here. I look up to tell him. He's started nodding off.

'It's not here,' I say quietly.

'Oh well. Let's watch some telly,' and he shuffles off to the lounge room.

I sit with him until he's asleep. Ken comes out of his room.

'Oh. Hello, Kate,' he says cheerfully. He seems to like me better as a visitor than as a sister. 'How's it going?'

'Good. How are you?'

'Good.' An awkward pause follows. Do we care enough to go further with this?

'How's the boarding going?'

'Boarding? Oh. It's good. I like it.'

'Are you staying there?'

'Yeah.'

'Well, that's good if you like it. I got some frankfurts for lunch but I'm going out.'

I'm stunned that he thought of it. He's very pleased with himself.

'Yeah. Will you get them ready for Dad too?'

He really is looking after Dad as he said he would.

'Yeah. All right. Thanks.'

'See you next time then.'

'Yeah. See ya.'

He's gone again. I like him for keeping his promise.

In my room here I'm completely at home. By myself in my own space. No-one, not even Kerry, will come in and see me with nothing to do. I tidy up although the room is already tidy. Gradually, in the aloneness, my relief and fears and sadness well up from inside and I find myself sobbing, wishing I still had Miss Molesworth to tell me that I made the right choice. And to be my friend.

Have I made a mistake moving from here to the place where Emily watches and dislikes? If I came back here, would it be like it is today or like it was before? I feel 'before' again and cry about the misery it had been, the failing of the dream. And my father. I cry with relief that he's all right. I cry because he's so old and because his life is nearly over and because I've let him down so terribly. I cry for Kerry, back in her prison. I know how she feels. She's hating it and she's hating me for causing all this.

Years later, when I understand that my father had been the one who'd done the letting down, Kerry and I each tell our truth and I'm free of the undeserved guilt and shame that I took with me everywhere as a teenager. That guilt and shame meant that I couldn't go to live with my aunty in case she learned my dark secret. That guilt and shame meant that I had to live in a hostel and be lonely.

I'm so afraid of my loneliness. How long will it last? How will I make it stop, make people like me? How am I meant to get a boyfriend who will save me from all this? At last the tears stop. I march to the kitchen and wash up the pile of dirty dishes, put the coke bottles under the sink where columns are mounting up again. I cook the frankfurts and take lunch to my waking father.

'Thanks, Princess. Oh, I don't think I can manage frankfurts.'

'Ken got them.'

I want him to want frankfurts. They're Ken's promise kept.

'My old tummy can't cope with spicy food these days.'

'What can you have? You have to eat.'

'I'll just have the bread. I don't need much to run on.'

'Is that enough?'

I want him to eat and get strong.

'Oh there's a jelly thing in the fridge. I'll have that if I get hungry.'

We have lunch in front of the telly and soon Dad's asleep again. I realise what a massive effort he has made to be cheerful for my visit. It's worn him out. He's just as frail as he was a week ago. I try to will some life and strength into him while he sleeps.

Then, 'Dad. Dad. I'll have to go now.'

'Mm? What's that?'

'I said, I'll have to go now, to get back in time for tea.'

'Oh. All right then, Princess.'

He stays sitting down, still groggy with sleep. I wait for him to finish waking up.

'Bye bye then, Dad.'

'You're off then, are you?'

'Yes. I have to get back for tea.'

There's an unexpected lump in my throat. Saying goodbye to him is always so hard.

'When will you come again?'

Now he's awake.

'Next Sunday. I'll come next Sunday.'

'Good. I want you to come back whenever you can. This is still your home.'

'All right. Next Sunday.'

'Good girl. So it's goodbye for now then.'

'Yes. I've got to go. Bye bye, Dad. Don't get up.'

'Oh. I can see you to the door.'

I walk so slowly to the door. I wait for him when I get there.

'You're happy in this hostel place, are you?'

He wants me to be happy even though I've hurt him so much.

'Yeah. I'm happy.'

'Don't get so happy that you forget your old Dad, will you.'

'No. I won't. Bye for now.'

'Goodbye, Princess. Be careful going home.'

'I will.'

'You'll be back Sunday?'

'Yeah. Sunday.'

Tears as I walk to the bus stop. Must get back in time for tea or I'll be in for it.

BEGINNINGS

Things get better at work. I still don't know what I'm doing but I'm doing it more accurately. The longer I leave it to ask what the quotes are for, the sillier I'll look so I just keep filling them in.

Denise's table in the canteen is mine too now. Her friends accept that I'm shy and they don't mind that my blush is wired up to my tongue. Until now my world has been so foreign to the one they talk about, it's hardly been worth the effort of trying to join in. Sometimes they would ask me questions but soon realise that conversations about me had nowhere to go.

'Where do you live, Kate?'

'Marrickville.'

'With your parents?'

'No. With my father.'

'Not your mother?'

'She's dead.'

'Oh. Sorry.'

There they go, being sorry. Why be sorry? What do I say next? Or they'll ask, 'Did you have a good weekend, Kate?'

'It was all right.'

'What did you do?'

'Nothing.'

They're much more interested in where I live now and their questions help me become more confident at talking. I take risks. I tell them about the dish mop rule and the book at the door. I test the experience of having their attention. It's not as bad as I expected it to be, but there's the blush and dry mouth every time I speak. They keep smiling. I risk making very short jokes. This came as a shock to them at first, but they always laugh and sometimes they look expectantly at me. Under pressure I can't do it.

'How about coming shopping at lunchtime?' Denise asks one day. 'You could help me pick out a present for my cousin. She's getting married.'

I don't want to. It will be to somewhere new and there'll be strangers and I might get lost. Besides what do I know about cousins! I don't want to offend Denise and I don't know how to say no, so we charge off together as soon as it's twelve-thirty.

At MacDowells we look at all kinds of things that I didn't realise were all sold in one shop. There are electric jugs and toasters and sewing machines and tables and chairs and brooms. In other shops we look at underwear like Nina's, posh Saturday night clothes and yards and yards of material. So many things to look at! Most of all I look at Denise to make sure I don't get lost. I haven't shaken off the feeling that I need permission to buy anything, that something awful might happen if I make an independent decision. I content myself with looking and dreaming. I might buy things later.

Denise buys a sandwich in a shop! There are so many kinds of sandwiches you can have and they're written on a blackboard. I leave the one I brought from home in my bag and take a chance. I buy one too, the same as Denise's. I feel very reckless but nothing terrible happens except that we have to rush to get back to the office in time.

Now I've had a glimpse of another way of spending time, another way of life. Denise's shopping trips are often to buy presents for friends or family or to look for the right material and pattern for her next dress. Other girls knit at lunchtime and some play cards. Now I have options too. Sometimes I spend lunchtime, with or without Denise, wandering around the shops seeing what else there is to buy, listening to strangers ordering strange lunches and copying their orders for myself. Chicken and chutney, salami and lettuce on rye. I'm testing my freedom through shop counters and sandwich fillings.

At the lunch table I make a lot of new discoveries too. They surprise me more than anything else. People gossip about who's in love with whom, who's going out with whom and who's hoping to. Nice teeth seem irrelevant but nice eyes are a help. Mr Mansouriani, they say, is in love with Pat. She hates him and loves Daniel who doesn't like her at all. Her friend Ann in the typing pool hates Mr Mansouriani, and Daniel too, but her boss, Merle, is in love with Mr Mansouriani. Merle is a spinster and so is her friend Phyllis, who's Denise's boss. Phyllis is in love with Mr Mansouriani too and so Merle and Phyllis have days when they don't speak to each other or to Mr Mansouriani. Sometimes Phyllis flirts with Daniel but that's to make Mr Mansouriani jealous. Daniel only goes out with Jewish girls so he never falls in love with anyone at the office, though he flirts like a Frenchman.

This isn't how love is meant to go! It's meant to be easy. Mr Mansouriani should fall in love with Heather who falls in love with him right back. Then they get married and live happily ever after in a nice house with children and a car. Merle and Phyllis find a man each, live happily ever after and be friends with each other every day. Love in the real world is so complicated and it seems to be getting a bit late for the two spinsters who seem almost ancient. They must be at least thirty.

I wonder what I'll be like when I'm that old. They intrigue me and I watch them when I can. They are confident but people make fun of them behind their backs.

My newfound confidence takes a bit of a battering when my job changes.

'Would you like to start counter work today?' Pat asks.

'You'll start counter work today whether you like it or not,' is what she means.

I'll have to go to the counter and see what people want! Talk to strangers. And everyone will see me going red and fumbling about.

'Can't I keep doing quotes?' It's worth a try.

'It's your job to do the bloody counter. No. You can't just do quotes all day. Other people have work to do too you know.'

Pat comes with me the first few times. She fills out a new form according to what the people say and then I fill in the quote forms. The fact that I don't know what I've been doing for the last few weeks begins to show as Pat leaves me to my own devices.

'Yes. Hello, dear. I'd like to cash this policy in.'

'She wants to cash her policy in.' I tell Pat, back at her desk.

'Well fill in the form and do a quote!'

'A quote.'

'Yes. Quote. What you've been doing for the last few weeks.'

Counter work is torture. I hope that all the people will come in while I'm around the corner, then Pat will have to see them. But she's wise to me. She comes to get me.

'Look, it's your job to do the counter, not just mine. When you hear the door bang, get around there quick. You don't keep people waiting.'

There's one thing she said that I remember well. If anyone on the policy is dead, I have to give the work straight to Daniel. I find myself hoping that CML customers will be dropping dead all over the place, happily winging their way to heaven, not to my counter. They can even drop dead right here at the counter. I won't mind.

Not that I like talking to Daniel. He's ugly and he stinks of tobacco and swaggers about with his nose in the air, looking down on everyone who he doesn't want to flirt with. I hope I don't get caught by a boy like him.

Daniel and Pat have a big argument and I'm the cause of it. Hopeless, daft, stupid me. I'll probably get the sack. I won't be able to pay board then . . .

Daniel asks me to help him with a customer. He's busy on the phone. Too intimidated to do anything else, I help. When Pat sees what I'm doing she explodes.

'Who do you bloody well think you are, Daniel? You do your own fuckin' work. I'm having enough trouble getting her to do what she's supposed to do,' she shouts. Like a fishwife, Mum Perry would say.

Soon Daniel, the smoking dragon, is shouting too.

I'm crumbling, humiliated, struggling with tears. It's all my fault.

Mr Mansouriani comes out of his office.

'Mr Zimmerman. Miss Walters. My office, please. Now.'

I retreat to the records and try to fill out quotes.

'Don't worry about it, Kate. They're always at each other,' says Heather, who I hardly know.

'What?' I blurt out without thinking.

'It's not your fault. They've been at each other for months.'

It's not my fault! Not my fault. Now I can't stop crying with relief. It's not my fault. Heather knows. It's not my fault!

Merle, or Miss Myers on occasions like this, the boss of the typing pool, comes to see what the problem is, or at least to be where the problem is.

'What's going on now?' she sings.

'It's Pat and Daniel at it again. Kate just got shouted at,' Heather explains.

'Hmm. Don't let them upset you!' Merle sings.

She strolls, as far as strolling can be done on too tight high heeled shoes, around to our department. Her nose goes first to compensate for the absence of a chin and her bottom sticks out to balance it all. She's off to watch the show through the window of Mr Mansouriani's office.

When Pat and Daniel come out they're both red and furious. Daniel struts to his desk and lights a cigarette. Pat powers towards me and seethes, 'Don't do a bloody thing for him.'

Miss Myers strolls into Mr Mansouriani's office and plants herself opposite to give him her very best unwanted advice.

'Gawd,' says Heather. 'She'll put her bit in then Phyllis'll be in there too. Poor Mr Mansouriani!'

Sure enough, Phyllis, Miss Samuels on occasions like this, is puckering up to her compact, making sure her lippy is perfect and her nose isn't too shiny for her to be of assistance. Yes, she's getting ready to help my boss too. She snaps her compact shut, pops it quickly away then parades by, nose in the air, smoothing her dress over her swaying hips as she goes. A few minutes later the two women come out smirking and whispering behind their hands. Mr Mansouriani sits at his desk with his head in his hands. I go back to work, my work, and nothing more is said about the argument.

Soon after this Pat leaves. She doesn't say goodbye. She just doesn't come back. I stay. Dorina replaces her. Dor, a ray of sunshine, whose curious name was made up especially for her by her father. She knows what my job is before I do. She explains it all to me on her first day in our department. It's so easy! I'm elated. I don't mind that our customers aren't all dead, though when they come in angry, complaining about the surrender value they've been offered, I wish they would wing their way heavenward. So begins a comfortable friendship and a love of work—except counter work. It doesn't matter. Dor shares that and the counter becomes a place where I can practise talking to strangers in relative safety.

Work life is getting better and hostel life will soon too. When I find out why the girls don't seem to want me around.

I sit in my room on Saturday night, like I always do, wondering what's wrong with me. Why don't I get invited out or even to other girls' rooms for a chat?

Sue Lipman barges in. She's an older girl who's getting married soon. She's popped into our room to borrow something of

Emily's. Emily's out.

'Oh! G'day, Kate. How are you?'

'Good,' I say, but my voice cracks and I cry. Oh bum! Now she'll hate me. I'm such a sook.

Sue sits beside me and puts her arm softly round my shoulder.

'What's wrong?' Softly, gently.

'Sorry.'

'No. It's all right. Tell me what's wrong.'

'I just feel so . . . so . . . lonely. I thought it would be . . .' snort.

'Gosh. You shouldn't be should you!'

'S'pose not. But I am. No-one talks to me or anything.'

'Ah. Well you know why that is don't you?'

'No. I don't.' Is it because I'm fat, like at school? Because I've got glasses? I'm shy? Bommy clothes?

'Well. I suppose someone had better tell you.'

'Tell me what?' Oh please. But don't let it be that I'm not good enough.

'You're friends with Miss Driver, aren't you?'

No. Well, yes. Miss Driver got me into the hostel and, although she's hasn't had much to do with me since, I know her better than the others do. I suppose she's a friend.

'Yes,' I reply.

'OK. The others aren't. They don't like her. Well, it's not that they don't like her really. It's just that she's the matron and she can throw you out if you do anything wrong.'

'I don't get it.'

'If they make friends with you, you might tell her what they get up to and they'll be in trouble, get thrown out maybe.'

'Pimp on them? I wouldn't!' I know about not pimping better than any of them! I'm a Burnsider.

'Well. That's how they think. You're friends with the enemy.' Sue smiles. 'See. There's nothing wrong with you.'

'Oh. Yeah. Well, what can I do?'

'I don't know. Give it time, I suppose. You can come and talk to me if you like. I'll be your big sister.'

She squeezes my shoulder.

'Thanks. But, when can . . .'

'Yeah. I know I'm never home. Well, give it time. They'll work it out. Don't get too sad.'

'All right. Thanks.'

'Come and talk if I'm ever home,' she says standing to go.

'Thanks.'

I wait. Nothing changes. I try to talk to Miss Driver about how to make friends but I can't see her reply as helpful at the time, though now I know it's true.

'Well Kate, I can't tell you how to do it. You have to do it yourself, in your own way.'

It feels like a dismissal. She's washed her hands of me. She knows I'm floundering but she can't tell me how to make things right. Miss Molesworth would have helped.

My loyalty to Miss Driver dissolves. When girls make fun of the rules, I laugh along with them. When they need help getting in late I'm willing to sneak down and open the door. I feel free to loosen up and disobey the letter of the law.

Gradually invitations come for visits to other rooms to see new clothes or to discuss hemlines or new boyfriends or listen to tales of visits to the bush to see families. My contributions are as a willing audience. I'm good at that and I learn about life this way. I make jokes and girls laugh heartily like they used to at Burnside. I feel alive.

Meanwhile I keep going home on Sundays to visit Dad and we fall into an easy routine. His hands stay where they should. It feels as if his dark side has gone. He's always sleeping now. His back is bent so far down that I'm sure he can't see much of his house at all. I don't like sitting around waiting for brief moments of conversation that make him know I've come to visit.

Today there's a knock on the door. Dad's asleep and Ken's gone out.

'Hello, Kate. Remember me? Cheryl, from St Mark's. Just

wondered if you'd like to come again some day.'

I make up my mind to go to that nice church next Sunday. I'm sure Dad won't be pleased.

He isn't but I'm determined to get away for some of the time I'm supposed to be with him. To appease him I say I'll come home on Saturdays and stay 'til after church on Sunday.

Leaving the girls at the hostel to their Saturday night preening is such a relief, even if I am just going home. They've got dates and plans for movies and parties. I haven't and they can't tell. But I've got Sunday, lovely Sunday.

Sunday with the wonderful singing at church and the service that I can be part of, all written in *the Book of Common Prayer*. I get there with only enough time to go in and sit down at the back before the service starts. I leave as soon as it ends. I only say hello to Cheryl if she catches me.

Cheryl is persistent.

'Kate, how about coming to the youth group,' she says when she manages to catch me one morning. 'Jane and Errol lead it. We just sing and have studies and fellowship . . .'

'Fellowship?'

'Yes. It's fun. It's just people our age.'

I know about fellowship and people our age. I don't want to go through that again. But I'm lonely and I want to have somewhere to go on Saturday nights, like girls at the hostel and the girls at work.

'All right. Thanks, Cheryl.'

Dad isn't pleased but I go anyway. This fellowship is much better than the Parramatta one. People are friendly and I don't struggle for things to say. I pretend I'm Denise and conversation becomes a bit easier. With girls. I'm still painfully shy of boys. They're sizing me up for a girlfriend or wife and I'm sure I'm inadequate, apart from my nice teeth and eyes.

So this is my pattern now. I work during the week and go home for fellowship, church and visiting Dad on weekends. I expect that I'll soon be surrounded by millions of friends and that adventures of all kinds will begin. Then I'll stop being shy of boys and I'll be able to smile at them, without my lips sticking to my best asset. Who knows what might happen then!

I've rung Aunty Dot and told her that I've moved to the hostel. No, I still haven't got a boyfriend. I will one day. Auntie thinks going to the hostel was a good decision. I really need to be with people my own age and although we're family and she loves me, I've made a good decision. I mustn't forget that I'll always have a home with her if things don't work out. It's hard for me to have a family like that.

My family keeps growing, mysteries unfold and new ones begin.

'Phone call for you, Kate.'

'Kate, it's Zelda.'

'Who?'

'Zelda. Your sister.'

Ken had told me that she's our half sister, whatever that is. But I don't want her calling herself my sister. Kerry is my sister. I don't trust Zelda but I hardly remember why.

'I thought you might like to come and have dinner with us.'

'At Dad's?'

I can't imagine her anywhere else.

'No. Here at Kensington. At our place.'

I'm beginning to feel more confident about doing new things now but the real reason for my accepting her invitation is that I don't know how to refuse it politely. She'll be angry at my bad manners and she's scary when she's angry. She'll slap me. We make arrangements for me to go to her house after work one night.

I knock on the door, hoping I'll remember what she looks like. What if I walk into the wrong people's house!

A woman in dark glasses answers the door.

'Ah Kate. Come in.'

Oh well, it must be her. The hair looks the same except those two white clumps at the front.

I follow my half sister to the lounge room.

'Would you like a drink?'

She pours some stuff that smells like a pub for herself.

'No, thank you.'

'Don't you drink?'

'No.' I don't know what to try or what there is to ask for.

'Uh huh. That's good. Don't want to get on the grog like me.'

'What do you mean?'

'The doctor says I shouldn't drink. Got cirrhosis.' She sips her drink.

'What's that?'

'Means my liver's crook. I shouldn't drink.'

'Um. But you are!'

'Yeah. I ought to stop. Still, we've all got to go sometime.'

What a weirdo. At least it's easy to keep the conversation going.

A man appears from nowhere.

'G'day, Kate.' We shake hands. 'Like a drink?'

'No. I already asked her that. She doesn't drink. This is my husband, George.'

'Smart girl. Pleased to meet you.'

'Go and dish up while we talk, will you, George?'

George goes to the kitchen to do as he's told.

'He hasn't been very well either but he's on the mend. Tell me, Kate, how are things at home?'

'I don't live there now. I moved to the hostel.'

'Yes. Dad told me, gave me your number there.'

There are some questions I just have to have answers to and this person seems willing to answer anything.

'He's your father too, is he?'

Zelda laughs.

'Kate wants to know if Charley's my father,' she calls out to George. George laughs too.

I'm embarrassed and confused. What's so funny? I feel my face redden.

'He had you kids very late you know.'

'When did he have you?'

'He was married to my mother before he met yours. A long time before. My mother was his second wife.'

'Second? No mine was his second.'

'No. Yours was his third. He was married in England, before he came here.'

'What happened to her?'

'Died I believe.'

More of the father I don't know. Zelda lights a smoke and sucks hard.

'And what happened to your mother?' Surely he hasn't got three dead wives!

'They got divorced. It was a big thing to get divorced back then but he divorced her.'

Divorced! My father?

'Why?' What about happily ever after? 'til death do us part?

'My mother, Ruth was her name, Ruth was an alcoholic. A drunk. She beat Dad up. Even put him in hospital a few times.'

My jaw drops all the way to the floor.

'Haven't you heard any of this before?'

'No. Dad doesn't talk much.'

'No, well, for a man to be beaten by a woman, well he wouldn't want to talk about it. It was hard for him and she made it as awful as she could. Oh yes, she humiliated him at the pub too, lots of times, so he couldn't go there with his mates.'

My face must show that I can't believe it.

'Oh yes. She'd throw her drink at him and shout all over the place and get stuck into him. A man couldn't fight back, not with a woman.'

No! This isn't how people are. Miss Molesworth wouldn't do that. No-one at Burnside would. No-one anywhere would. Would they?

'So, they got divorced. He divorced her. He had a good case.'

'Then he met our mother.'

'Yes. Well, much later and you know the rest.'

I don't feel like I know anything much. Not about my father.
George calls us to dinner. While we eat I try another question.

'Who was Nanna?'

'Nanna was Jack's mother.'

'Who is Uncle Jack though? How does he fit in?'

'Jack and I were married once but we got divorced too. Must run in the family eh?'

'I'm not gunna.'

'That's what Jack and I said.'

'Well, why did you?' Did you beat Uncle Jack up?

'Oh, it's hard to explain. We had our troubles. You don't want to know about that.'

Yes I do!

A short silence follows while I try to weave all this into the family I knew I had. I get my next question ready. I'm going to sort the family out now, while I've got the chance.

'Who's that girl, Elsie, who used to live with Nanna?'

'Elsie? She's my daughter. Mine and Jack's.'

I'm only just keeping up.

'So, if you're my half sister and Elsie is your daughter, then I must be her . . . her . . . What? It would have to be aunty wouldn't it? Am I her aunty?'

'Yes. And you're a great-aunt too. Elsie has two boys now.'

My brain's working overtime. Dinner is finished when George says he's going 'to the local'. He says he'll wash up when he gets back.

Zelda and I talk on, Zelda sipping away at drink after drink.

'I'd better go,' I say, imagining getting home before someone puts the chain across the door.

'No. Wait 'til George gets home. He'll drive you to Redfern.'

'But I'll miss the train if I wait.'

'It'll be quicker if he drives you.'

I wait, knowing I'll miss the train. Zelda rambles on and I sit worrying about being locked out. At last George comes home and Zelda tells him to drive me to Redfern.

'Geez! I'm sorry, love. Can hardly stand up! Drank a bit too much for driving.' He falls on the lounge. 'Shoulda told me before I went, love. Can't drive anybody anywhere like this.'

'Sorry, Kate. Will you be right on the bus?'

What's the use of telling them I'm scared of going out so late in the dark and getting home late and being locked out.

Zelda comes close to give me a last piece of wisdom before I leave.

'If any bloke tries anything, just raise your knee. Hard.'

She mistakes my silence for understanding.

'Goodnight. Ring me sometime and we'll do this again.'

George sees me to the door and says he'll watch 'til I get to the bus stop. I walk quickly down the dark street and wait at the bus stop. I hope a bloke won't try something so I have to raise my knee. I'm cold and frightened and by the time the bus comes I'm trembling.

'Redfern, please.'

'You're out late on your own,' the driver says as he gives me my ticket. 'Been visiting your girlfriends?'

'No. My half sister and her husband.'

'Couldn't they drive you home? A young thing like you shouldn't be getting around here by yourself at this time of night.'

'They can't. He's too drunk.'

'Oh for pity's sake.' He sounds angry. 'Sit there,' he says pointing to the seat behind him.

'You be careful,' the driver says as he lets me out at Redfern.

I stand on the station at midnight. I stand rigid, too scared to look at any of the shadows in case they hide blokes about to make me raise my knee.

In the train I sit stiffly, suspicious of every person who gets on and off. I refuse to cry and I know I'll never visit Zelda again. I hope they haven't put the chain across the door at the hostel.

They have. Will I try to get to Dad's house? No. It's too late and I'm half-asleep. I'll do what the others do when they're locked out. I find some dirt and chuck it at Janet's window, not too hard. I don't want to break it. Nothing happens. I'm about to chuck a stone when I hear the chain slide across the door. The porch light goes on, the door opens and there's Miss Driver, bleary eyed in her dressing gown.

She's going to chuck me out. I'll have to live with Aunty Dot after all.

'Where on earth have you been?'

'At Zelda's.'

'You know you have to be home by ten-thirty! It's a quarter past one!'

'I missed the train.'

'The train! You got on the train at this hour? Haven't they got a car?'

'Yes, but George drank too much.'

'Kate, this is dreadful. A young girl should not be traipsing about in the dark by herself. You'd better think very seriously before you go out to Zelda's again.'

'Yes, Miss Driver.'

Next morning we whisper about my being locked out. My friends imagine what fun I must have been having to get home so late! They don't believe it was just Zelda and I. They realise that I'm one of them and I realise that Miss Driver cares about me but that that need not set me apart from the others. The girls think my family is almost as curious as the way I've been brought up. I agree about my family. It's certainly not what I thought families were like. Not even mine.

NOT VERY CLOSE

'Phone for you, Kate.'

'Hello, Kate. It's Ken.'

Ken never rings me. We talk at weekends and that's enough. Is something wrong?

'I thought I'd better tell you that Dad has to go to hospital for an operation.'

'What? What for? What operation?'

'Oh, some men's thing. I don't understand the medical business. Anyway, can you go and see him?'

I'm forced to admit that my father is sick, not just tired. I wonder if he's dying. Fear. I don't want him to die. Not now. Now that we're friends and safe.

I go to the hospital. It's the night before the operation.

'I'm glad you came, Princess. Didn't know if you'd have time after work.'

'Yeah, I had time.'

We sit quietly. He holds my hand, safely. I wonder what to say. His hand has veins like threads of navy blue cotton under tissue paper skin. I'd better not hold on too hard.

'What's wrong with you, Dad?'

'Oh, just my waterworks. Needs some plumbing done.'

We laugh, weakly.

'Will you be all right again then? After the operation?' Please tell me you will.

'Right as rain. I'll be home again in a few days.'

We sit quietly. Something makes me look at his face. Tears are rolling out of the corners of his eyes.

'When's Kenny coming?' he asks at last.

'He said he has to do overtime tonight.'

More tears.

'Will you ring him and ask him if he'll come and see me tonight?'

'He's coming tomorrow.'

'I need to see him tonight. Ring him, Princess. Please. Tell him he has to come tonight.'

His voice is urgent, pleading to make my brother come. Tomorrow isn't soon enough. Tomorrow will be too . . . The tears scare me. He's so vulnerable. Like a child. A pleading, broken child.

'But he really, really wants you to come tonight,' I tell my brother. 'He's crying 'cause you're not here.'

'I have to work.'

'You've gotta come. He wants to see you tonight. He's really upset. He's crying.'

I plead now. If only I had the control over Ken that his boss has.

'All right. Tell him I'll come after work but it won't be 'til late.'

My father cries with relief when I tell him Ken will come late.

He cries again when I tell him I have to go, to get the train home. I tell him I'll come back again tomorrow.

'Don't worry about tomorrow. I'll be too groggy after the operation. You go home and get some rest and remember your old Dad loves you.'

I'm struggling to pretend that the operation will make everything all right. My call to the hospital the next day isn't much help.

'Mr Shayler is doing as well as can be expected.' No more information will be given over the phone.

Soon after, Dad goes into a nursing home. I know he'll hate that. I go to see him there.

'Down the hallway and turn right. Room nine,' a busy nurse directs.

A shout and a cry draw my attention to room three where a nurse is spanking an old man. She shouts at him about how bad he's been as she whacks his hip with a slipper. Where am I? Where's Dad? What is this place?

I hurry to room nine and find Dad safe, cocooned in his bed. I can only see from his chest up. He looks tiny, fragile.

'Hello, Dad. I'm here,' I whisper close to his ear.

'Is that our kids making all that noise?' he replies.

Is he joking? What am I supposed to say?

'Dad, it's me. Kate.' Louder this time. To break the . . . whatever it is. 'Wake up. It's me. You must be dreaming.'

'It sounds like ours. Both of them,' he says.

He seems to be awake but where is he?

You've got three kids and we're . . . I'm not . . . No. Oh no. Not dark things here! I shouldn't have come. You lousy . . . I won't . . .

I just can't make sense of this.

'We can't let the kids go careering round like that! I'd better see to them.'

He really thinks we have children, like I'm the . . . oh, he thinks I'm my mother!

'Dad, it's me. It's Kate. Your daughter. There aren't any kids. We're at the hospital.'

'Better go and see to them.'

He tries to get up but the sheet holds him captive. He lies still, eyes wandering around the ceiling. Soon he's asleep. I sit beside him angrily. I don't understand anything. Why did he have to say such stupid things? Why couldn't he just be normal? Was he doing it on purpose? I'll wait until he wakes up again. Perhaps he'll know me then and we'll chat about what it's like here. He doesn't wake up for long enough to talk. I have to run for the train.

'How was your Dad today, Kate?' Miss Driver asks.

I tell her what had happened.

'Sounds as if he's quite ill.'

'Why?'

She explains that he might be having a second childhood and that that happens to some old people when they're near their end.

'Is he going to die?'

'Er. I don't know. You'd have to ask at the hospital. Ask them to explain what's going on.'

'They don't tell me anything. I'll ask Ken.'

I don't want to ask anyone. I know what they'll say and I'm scared.

Shortly after, dressing for work, Miss Driver calls out, 'Kate. Phone call!'

I never get calls in the morning.

'It's Zelda,' Miss Driver whispers as she hands the receiver to me. 'That's you're step-sister, isn't it?'

'Yes,' I whisper.

I know my father is dead. Zelda's words only confirm it.

We sit in the front row of the chapel. I can't look at the coffin lying quiet and lonely out the front. That coffin and I are all that exist in the world. I want to rip the lid off and scream at my father to stop mucking around. To get out. To come back. To stop being old and frail and . . . and . . .

Watery organ music intrudes. I hate it. It's too sweet for this, too sickeningly sweet. I'm angry. I cry but I mustn't cry. I must be strong and mature. Kerry is sitting beside me. She tries not to cry too but the pressure is building and that awful sweet music brings us both to breaking point. Kerry sobs first. I join her.

'Hold her hand,' Zelda hisses at me.

'What?'

'Hold Kerry's hand.'

'Why?'

'Just hold it. It's what you do.'

There's venom in that hiss. Is she angry because I don't know how to behave at my father's funeral? I'm trying to do it properly, trying not to cry when everyone is looking, judging. I hold Kerry's hand. She gives me a look that means she doesn't understand why I'm grabbing her hand either. She goes along with it though and holds mine back, tight. It feels false. We don't touch, normally. I sob. Nothing is right here. I'm glad to let go of Kerry and find my hanky.

I sit numb through the service. I don't know or care what anyone says. Finally the curtain parts. The coffin grinds slowly through the gap. I come so close to jumping up and shouting, 'No. No. Don't go. Don't leave me.'

Later Kerry is angry.

'You killed him!' she shouts at me. 'It's your fault he's dead. If you hadn't left him he'd still be here. You broke his heart.'

I know.

'Sorry to hear about your father,' people at work say.

'Oh it's all right. It was for the best.'

I've heard that on TV. It lets me stay tearless in public, not fragile and needy. I focus on work. I don't think about Dad. There's emptiness again. Don't think about it.

The tears I shed in private are born as much of confusion as sadness. I don't want to feel the depth of grief that's there when I'm alone. I've hated my father and wanted him to die so many times in the last nine months. I've loved him too and wanted him to last forever. I feel so empty now. It's best not to think.

'Sorry to hear about your father,' Cheryl says as we walk home from fellowship. 'Will you be all right?'

'Oh yeah. I'll be fine.'

'I hope you don't mind me saying so but you don't sound very sad!'

I wonder what to say. Isn't this the right way to be, to hide your grief in public? Not to make others uncomfortable by bawling your head off whenever you feel like it?

'I get sad sometimes,' I tell her, so she'll think I'm normal.

'Well, I mean, he didn't bring you up did he,' Cheryl continues, as if I hadn't spoken. 'He was just a sort of visitor really. I mean, you weren't very close.'

Not very close! My father just a visitor!

How could Cheryl understand who my father was. He gave me an identity, prevented me from being nobody, gave us family, lived for us. He was my father.

'He was the only person in the world who loved me and now he's gone.'

'Oh!'

'I'm scared, really scared that there isn't a single person in the world who loves me now.'

Cheryl drew in a shocked gasp. I was glad it was night time so she couldn't see my chin trembling or my tears.

'But I love you, Kate,' she said. 'Lots of us do at the church.'

'Oh. Uh. Thanks.'

That love didn't fill the void. I didn't believe it or understand it then. As far as I knew, you could only be loved by family and I didn't have one. Not really. Not any more. It had fallen apart.

A new loneliness filled the gap left by the old father who I loved and hated, needed and wanted to die and missed so terribly when he did die. I buried the darkness of him and remembered only his love for many, many years.

And nightmares of wolves contained the darkness. For many, many years.

EPILOGUE
THE END OF THIS CHILDHOOD

My mother has been dead for thirty-four years. I'm an adult now. I'm reasonably comfortable, successful. I'm going to see my mother's grave to get information, to see what the grave is like. It's not that I need to go.

I search my memory for the name of the cemetery. Something about meadows and Mars. Fields. Field of Mars. Yes. That's it. I remember my father saying it to me when I was a kid. It had sounded like fields of flowers or fields of stars. Fairy memories. Flower memories. Two little kids skipping about between towering gums. Drifting back through my past.

I ring the Field of Mars Cemetery. My mother's grave is in the Protestant Section. They tell me the grave number. I'll drive to the cemetery for a look then I'll come home and write to Kerry. Must ask if she's found our brother yet and tell her I haven't.

The cemetery is profoundly ugly. Where are the trees and the fairies and colours? There's barely a tree in sight. The flowers are mostly plastic, faded things in jars that lost their sparkle years ago. Row after row of concrete rectangles jammed together, watched over by mouldy, decaying angels. They're at eye level now, so I can see them for what they really are. Cold, concrete lumps, not fairies who look after flowers and fly among stardust.

Preoccupied with the ugliness of this place and finding numbers on the graves I'm not ready for what I find.

Gold letters of my father's name. Glaring at me.

Oh no. Not you. I didn't come here for you. What you did was . . . Go away.

Anger boils. I want to kick the bloody gravestone over. How dare he defile the grave of my mother, the saint! How dare his gold letters shout false saintliness to the world!

Drowning out her very existence.

Where's my mother?

Where's Mummy? I find myself asking. Where's my mummy. I want her. I want my mummy.

As the child struggles with the adult, the tears roll down and I fumble to find the tissues I brought, just in case.

Oh, where's Mummy? Someone tell me where she is.

I feel weak. I sit on the grave and look for my mother's name. Yes, there it is, below the gold one. Norma Shayler's name is here but her gold has worn away.

'Beloved mother of Kenneth 6, Katherine 4 and Kerry 2.'

The child who is me sits sniffling. Stares at her mother's name. It's so near her own.

Right. I stand up. It's time to go. I've seen the grave, seen my mother's name on it. Now it's time to go back home. This is just silly, this sitting around crying.

But the child is bound to the name on the grave, no matter how dull it's become. She demands that we stay.

I have to sit down again. I choose the grave opposite my mother's. Corporal Binns' faded letters can just be seen. I chuckle at his name. What if Eric Bogle had chosen Corporal Binns' graveside to sit beside instead of young Willie McBride's. I hate war. It's obscene. I wonder how Corporal Binns fared on the battlefield. I know these are distractions but I need space between me and the other grave.

The child is restless. She won't tolerate diversions any longer. She draws my eyes back to the gold and the anger.

I'll deal with you later, another time. Stay out of my way. I'll think about Mummy. The word, just the word 'mummy' sets up the flood of tears again. Another handful of tissues. Mop up the sobbing.

'Mummy. Mummy, oh Mummy.'

Where is this coming from? This is not me. I don't have a mother. I'm thirty-eight years old and I do not need . . .

The caretaker wanders lethargically by the end of Row H with his broom. He stares at me but I can't stop the child sobbing. He walks slowly away.

Pull yourself together, I tell myself. This is not how grown women behave. It's embarrassing.

'Go with me, Kate. Go with me,' demands the child who I am inside. 'Go with me. Back to Mummy.'

The woman is too worn to refuse.

'All right. I'm coming.'

'Oh Mummy, I miss you. I miss you so much. Come back.'

We sob some more. Pause to catch our breath. Go back again.

'Why did you go? I needed you. Why did you leave me?'

How could I be breaking my heart like this? After more than thirty years? I can't stop it though. My heart will break. Will literally crack apart inside me.

I distract myself from pain by pulling weeds out of Corporal Binns' grave. But there's the child wanting to get things right. To sort it all out. She drags us back to Norma Shayler.

'You were my friend, my dear, dear, best friend and you went away and left me. I was all alone. I needed you and you went away. You weren't there to rock me, push me in the pram, hold me close. I missed you so much.'

All the tears are wrung out of me. I sit feeling. Breathing heavily.

'You went away and left . . .' No. Don't go back there. Rest.

'Just as well you brought the tissues,' I say aloud to myself, to assure myself that I am a grown up.

The slow man with the broom wanders by again, watching. He looks away, grinds his cigarette butt into the ground and moves on.

'Just as well you came alone,' I tell myself between the trumpeting of blowing my nose.

'Alone' does it this time. I sob.

'I was so alone without you. So lonely, Mummy. I missed you so much.'

More tears roll out between me and the child.

After a while I stand aside and look at us. Am I actually telling a grave that I miss my mother? Telling it that I've been so alone since . . .

It's afternoon but a dawn, a glorious golden dawn folds out around me. I realise so much in this moment! I say to Norma Shayler, aloud, with the faltering voice of new understanding.

'I still miss you, Mummy. I still need you. I need you to love me, to tell me who I am, to make me good.'

I sit with my need for her. I feel my new awareness. It comes with a lonely knowledge that I've never known love, whole love, since my mother died and took hers away. I can see so clearly now, here, that many of the friendships I've pursued and treasured or been disappointed by, have been out of longing for her, my mother. That's who I've been missing, who I've been searching for. Searching for love like hers that made me whole and perfect.

'You knew me.'

She knew the wholeness of me, knew my roots, my body, my person, my self. Knew like no-one else does or can. Knew without explanation, without words, without questions.

'Oh, I wish you were here! Remember our pram. You took us out to show us the world and then you left. I was perfect then, when you knew me. If you were here now you could tell me what to do about all the things that trouble me and I could tell you all the things I've done since you left. Work. Uni too. I'm a teacher.

They're the good things. And my friends too. But, oh, I've made some dreadful, terrible mistakes. Haven't found a nice boy either. I might be like you. A late starter.'

Now my tears are gentle and slow. I won't break. She understands me. Loves me. Forgives me. Knows my wholeness.

'You're not here,' I tell her calmly, 'so I'll have to get on without you, to keep getting on. It's lonely but I'll be all right.'

The sobbing starts again. I let it out, not fighting it. It feels like the relief of a warm soapy bath now, not torture.

The crying subsides and I think quietly to myself, 'I've made it this far without her, so I can keep going, mistakes and all. She loved me. She knew me. She knew I was good. I was always good. I will take that with me from here.'

Now I want to laugh–cry. They're usually separate things, laughter and tears, but today is not a usual day. Today laughter and tears are one. A smile spreads across my crying face while the heavens boom out my understanding, 'My mother loved me!'

'And I was always good,' reverberates through the universe. I laugh at the joy and the power of it.

'My mother loved me,' I tell myself quietly as the ripples spread across galaxies. 'And I was good. I was always good.'

I sit exhausted, grateful that Corporal Binns doesn't have visitors today. I'm utterly exhausted. I suppose I should go but I'm afraid of the last goodbye. Afraid to leave the one who knows me. I try.

'Goodbye M . . .'

No. I can't do it yet. More tears flow gently and breathing is heavy but easy. I rest. I look at my watch. I've been here for four hours. I try the last goodbye again but it still gets stuck.

'I'll be all right you know,' I tell my mother. I try to feel what being all right will be like now but it's too early for that.

'I will be all right. I really will,' I tell her.

I breathe deeply.

'I'm thirty-eight. I'm not a child and I'll be all right. It'll be hard and lonely sometimes but you loved me. I am lovable. I am

345

good. I'll take that with me and so I'll be all right.' Another deep smooth breath. The child is quiet. I, the woman, stand up.

I begin, 'Goodbye . . .' but my eyes wander too far up the headstone and I see the obscene gold.

'I'll deal with you later, Dad. I was always good. You weren't. Not always. But today is too big for darkness. I won't let it in.'

I let my eyes drop to the dull name.

'Goodbye, Norma Shayler.'

No, say it properly.

'Goodbye, Mummy. I'll be all right.'

What about my father? My father who stole my childhood, who never stopped loving me and who left me twice? What about him?

I wrote this story, my story and I found us both there.

The woman who found words for this childhood found the perfect child she was. She found her father's goodness alongside his loathsome darkness. She walked through the darkness with the broken child, cried with her, comforted her and mothered her. And finally understood her. She still mothers her and knows that she was always good.

Dad can have his gold letters. Perhaps he deserved them, perhaps not. There are no excuses for the bad things he did. He wasn't all bad though and he wasn't all good.

I was a perfect child once and my mother loved me.

I was a perfect child once and my mother and father loved me. That's harder to say, but there it is. They loved me.

I always deserved love.

I wish I'd known.

I do now.

It is no Secret
The story of a stolen child
Donna Meehan

One 60-year-old white lady came up to me with tears rolling down her cheeks. She held my hand and said, 'I was one of them. I took the children away from their parents. I am sorry. I thought we were doing the right thing.'

I wasn't angry. My heart was filled with love. I hugged her and said. 'Thank you for coming.'

At the age of five, Donna Meehan was taken away from her large and loving Aboriginal family at Coonamble NSW and sent to be the only child of a white family in distant Newcastle. Tiny and vulnerable she had to try to make sense of her strange new world and the loss of everything she had known and loved.

Despite the true and enduring love of her adoptive parents and of her soulmate husband Ron, the loss of her sense of belonging brought Donna close to suicide. Only when she traced her birth family could her healing begin.

It is no Secret is an honest book with much sadness in it, but thanks to Donna's resilience and forgiveness, it is ultimately uplifting. This is a story about hope and grace and the indomitable strength of the human spirit.

Orphans of the Empire
Alan Gill

This is the shocking yet compelling true story of the thousands of men and women who came to Australia as child migrants and so called 'orphans'. From the convict era to recent times it traces the decades of misery in the child migration schemes which seemed 'right' at the time but which have now come back to haunt both the Australian and British Governments and many religious organisations.

Drawing on years of painstaking research and many hours of interviews, Alan Gill has written of the horrific abuse of destitute children in the 'care' of their guardians. He also reveals the deliberate destruction of documents which has increased the immense difficulty already faced by the grown 'orphans' in trying to find their true identities. Here, too, are accounts of heartwarming acts of great kindness.

Orphans of the Empire examines the politics of child migration at government level and the denominational numbers game played by the churches. He suggests that the import of children may have been motivated by a desire to swell the numbers of 'the faithful' and possibly gain building grants rather than by a wish to help the underprivileged.

'. . . unusually affecting, hard to put down . . .'
Geraldine Doogue, *Life Matters*, Radio National

'This is a book all Australians should read.'
Sir Ronald Wilson